ENDORSEMENTS FOR A WOMEN'S GUIDE

'*A Women's Guide To Saving The World* is a great anthology of women writers, and serves as a call to action none of us can afford to ignore.'

The Ecologist Magazine

'As this inspiring book shows, all over the world, ordinary women are using their positions as teachers, artists, computer programmers or community workers to make their voices heard. And all over the world the glass ceiling is shattering as women seize the high ground in politics, business and academe – and not a moment too soon. There may be less than ten years before we reach the tipping point and trigger runaway climate change. Women are needed to make the paradigm shift – we can show the way.'

Nicky Gavron, Deputy Mayor of London

'In 1973 E. F. Schumacher wrote *Small is Beautiful,* which laid out a clear path for those seeking a future that was opposed to the exploitation of nature, the desecration of spirit and the violent processes of economics. The women who have written these stories have taken that opposite pathway, each, in isolation, gives testimony to their struggle but, as a collection, an amazingly strong manifesto emerges. We are at a tipping point in our culture, a period of chaos where previous, male dominated systems will restructure. It is time for that rebalance to happen and for the voices of women to converge with those of men to shape a world of equality and quality. This is a wonderful contribution.'

Ian Roderick
Director, Schumacher Institute for Sustainable Systems

'It is good to be reminded how these problems are taking priority within the thinking of both sexes, where we can spur each other on by confirming each other's deepest concerns on the issues involved. Then all the sooner may events occur which might really start to change the world.'

Alexander Thynn (Lord Bath)

'In the clamorous debate about how to 'mitigate' or 'alleviate' the devastating environmental impacts of the global industrial system, it must always be remembered that the root cause of the problems we face is an unjust, oppressive system of patriarchal power based on military force. Karen Eberhardt Shelton's timely book brings together the voices of women across the world who are forging an alternative to this obsolete mindset, a new order based on compassion, intuitive wisdom and tenderness – this is the voice that we must now heed to find a way out of our apparently terminal dilemma.'

David Midgley, co-founder of the Gaia Network and
Director of Schumacher North

'Climate change is a great challenge, but also a great opportunity to work out a way of harmonious co-existence with Planet Earth. To do this we need all the inspiration we can get, and the women featured in this book show what individuals can achieve with passion and commitment. *A Women's Guide to Saving the World* brings together over 80 such women – including activists, healers, writers, teachers and artists – to tell their stories and to remind us how we can all make a creative contribution to the future.'

John Elford, Green Books

'Karen Eberhardt Shelton has brought together an amazing array of women's insights and experiences that make for an absorbing read. Sometimes it can feel like the global social and environmental issues we face are too overwhelming a problem to tackle. But here is a wonderful source of inspiration from women who believe that *together* we can make a difference. These women, like many of our ethical entrepreneurs, have something important to say. We owe it to ourselves, our mothers, and most of all our daughters, to listen.'

TRIODOS BANK, Bristol
(the ethical bank)

'I am delighted to see the publication of *A Women's Guide To Saving The World* because I feel the world will continue to suffer from the highly disruptive, reductive Cartesian paradigm unless a new, in-your-face **wake up call** is not forthcoming. At present, we humans are an aggressive, clever, self-obsessed ape arrogantly acting like an invasive and virulent disease likely to destroy its host. Where is our intelligence, our *'sapiens'*, our humility? Woe-man! This inspirational *Women's Guide* offers an antidote. It is from the heart and carries a plea for the human animal to be serious, to be mature, to move past tribalism, to deepen our respect for all life – plant and animal – and to enhance the Whole. It is a timely imperative we'd be well advised not to evade.'

Mike Dodd
(internationally recognized potter*)*

'To produce a book with this title is an excellent idea. The writing of environmental activists who happen to be women, along with so many others, should enable them to serve as role models for talented women everywhere to emulate.'

Edward Goldsmith
(founder of *The Ecologist* magazine)

'*A Women's Guide* is an out-of-the-ordinary, watershed project; a significant symbol of the folly of perpetuating the male dominance of human society with the possible consequence of the destruction of all life on earth. The women here have been gathered together to make a concerted appeal to humanity to come, however belatedly, to its senses and try to save itself and the resplendent but all too fragile earth it has inherited.'

Jim Prowting
*(*top-ranked veteran orienteer and acclaimed orienteering mapmaker)

A WOMEN'S GUIDE TO SAVING THE WORLD

Karen Eberhardt Shelton

Book Guild Publishing
Sussex, England

First published in Great Britain in 2008 by
The Book Guild Ltd
Pavilion View
19 New Road
Brighton
BN1 1UF

Typesetting in Times by
IML Typographers, Birkenhead, Merseyside

Printed in Great Britain by
CPI Antony Rowe

A catalogue record for this book is available from
The British Library.

ISBN 978 1 84624 200 7

This book is dedicated to my mother, Elizabeth Eberhardt, and the Quaker Trust she established during the last twenty years of her life. The Trust, sadly, has been dissolved, but a memorial plaque commemorating her work and the Alternatives to Violence workshops held on her Trust property in California was placed on the wall of a school in Vietnam by Vietnam Veterans for Peace. My fervent hope is that this book will make it possible to establish an Eco Trust in her memory.

CONTENTS

ACKNOWLEDGEMENTS

I feel indebted beyond measure to all the good and thoughtful women who offered their fervent messages of care and concern completely free of charge and unfettered by legal issues. Without their willingness to Speak Up, there would be a vacuum in the niche this assortment of wake up calls now occupies. I thank you all most earnestly from the bottom of my heart.

For their valuable support – financial, textual, moral and other – my genuine gratitude to the following:

Mike Dodd, Hans Richter, Tracey Amhoff, Teddy Goldsmith, Jean Schulz, Nicholas Evans, Zac Goldsmith, Andy Rees, Roger Pull, Ian Forster, Del Eberhardt, Carole Jones, Michael Henry – and in particular, Helen de Castres for offering her original iconic female sculpture to be used as the image on the cover.

My lasting respect and devotion to **Book Guild** for their humanitarian approach to running a publishing company. In light of their consistent kindness and integrity, they have been a genuine pleasure to work with – all the more so because of their location in *green* and enlightened Brighton.

INTRODUCTION

Karen Eberhardt Shelton

What, how, why, where, when … To me, them, whom, what, it, they, them, us we, you, ours, everybody, *everything, everywhere, all …*

What's to save? Why women?

Usually the idea for a book is sparked by something timely or ungodly or unearthly; an encounter, a sense of destiny, headlines, history, family trauma, or maybe just a reaction to a small and pertinent item that germinates in some unexpectedly fertile loam and starts growing.

I can't really remember where the idea to produce *A Women's Guide* originated—it probably formed as soon as humans started writing things down and passing along information about what they were doing, thinking, feeling, and in my own life has evolved into a certain side-stepping of men born of a weariness and frustration about how it has all been going for the past 10,000 years or so. As Archbishop Desmond Tutu put it: 'We men have had our turn and made a proper mess of things. We need women to save us.'

By telling their stories, women can make a difference. Columnist Libby Purves declared in one of her columns: 'Humans need stories. Statistics bore us, generalizations offend, social science irritates by reducing our lives to formulae. Only stories connect with universal instincts, and to make a story, you need individual lives. True or fictional, history or myth, we crave the personal.'

I've been a reader, explorer and storyteller since childhood, and wish at some point I'd also studied history and some of the sciences in which you learn about cells, genes, DNA—the stuff of all life. I've been a Quaker too, a lover of animals, and someone who put her palms on the altar of earth and said, 'I accept—without you, there is no me.'

And now, as a mature and experienced woman, I find it harder than ever to continually be reminded about invaders, inventors, rulers, warriors, kings, heathens, jailers, theologians, inquisitioners, judges, bosses, chairmen, presidents, scholars, philosophers—99 per cent of them men—methodically prodding me to reflect on why the world is the way it is. After September 11 in the USA when Bush and Blair subsequently

1

launched a major weapons flyby against Iraq, I felt a profound sense of *Dear God, is this never going to end?* It should, it must! Why doesn't it? What *can* we do to make a difference, interfere, change course, challenge dogma and the status quo, effect a positive outcome?

I think of women throughout recorded time who have made a difference—Boadicea, Hildegard von Bingen, Joan of Arc, Florence Nightingale, Indira Gandhi, Helen Caldicott, Mother Teresa, Jane Austen, George Eliot, Annie Besant, Madame Curie, Marie Stopes, Anne Frank, Eleanor Roosevelt, Queens Elizabeth I and Victoria, Edith Cavell, Catherine of Sienna, Amelia Earhart, Helen Keller, Arundhati Roy, Aung San Suu Kyi, Wangari Maathai—I can think of only a few historically great women—small names, big names—but not many of them, and so few in relation to men. Women have mostly stayed at home—pregnant, cooking, washing, minding … And when they've found a way to speak up, aside from that riveting few, it has mostly been with subtle strokes and guarded effort.

One of my primary concerns is the vast size of the human population; try working with a group of 15 students, then expand the classroom to 40, and see the difference. A village of 2,000 manages beautifully, but cities of 100,000 and more fray along the seams. A world of 2 billion might be manageable; enlarge it to 6 billion plus, and it becomes a scene of out-of-control lemmings.

If you think you can take your next breath without the natural world, you're deluded. If the solitary individual speaks up, we'll never listen. But if many voices are raised, a pondering pause ensues. I don't expect this book to change the course of history, but in my sorrowful, worried, loving, observant interior, I must do my tiny part to make a difference, and this book is that gesture. Don't mock the power of women who cry from the heart. Each little message here carries a seed that can be planted, nurtured, spread, enlarged, repeated … *infinitesimal increment*. We are the grains of sand that build the contours of a fresh new beach.

In everyday terms, there's a frightening poverty of awareness, a clamp on human potential—we're being strangled into silence and compliance by a system that withholds freedom of thought. We are constantly *self-referencing*, thinking primarily in human terms of what's best for *me*, my wants and needs, instead of taking into account the interconnectedness of all life and the needs of everything around us. Consequently, I've invested in this project as a way to draw out ideas and beliefs based on a concern for action and change, a sort of *what I would do, what we can do … this and this*. I approached women across the board and asked them to invent personal narrations describing what they would change, what they see as remedies, what they want to happen—in terms of *saving the world*, turning around our downward slide toward environmental and cultural catastrophe. The question I asked these women to address was, '*If I could wave a magic wand and make the world a better place, and offer that wand to other women to do the same, what might come of it all*'? I asked each participant to be as specific as possible about how, what, why … '*I want to see food produced as locally as possible in this way and for that reason—NOT doing this is screwing up the world because …*' in the most impassioned, immediate, personal, and colloquial way they could muster. 'Please,' I pleaded, 'avoid formality.' (Although, as it turned out this wasn't avoidable in every case.)

'Please,' I implored, 'write as if your heart is bursting, and you're talking to a society that hasn't yet caught on'—which it hasn't, or there'd be no need for such a book. If each contributor grasped the extent of the need for 'saving the world', she'd see why adding a dose of her own medicine (as part of the solution, not the problem) could be of benefit. Solutions and antidotes need to reach the Mainstream where they'll have a chance to influence ordinary people and nudge them toward restorative and life-enhancing behaviour.

I continued: 'If you have a major concern, it's important to share that with others. (I call it, simply, Speaking Up.) Describe what your heart knows; let it burst into flame. Pretend you're Joan of Arc tied to the stake, faggots piled around you ready to be lit. You'll be cinders soon; this is your last chance to Speak Up, raise your voice, make a plea for common sense. What final words would you utter? Why don't more of us feel a sense of urgency about how we live, where we're all headed? There are *so many* wrongs, so many failings—a brown cloud of pollution which can be seen from space, covering the whole of Asia. Why? Because humans build dams and roads and houses and more humans, with never a care for the "others". Speak up for all the others! Reflect on how globalisation is affecting the world. "As we pursue our own needs because we can do it, everything else around us takes a hit." Sold down the dead river. (Brian Clarke, *The Stream*, winner of the BP Natural World Book Prize). Why accept? Let's rebel! It doesn't wash to busy ourselves with the "usual stuff"—the need to deliberate on what we can say or do that will effect a positive outcome is too urgent. As women with a huge investment in the future, we can pull together and make a statement—add to the debate, encourage debate, *force* debate, and like Arundhati Roy in India who

3

spoke up and risked imprisonment as the alternative to being "silenced", we too can be vocal.'

So please, read on. Search your soul, check your priorities, ask yourself where your commitments lie in relation to sharing one small, finite planet with everything that lives. What would *you* speak up for? *What* would you change, *why* would it be a good thing, *how* would it work, *what* difference would it make, *who* or what would benefit? Share it with your family, your neighbours, your MP. Live your own story about how you'd fix the world; do what your *heart* knows, share concerns about issues that are eternal. Reach out simply and directly, treat the rest of your life as a unique opportunity to lay your convictions on the line. If *you* don't speak up, who will? Help create a compendium for a shift in outlook and attitude; write out your recipe for healing—now—don't put it off till tomorrow. By the time this book is in print, the earth and its cargo will have suffered further insults/assaults. Global Warming may have increased by another degree. Speaking up is one way to proclaim that we do not see the world as a machine to be dominated, but rather that we are part of nature, not separate from it, and it's complete insanity to kill the earthly components our lives depend on. And finally, without cooperation we cannot survive. Let this book serve as a testimonial to our common commitment to honour the Life Force binding together all of creation.

If you know of someone who is on fire with a 'cause' and might want to form a community of like-minded women, get in touch with her, talk to anybody who will listen. Make time to address your priorities—because you care. Eventually, why not cards, a calendar, posters, talk shows? Let us set in motion the Hundredth Monkey Syndrome! And to celebrate, have a big party on your village green. Now, go out and create some ripples!

Karen Eberhardt Shelton

A bit about me: I grew up in California, went to school in England, travelled the world. I come from a Quaker/activist background, have responded to 'causes' my entire life. In 1989 I lived with my daughter in Sussex, and in 1999 moved permanently to England, kept house in Somerset for nearly four years, and for three of them wrote a total of ten stories a month for the *Western Daily Press* in Bristol and the *Mid Somerset Times* in Wells, plus occasional pieces for other publications. In

2002, *The Message* came out—a book of poetry by myself and Jay Ramsay. I've always been a writer, poet and photographer and during lengthy sojourns in Australia, New Zealand, India, Switzerland, both the east and west coasts of America, and elsewhere, have focused my literary skills on the need for co-existence with this finite environment. After 9/11 (when I worried that maybe my father and his wife had perished in New York), I decided to compile a list of messages, a book made up of the concerns and considerations of other women who, like myself, are deeply aware of the interconnectedness of all living things and worried that we are running out of time. Women who, along with Pulitzer Prize winner Edward O. Wilson, are attuned to the Gaia notion of earth as a single organism, and similarly feel that 'what humanity is inflicting on itself and Earth is a result of a mistake in capital investment … we expect progressively increasing payouts from a finite resource that is being decapitalised by over-harvesting and environmental destruction … Why, our descendents will ask, by needlessly extinguishing the lives of other species, did we permanently impoverish our own?'

ONE WOMAN'S VIEW

Susana Ager

Susana lives in Somerset and takes in rescue birds and other animals

I do believe it is important for our survival that we nurture animals and plants. The loss of just one species upsets the balance of nature. Today, far too many plants and animals have disappeared because of man's negligence. It is too late for this generation to change their ways, so it is up to us to teach the next generation of the importance of such nurture. For this, a review of what we teach children in school needs to be undertaken.

Too many myths from the past are perpetuated. For example, the old view is that the fox kills just for the sake of it. So he deserves vilification and death. If you needed food and lived from one meal to the next, when a surplus presented itself, would you take just one item from the supermarket shelf? No, you would think of the future and the next few meals, and stock accordingly. So does the fox when he culls all in the hen house, hoping to have enough time to carry his booty away and bury it for another day to feed his family. Too often human morality is imposed on animals. The dog that bites does not do so out of spite but most probably out of fear because he has not been handled with compassion.

Children need to be taught how to live, how to make the best use of the food that is produced using simple skills in cookery, boys as well as girls. This was once routinely taught in school, but has now mostly been abandoned in favour of other more trendy subjects. Too often, in schools it is the academic child who is most valued, but it is the practical aspects of life that are more important than academic achievement. Footballers, pop stars and film stars are increasingly hero-worshipped as those who our children aspire to be like.

We must stop and think and take stock about what we are doing. The supermarket shelves are bursting with goods, so much junk food—too much ever to use, which means much must go into landfill. There are fruit and vegetables out of season, most available all year round and coming in by plane from all corners of the world. At what cost! I know from my own garden that fruit and vegetables picked in season taste so much better. Peaches and melons picked before they are ripe and stored in gas to delay the process of ripening often just taste of cotton wool. We deprive people in the Third World who should be growing crops for themselves, not luxury items for the greedy western world.

This year I am very conscious for the first time I can ever remember that I have not seen a single wasp on the plums and apples in the garden. What has happened to them? They do so much good at the beginning of the growing year, with pollination and eating various destructive insects. I wonder what the consequences will be for us next year!

Energy must be conserved. The *few* are taking more than their fair share. We seem incapable of sharing fairly. It is so sad, when we live in such a wonderful world, surrounded by the beauty of plants and animals. The skill and expertise of so many people can be breathtaking. People are amazingly clever, but then there is the dark side; the poverty, war, death and destruction, the opposite side of the same coin.

Why must the human race be so destructive? Even our religions speak of kindness and tolerance but often show the opposite. Most people want to conserve our plants and animals—it is just a small minority who could not care less and an even smaller minority who have the means or the power to change things for better or worse. It is said 'what goes around comes around' and that 'evil gets its just desserts', but sadly, it is the bad who often prosper and the good who struggle to survive.

We waste a huge amount of time being negative, fighting over land or over control of each other. In the long run, we own nothing. Everything we have is on loan for, at most, only as long as we live. That lovely piece of furniture or beautiful house and garden is ours to nurture for a relatively short time. Why can't we make the most of the time we have by not spoiling our earthly home?

How do we change the world? I'm not optimistic, but how can it happen unless we change our attitudes? It must be up to parents and teachers to educate our children, to help them understand what a wonderful world we live in. It is incumbent upon us to protect and nurture plants, animals and the environment. If we do not do this, we will be the losers, and in the end, we too will become extinct.

FINDING FREEDOM

Thea Anderson

Thea is 27 and was brought up in Leicestershire and now lives in Brighton.

Here are my thoughts on saving the world!

When I look around, I see us, in our western world, living under so much *pressure*. I want to scream, 'Look at what we're doing to ourselves!!' We're causing ourselves so much unnecessary misery, suffering and even death. And all I believe we could do with is a little more awareness. I would like us to throw away what isn't helping us any more and find our freedom.

First, there's the baggage we're carrying around from childhood: our survival patterns. I reckon, from taking a good long look at myself and talking to others, that there are so many ways we all behave, think and feel, and pressures that we put upon ourselves that are caused by these. I think when we start looking we'll find patterns of behaviour we have copied from our parents and possibly parts of ourselves we have denied for them (even if we've had a wonderful childhood). All to ensure their love—to ensure our survival. And sure, it can be complicated and this stuff is often subtle and buried in the unconscious … I'm not saying it's going to be easy, but it's *so* worth it! If some of who we are is governed by these potent, old lessons, then to look at them, become more aware of them, can give us so much of our power back. We can then decide, as adults, whether or not we want to feel or behave in such a way any more and this is so liberating. I had learned to live in my head, not to trust my emotions, and also, as is the case with many women, to *give* regardless of my needs or reserves. All this resulted in pressure, stress and illness. And this is the misery and suffering I am talking about which manifests in countless ways for countless people. I am learning to trust my feelings as a source of guidance, and to listen to my needs. There are many types of therapy now to suit all.

So, it's about freedom. Freedom also from external pressure; the demands our society makes on us. They too are so many and sometimes subtle: 'work harder', 'earn more money', 'look sexy' and 'practise twenty different sexual positions a week!!' The pressure is definitely on us

9

all but I feel that it's particularly on women and the message is clear: that we are not innately perfect and must beautify every inch of our bodies. It's powerful stuff, tapping into our insecurities. But in reality it is just companies trying to sell to us and we don't particularly need a different type of shampoo for every season. In fact, they need us more than we need them. There is nothing wrong with caring about your appearance, but I think we've gone past that and created stress, debt and disease. I would love us all to maintain our awareness and make decisions based on the fact that we know each advert is competing for our cash: to think about it and question (something I don't think we are taught much about in school).

I feel there is so much about being a woman that is shamed: our bodies, our emotional intelligence, intuition, sometimes even compassion, and certainly the wisdom inherent in age. Adverts tell us that periods are unclean, but ancient cultures worshipped this as women's power time. I would love for women to be able to come together and give each other support to explore new ways. And whilst we (men and women) strive to be all we are told we *should* be, what happens to those other parts of us? Well, there is no *should*! What if we begin to believe we're free to express ourselves in any way that is right for us, even against our conditioning? We can begin to live without these pressures and stop trying to please and fit in with our internalised parents, peers and society. I really feel that if we begin to realise that many of these pressures aren't real, then we can begin to really live our potential. I am sure we all have a wealth of hidden talents and abilities. I also know that we all know what is right for us; we've just forgotten to listen. We have the right to find, own, honour and express our unique voice. And we will survive (against our greatest fears). The irony is that it's our survival patterns and programming that are killing us. It's going to take some courage but I have no doubt that we can do it.

CHANGING THE WORLD BEGINS AT HOME

Judy Baker

Judy, who recently moved to California, does art therapy and clinical psychology

How would I make the world a better place? I have so many concerns that I don't know where to begin—chemical farming, genetically modified foods, the poisoning of our water, animal cloning, rote learning, fee-based recreation on our public land, scraping and scouring the earth to make way for roads and housing developments. I read through this list and weep, while inside I'm screaming! It all feels so *huge* and out of control. I ask myself, *what bit of good can the action of one little me make in turning the tide, in bringing insight and compassion into big government and corporate business, who seem to be in charge of it all?*

Yet, that's just it! What I do, that one little me, *can* make a huge difference because of the ripple effect of taking action, as in the 'hundredth monkey' theory, where just 1% of the population of the earth can tip the scales toward positive change.

Two groups which give me great hope for a more sustainable future and concrete methods of how to live more sanely are the Bioneers (www.bioneers.org) and the Cohousing Network (www.cohousing.org). Both are groups of people with great vision who honour the earth and humanity so deeply that they work together to find ways to live more gently, tread lightly and use resources sparingly and creatively. Groups of scientists within the Bioneers organisation develop new systems for biodiversity in farming, permaculture principles for water harvesting and conservation, revitalise habitats for wildlife, and clean extremely polluted waterways. Cohousing groups create villages where people of all ages share skills, tools and resources on as little land as possible, maintaining large shared green spaces for recreation and gardening.

These two groups have provided me with great inspiration for altering my own way of living. They remind me that solving big problems can happen when like-minded people come together. Their actions and intentions create that wave of momentum that ripples out into the world, leaving change for the better in its wake.

In our own household, we have begun by eliminating all toxic substances for cleaning and garden care. We recycle diligently, down to the smallest scrap of paper. Kitchen waste becomes compost for the garden. We have begun vermiculture (worm composting) to increase the number of earthworms that go into our small vegetable garden. Herbal plants are scattered throughout for both cooking use and food sources for birds and butterflies. Our entire landscape is drought tolerant and wildlife friendly.

This past summer we developed parts of that landscape with permaculture principles in order to harvest much-needed rainwater runoff in order to cut down on supplemental irrigation in this arid, high-desert region of Arizona.

As much as possible, we purchase clothing, household goods and materials that have been recycled, eliminating our total dependence on new items, and helping reduce the glut of consumer goods, which take precious resources to manufacture. All appliances in our home are energy efficient, not only to reduce our utility bill, but also so we'll know we are taking less from the environment to produce that energy.

We support organic foods and humane animal treatment by purchasing organic fruits and vegetables, hormone- and antibiotic-free dairy products, eggs and poultry, and buying from local farmers as often as possible.

Though we do not currently live in a co-housing community, we fully support the concept and envision a time when we will either join or help transform an existing residential city block into a co-housing community modelled after the N Street Cohousing Group in Davis, California. There, all the fences were removed in order to join the backyards into one large shared green where children play and neighbours share tools and meet for spontaneous conversation. Together they purchased a house at the end of the block to turn into a common house where they have group dinners and take turns doing the cooking, and where the children play games, guests have a place to stay, and someone is always available to keep an eye on the children.

Our intentions, values and resources are shared with our own small community of friends, who then share with *their* family and friends, and so on. The ripples move out into the world. For my own part, I am now beginning to teach these values to my three-year-old granddaughter so that she will continue to expand the ripples through her generation. Changing the world is not a one-time event, but rather an ongoing process of bringing what is out of balance back into equilibrium. My contribution begins with creating that balance in my own beliefs, intentions and actions, and sharing those with everyone who comes into my life.

ON THE TRANSFORMATIVE
POWERS OF MUSIC

Elizabeth Jane Baldry

Elizabeth is a professional harpist and filmmaker who lives in Devon

Once upon a time in my childhood, I was crossing a field in a car driven by my father. My little brother was playing in the field, which happened to be the home of an enormous white bull. A chirpy little lad, my brother decided it would be a joke if he started waving and laughing at the bull. With gut-wrenching horror, I watched as the bull turned to observe him, and then, irritated by his manic behaviour, began to paw the ground and lower his head ready to charge. With complete presence of mind, my father leapt heroically out of the car onto the roof. In a huge, powerful and magnificent voice he began to sing that old patriotic hymn, 'Land of Hope and Glory'. The bull paused, turned away from my brother and looked at my father. For a heart-stopping few seconds, he just looked and listened to the singing. Then he seemed to shake his head in disbelief as if to say, 'What crazy creatures these humans are,' and proceeded to eat grass, as calm as a lamb.

This was my first memory of the mighty power of music to change and transform. Now that I am a grown woman with sons of my own, I find myself earning a living as a classical musician, a harpist in fact. I was drawn to it from an early age; its sound uplifted my spirit and called to me. On a daily basis I witness the power of music to transform and heal the human spirit.

We all know the ecological destruction facing our precious world today. It's not the world at fault. This is a human crisis. The dualistic thinking rooted in our western culture is to blame. We think of man and nature, instead of embracing nature as part of ourselves. We have God separate from man and earth, instead of honouring the goodness—the divine spark if you like—within the human heart, alongside reverence for nature. If, as indigenous people still do, we embraced reverence for the balance of nature, and saw the divine within every rock, every blade of grass, every contour of the land and meandering of a river, we would not violate that divinity. Whatever one's personal belief system, the religious impulse is a fact of human psychology. When that impulse is directed to an external God, we cease to view nature, including mankind, with reverence. We exploit our fellow human beings and desecrate the earth. This is what I mean by dualistic thinking.

So what has this got to do with music? In my performing life, I continually hear lamentations of regret by people who proclaim they are tone deaf, they would love to play a musical instrument or sing, but fate has been unkind to them. This is also a symptom of dualistic thinking. It is the artist versus everyone else, the musician or artist as somehow special or different. The erroneous belief that creative people are in a separate category to the rest of the human race is a bitter tragedy resulting in countless unfulfilled lives. I have seen completely tone-deaf people, even late in a hard life, develop musicality. I absolutely know from empirical observation that we are all artists, all musicians. Music is laid down within the mechanics of the brain as we are formed in the womb. Cave paintings dating back 40,000 years show Palaeolithic man enjoying music. Music is our fundamental nature. I am a musician, and so are you.

I am a great lover of myth, and amongst my favourite creation myths are those where the entire world is sung into existence. Our forefathers who created these myths showed an intuitive understanding of the harmony and balance of nature and the profound significance of music. Aboriginal tribes even have melodies dictated by the contours of the land. All of nature is simply energy in harmony, rhythm and balance. Music is sound waves in harmony, rhythm and balance. There is a connection between the music in ourselves and the harmony of the world. The entire universe is one great song—a uni-verse. The earth suffers from our ignorant misunderstanding—we have created the chaotic poisoned world in which we now have to live, but we can heal it. We need only heal the lack of harmony within ourselves.

Music is the fastest way to healing; it expresses emotions impossible to put into words. We bury the dead, we get married, we lull a baby to sleep with music. Music profoundly connects people when they play or sing together. Music is the most potent tool we have in our passion to heal the world. Although I am myself a harpist and have had the opportunity to observe the legendary healing powers of the harp recorded throughout human history, I recognise its impracticality—it is an expensive instrument requiring years of devoted study. What we need for our healing is an instrument that is portable and completely free. We all carry this instrument with us throughout every day of our lives—it is the human voice. The vibrations set up within our bodies as we sing can be scientifically measured. As we sing, we shift old stuck patterns within us, blow away the cobwebs, raise our spirits. *Who has not felt the joy of community singing? When we look back on an age before the ubiquitous wallpaper of muzak, we see electrifying working songs, especially amongst women as they weave, spin, sow the seeds and reap the crops. This was before the disabling concept of the musician as somehow apart from the common man. Once upon a time we all sang without inhibition. Some anthropologists even believe that man was singing before he developed speech, because the singing voice travels over larger distances than the spoken voice.*

I have a fantasy in which world leaders from countries in conflict come together and sing prior to their diplomatic negotiations. How much more effective would this small act of co-creation make their life-and-death discussions, once they had experienced the intimacy that sharing music creates! Political leaders unable to participate should arouse our suspicions. Shakespeare wrote:

> The man that hath no music in himself,
> Nor is not moved by concord of sweet sounds,
> Is fit for treasons, stratagems, and spoils;
> The motions of his spirit are as dull as night,
> And his affections as dark as Erebus:
> Let no such man be trusted.

Imagine if the President of the United States spent time with rainforest tribes, singing to their babies. How soon would he use the vast powers at his command to prevent the desecration of the forests to raise cattle for beefburgers? Imagine if the owners of child slave labour factories in the Third World sang nursery rhymes to their little workers. How quickly would they connect to those children and improve their nightmarish working conditions? Imagine if, as in Plato's time, music was absolutely central to our education systems as well as our everyday lives, celebrated as the core of human wellness instead of a pleasant extra for the better-off.

Surely nothing else could so lift us above the pathetic accumulation of material objects and the need for power. All this I know is currently unrealistic, but every one of us can begin to sing around our houses, in the car with our families and as we stand in bus queues. I sang when I was in labour and it eased the birth. We can sing vibrant songs to the mountains, deep groaning songs when we are in pain. All around us we see the advancing monster of world destruction, but through music, we can stop that charging bull, and sing the world back to health.

HOW TO BE A CITIZEN IN THE TWENTY-FIRST CENTURY

Elise Boulding

Elise is a peace activist who lives in Needham, Massachusetts

Do you love Gaia, this planet we live on? Of course you do! We all love our planet, but we know so little about it. There are six billion of us humans living in ten thousand societies,[1] each with its own history and way of doing things. We each speak one of five thousand languages. We are penned up in one of the 190 states that keep us from moving around as freely as we might like. Most of us know little about all the other life forms that crawl, walk, swim, fly or stay rooted in the earth.

And just think, no two of us are alike. Each of us hears, sees and experiences the planet differently. That difference is important—we all need space to be whom and what we are. But we all need other humans, need someone to care about and help, someone who cares about and helps us. We can't go it alone! As the Earth Charter,[2] which I hope you have all signed, says, *all life is interdependent in Gaia*. We are one body.

Yet humans sometimes get to fighting over their different needs. Fortunately, through most of history the story has been one of learning to deal with such differences through cooperation and negotiation. But now we are in serious trouble. Our species has reached a stage of development in which we have generated complex national and international socio-economic and political structures with super-sophisticated technologies for fighting destructive warfare, but woefully inadequate means for cooperative problem-solving.

That is why, over fifty years ago, something new came into being: the United Nations. It was founded by 'we the peoples of the united nations determined to save succeeding generations from the scourge of war'.[3] Note that the United Nations was not founded by *states* but by *peoples*. That includes you and me. But in fact, the UN charter was signed by states, and today the UN is run by states that vary widely in the extent to which they are willing to engage in the kind of cooperative problem-solving necessary to deal with their serious differences.

While creative social technologies of peacemaking to resolve differences, and particularly conflict transformation, have developed to the point where complete disarmament should be possible, some states have preferred to concentrate on military technologies and to rely on force to preserve what they perceive as their national interests. These states don't like to sign treaties limiting their freedom of action.

How can the UN get back on track, empowered to end the scourge of war? Why not claim our citizenship in the UN itself, as 'we the peoples'? This involves a new model of citizenship still rooted in love and loyalty and a sense of civic responsibility, but also taking into account three important levels of participation in our complex modern world.

It begins locally with participation in one's own community, one's own ethnic group or culture among ten thousand societies. At the next level, that love, loyalty and sense of civic responsibility extends to all those who live within the borders of one's own country. It resonates in the symbols of citizenship—the flags, the Constitution, and the institutions and processes of government of one's country. But it also values and embraces the entire sister entities within the borders of the country.[4]

At the next level, that love, loyalty and sense of civic responsibility one feels for one's own country and its entities needs to be extended to the UN itself with its 190 states and six billion people.

This third level of citizenship—our UN citizenship—has got to be recognised and explored. It is *terra incognita* for all of us. Yet given that states are reluctant to sign treaties limiting their powers to make war and their ability to exploit the planet in the national interest, our survival may depend on activating the citizenship implicit in the words used in the founding charter of the UN: 'we the peoples'.

What weaves the local, national, and United Nations dimensions of our citizenship together in a common fabric is the existence of 25,000 international non-governmental organisations (INGOs). These organisations bring concerns for peace, justice, humans rights and the environment from all our local NGO chapters to the national and the United Nations level. There are specific access points for INGOs at the United Nations, especially during General Assembly sessions and at conferences and commissions and hearings on critical world issues.

These INGOs were a new happening of the twentieth century and are still in a development mode in the twenty-first. International INGO offices are still learning to relate to local situations; figuring out how to learn from locals; and developing methods to learn from and cooperate with each other in the still-new action sphere of international non-governmental bodies. This is all part of a wider learning process as the new concept of citizenship evolves.

An important aspect of learning how to exercise this new citizenship involves overcoming a vast public ignorance about the United Nations that exists in every country. Within the United States, the concept of a national citizenship, encompassing active awareness of the diversity of people's needs, already requires a major new educational effort. The added challenge of learning how to work within the United Nations is daunting to say the least. But if we want to enable the development of a workable United Nations system of governance to solve the many types of economic, cultural and environmental conflicts already being faced within the international community of states, we have no alternative.

The UN itself tries hard to educate its world citizens about the extraordinary diversity of this world, as well as the functions of the UN itself. The programme of the *United Nations Years and Decades* declared by the United Nations General Assembly creates the occasion and materials for learning more about our diversity. The years 1993 to 2003 represented the third Decade to Combat Racism and Racial Discrimination; 1994 to 2004 was the International Decade of the World's Indigenous Peoples; 2001 to 2010 is the International Decade for a Culture of Peace and Non-violence for the Children of the World; 2001 was the Year of Dialogue Among Civilizations; 2002 was the International Year of Mountains. Each of these year-long or decade-long projects (many are not listed here) established by the UN were intended to educate and mobilise the peoples of the UN to work on these world problems. Each offered wonderful opportunities to activate our citizenship in the UN by developing local versions of these projects in our own communities.

The current Culture Of Peace Decade offers the best alternative to the 'war on terrorism' approach to non-state violence. It can be taken as an invitation to young people (and to mid-career people as well) to actively take up UN citizenship. Service in the UN volunteers programme can involve participation in UN peace-building activities around the world. Here is a way for young people to learn about the rich diversity of lifeways and languages around the planet; to explore the poetry and music and dance of human life; to thrill to the biodiversity of the rivers, mountains, valleys and oceans, the deserts and the plains—in short, to fall in love with the world that so badly needs loving.

If our young people are to grow up to be active UN citizens, they need to know how the UN works. We are all so ignorant about this critically important body! When I was in high school (back in the mid 1930s), every graduating senior had to take a course in Problems in American

Democracy. Now we should be instituting a course for graduating seniors in Problems In United Nations Democracy—with special community-based adult education courses on the same subject. Just getting the hang of the structure is important.

What does the UN system consist of? Six major United Nations operating organs, thirteen associated bodies, sixteen specialised agencies, five regional commissions, and fluctuating numbers of peace-keeping and observer missions, as well as twenty research institutes, other divisions and special programmes which continually evolve to meet new needs in various parts of the world. There are also two United Nations universities (one in Japan, one in Costa Rica), and about fifty worldwide Information Centers, plus special offices where field programmes are located. The research institutes publish their own newsletters and research reports.

What a difference it could make if all disarmament activists read reports of the United Nations Institute of Disarmament Research (UNIDIR). Suppose development activists all read reports of the United Nations Research Institute on Social Development (UNRISD). These are just two valuable United Nations research bodies. It is a tragedy that all the creativity and problem-solving activity that goes on in the United Nations is unknown to most civic activists, while the inevitable bureaucratic inefficiency is more highly publicised. So many missed opportunities for support of important peace, human rights, development and environmental initiatives that, if carried out, would make the United Nations a more effective body! Also, we should all be reading the quarterly *UN Chronicle* published especially to help 'we the peoples' to know 'what's going on'.[5]

There are many ways to work for peace, and each of us must choose the peace-making path we personally will walk. Personal commitment needs emotional involvement. If we can draw on our love of community in developing a more inclusive love of country, and our love of country in developing a more inclusive love of the multi-state United Nations, then we can indeed become very worthy citizens of this beautiful planet that is our home. We can be working each in our own way through the networks available to us to make that planet a 'homestead of peace',[6] as the teaching of all the world's faiths ask us to do.

Notes

1. The 'ten thousand societies' is the term referring to the existence of thousands of ethnic groups around the world. The term sometimes appears in UNESCO publications.
2. The Earth Charter is a declaration of fundamental principles for building a peaceful global society, with special emphasis on the environment. The Earth Charter Initiative collected signatures of individuals from around the world and was presented to the United Nations General Assembly in 2002. You can contact the Earth Charter secretariat at P.O. Box 319–6100 San Jose, Costa Rica; website: http://www.earthcharter.org
3. These are the opening words of the United Nations founding charter.
4. Ethnies are identity groups sharing a common culture, language and history.
5. The *UN Chronicle* is published by the UN Department of Public Information. Request subscriptions from UN publications, room D G 2–0853, New York, NY 10017.
6. 'Homestead of peace' is a term from the Koran.

IT'S DRIVING ME CRAZY!

Irena Basham

*Irena is of Polish origin and lives near Bristol, where she works for
Triodos Bank*

Va va voom. Vorsprung durch technik! Marketing expensive cars for TV
ads is very powerful. We see young men drool longingly at top-of-the-
range sports cars, sometimes with scantily clad women lying seductively
across bonnets as they walk or drive by. Settle down for an evening's TV
viewing and I can virtually guarantee you will see at least one sizzling ad
for the next top-of-the-range motor vehicle.

Yes, I understand the need to have cars for family transport, outings,
out-of-town shopping malls and supermarkets, but I ask myself, why on
earth do we need to see, almost on a daily basis, an ad telling us why we
absolutely should buy this or that car?

Of course I am pleased to live in a free country and appreciate the good
lifestyle we have, but it infuriates me that not one car manufacturer
advertises its vehicle as being 'eco-friendly', or encourages drivers to use
premium petrol or diesel to help alleviate the pollution constantly being
spewed out by exhaust pipes. (Although this is now changing.)

Why doesn't the government use its marketing skills to encourage
people to cycle more, walk children to schools, shop locally instead of
patronising huge supermarkets—to try to regain something we have lost
in our communities? What is the point of local councils threatening to
install car tolls in town centres and widen roads (particularly motorways),
when all they have to do is develop a more user-friendly bus and tram
service—preferably trams, as they don't pollute the air the same way
buses do? I have seen trams function successfully in Sheffield and Leeds,
so cannot understand why Bristol, the city I live in, still doesn't have any.

Yes, I feel hypocritical when I drive to work. It's a 10 mile journey each
day, but I try to do my bit by filling up with cleaner petrol each time my
tank runs dry, at a cost of perhaps £1.50 extra. I don't feel the need to keep
changing and upgrading my car for a newer model.

We all know there are far too many cars on the roads. Some families
with four or five members have the same number of cars parked outside
their homes. So my argument is this: If car manufacturers spent more time

on producing cleaner cars and the government put restrictions on their advertising, as the years go by, the air would become cleaner, people wouldn't be quite so materialistic and maybe we'd all become more aware of what damage cars do to our environment. I'm sure we'd all feel better breathing cleaner air and into the bargain, we wouldn't feel so powerless and duped at the hands of all that clever advertising.

A VIEW FROM THE SOUTH

Margarita Marino de Botero

Margarita lives in Colombia, South America, developed the Green Campaign, and is a consultant for the UN environment programme

It is not easy to think of how to improve things in the world, as I had never paused to think about what inspires the lives of some who dedicate long hours and sleepless nights to reflection and how to work for other lives and life itself.

Taking a good look around us, we see images of solidarity and pictures of the vigorous and intense beauty of the work of humankind everywhere. We live among millions of marvellous initiatives and acts of love, fervour, and tenderness for humans and nature, even though often these acts are not known or acknowledged by our nations or societies. Political grandeur does not portray the work of contemporary diversity, different modes of feeling and thought, and people all over the world whose task is mainly to survive. Political power certainly pays no attention to the enormous inequalities of humankind.

The media pays more attention to triviality than to observing the day-to-day existence of many women who are neglected in their dignity and the formidable contribution of their lives to put their best endeavours to work for peace and prosperity. Their striving to speak up and have the option of making a difference is a mountainous effort in a world where these acts are so poorly recognised by societies.

Many of our efforts aim to promote the intense trust we put in the labour of humankind as it struggles among situations of poverty and deprivation; we try to defend the cultural luminosity embedded in its myriad visions, in its local work and community knowledge.

A Women's Guide to Saving the World is meant to be a way to enrich our world with thoughts, words and deeds—to learn how to look at the work of others, to change humanity's attitude towards nature so there is respect for all species—to create a human chain of solidarity. To not be disheartened by the images of horror, famine, and harsh injustices in everyday life, everywhere.

We and other millions of people have not yet found the words or learned how to express all the anger and fury over the situation of permanent disregard for justice and equality shown by governments and leaders. But if we don't *speak up*, who will? Words we do use are so often said and lost in the air. Maybe this time something will happen differently.

What stimulates people to dedicate their best faculties to the repair of daily injustices? Why expect to accomplish some good among millions of people? Why devote oneself to the spirit of truth in order to develop a higher consciousness within the intellectual and spiritual possibilities of humankind? Why strive for hope in the midst of chaos? From whom will come the inspirations and highest dreams, and why this eagerness to inspire future generations?

We may not know much, but deep inside we sense that the best counsel is in learning to see deeply into nature, and to culture harmony, joy and splendid beauty. We sense that having a life purpose is a gift of nature and the power of thoughts and ideas is the only long-lasting power. We are what we dream we can accomplish, and that reflects on what we do with our lives.

The best advice is to never limit your aspirations for the justice of humankind and always hunt for humanity's best qualities and values. The finest recipe I know involves learning to see honesty and beauty in acts of solidarity all around us, even when they're invisible to others. A recipe for healing lies in living to understand and to develop a sense of observation and care.

Women are at their best when their hearts aren't compromised in their work for others. Nothing ever worked that is not full of honesty and enthusiasm. Never tire of repeating the truth. A task left *unfinished* is the best call for a new enterprise to be tried. Overcoming obstacles with a smile means learning to find understanding, strength and the power of sharing happiness when encountering good deeds.

Certainly something must be done to change us for the better. The best approach is to increase awareness of acts of human rationality. We need to value all knowledge, keep away from all dogma and *specific* systems of knowledge that filter out wholeness. We need to feel content in our understanding of other people's understanding and others' thoughts and feelings. Everyone can be an educator of some kind, an artist, a creator of good, can find a way to open space for this to happen. This is within the power of every human, and in the end, is greater than any material richness.

Women from the beginning have had a leadership role in the environmental movement. Perhaps this is due to the fact that no one else can perform a caring act like a caring woman. Now let us all *care* as one!

TREAD LIGHTLY

Rosie Boycott

Rosie is a writer and crusader for many causes, and has homes in London and Somerset

The study of climate change is advancing every minute and every minute we're learning new, scary facts about the changes happening to our planet. Those who deny climate change are shrinking in numbers as fast as the sea ice is melting.

I don't know if you've had a chance to read George Monbiot's latest book, *Heat*. In it he demolishes the claims made by 'deniers'. In a brilliant piece of investigative reporting, he sources all stories that say it isn't really so bad or maybe it's just due to normal fluctuations in climatic conditions—and goes back to one of the sources of the problem: Exxon Mobile. Monbiot explains how Exxon has paid for a variety of bogus scientific establishments to produce reports which skew the facts in the oil giant's favour, and he manages to source some of these false ideas back to the columns of journalists like Melanie Phillips on the *Daily Mail*.

A while ago, when I interviewed environmentalist James Lovelock at the Hay Festival, he said categorically it was 'too late', we'd already tipped over into a point of no return. Personally, I don't believe his level of fatalism any more than I believe there's nothing to be done.

According to the world meteorological organisation, '*The increase in temperature in the twentieth century is likely to have been the largest in any century during the past 1,000 years ... Carbon dioxide and methane in the atmosphere are higher than they've been for 650,000 years. Carbon dioxide levels have been rising faster over the past century than at any time in the past 20,000 years.*' The only means by which these greenhouse gases could have accumulated so quickly is through *human action*. Carbon dioxide is produced by burning oil, coal and gas and by clearing forests. Methane comes from farms, coal mines and landfill sites. Both these gases let in heat from the sun more easily than they let it out, and as their levels in the atmosphere increase, so the temperature rises. And this is having catastrophic effects on the planet.

Sea ice in the Arctic has shrunk to the smallest area ever recorded. Scientists watched the huge Larsen B ice shelf in the Antarctic collapse into the sea. Photographs from space show the disappearing ice, loss of forests, and huge dust storms being created in growing deserts. Pictures show creatures in the wild that are already disappearing and will probably become extinct in our time. Think of the polar bears without sea ice to save them from drowning. Rising sea levels are going to wipe out the homes of millions of people. Already, islands in the Indian and Pacific oceans are being evacuated and residents are having to abandon homes their forebears lived in—because of rising water. In Bangladesh, 15 million people live less than a metre above sea level; in India it's similar for another 8 million. These are poor people without support who will be forced to move to higher ground. Lovelock said too, '*Immigration is going to be one of the huge, early problems which no politician wants to look at. Where will all those people go? They can only head north.*' Many of the world's richest cities, from London to New York to Rotterdam will be affected too.

Climate change also has a bearing on the food supply. Farmers are having to adapt to new growing conditions, most of which lead to lower productivity. According to the United Nations, more refugees are fleeing because of environmental factors rather than the effects of war.

Changes are happening everywhere. Oceans are becoming more acid, coral reefs are dying, fishermen are finding warm-water fish in cool-water regions. Ocean currents are changing in ways that could mean the Gulf Stream might slow down or shut off altogether. New facts and data come in every day that reinforce the sense that we are running out of time. It's not just a 'scare' story any more. Unless we act quickly and with all seriousness, the world our children will inherit will be very different from the one we know now.

We have only ten or fifteen years to change our policies and put new technologies in place. If you're under thirty, why save for a pension? If you care for your children, stop driving 4×4s, stop jetting off to holiday homes on airlines offering flights for a fiver. If you're educated, aware, and you care, stop assuming things will be more or less the same fifty years from now.

The truth is, we cannot control climate change without *pain*. Any politician that says differently is lying. It's all very well to have a consensus to heal the planet, but climate change is so serious, long lasting and transnational, that in reality, no one leader or single country can tackle it. I'm afraid I don't trust politicians and what they say, especially since their words and actions show they're not doing anything like enough to tackle the issue. Why should airlines be exempt from paying tax or VAT on fuel, and also be exempt from the climate change levy? We *all* know that every single plane spews huge amounts of carbon into the atmosphere.

We all know it's not a just a matter of turning off the lights before we go to bed—we're past that, but sometimes when I listen to politicians speak, I'm amazed at the way they make it sound so easy. They're all living in the short term, worrying about their re-election chances rather than the long-term chances of the planet.

The trouble started a long time ago. In Genesis, the Bible says that God gave man the world and dominion over plants and animals and all that moves and breathes. Christian theology has supported, permitted and even encouraged wholesale exploitation and manipulation of nature for the sake of humans. It was God's will that man should bring nature under his control. In God's eyes, human beings had special status; we were more important than other creatures and thus had the right to use the earth as if it were wholly ours. Our only task was to find out how to do this most efficiently.

I'm sure the good men of the Industrial Revolution thought what they were doing was right. In their view, mind and matter were separate, and mind could always dominate matter. When there were far fewer people on the planet and the scope of our technology was relatively narrow and local, this didn't matter too much. But as human inventiveness, product-ivity and the reach of industrialisation increased, so did that sense of 'specialness'. This is a mindset that now has to change. Centuries of believing we lived on a planet with an endless capacity to support and feed us, regardless of how we treated it, is plainly wrong.

I find it extraordinary that the concept of Gaia, first put forward by James Lovelock in the 1970s, should have taken so long to be accepted by the world's scientific bodies. Gaia is a simple concept. It basically posits that the earth is an entity all its own; not some lifeless blob on which we all live, but a complex body in its own right, which regulates its temperature and climate and provides the basis for the existence of all life. It is a hugely complex and interdependent organism which we still barely understand. And it is brilliantly resilient too in the way it absorbs and processes everything we do to it and still preserves its strength and vitality. And we take it all so very much for granted. We have trusted science to come up with answers for every problem, in spite of the way we keep demanding cheaper food and clothes and all types of consumer goods—more holidays, more roads, more cars—an endless catalogue of more and more wants.

29

But it's this very mindset that has to change if we are truly going to shift our destructive ethos and the politics that go with it and actually save what we're so richly endowed with. So it's a vote loser if airlines are taxed and the amount of food we import is curbed, along with the amount of meat we consume in order to stop the rainforests being cut so grain can be planted instead to feed the cattle that end up in Big Macs. It's still a vote loser to say every household can only have one car, or maybe even no car if you live in a town. But if our mindsets begin to change, these things will take on a different importance and begin to happen. The list of changes needed is very long and I'm sure you can think of many things that could be added.

Ultimately, it is the way we perceive the world and ourselves within it that determines how we behave. Change our perceptions, and everything else will follow. Trivial things like turning off that light, not booking that cheap airplane seat when you could have gone by train, switching off the 'standbys' on your computer and TV are small things and can never be a substitute for the kinds of controls governments need to implement.

I always remember my father talking about the morality that held sway during the war; there were many things you did not do, not because you thought they were or weren't going to bring about some vast change, but because that was the way you looked at the world and the way you were expected to behave. In short, it was a moral *attitude* that was adopted for the common good, and it wasn't, as such, a gigantic sacrifice. So the question now too is a *moral* question, because it's about how we conduct our lives and how we are *seen* to conduct our lives so that our attitudes in turn influence our political leaders.

Even so, you may still ask what difference it makes if I bother to switch off the light if I know that my neighbour is not bothering to switch off hers. I can only say this: it is a *moral issue* if we want to be able to look our grandchildren in the eye and claim with all honesty that we *did what we could, based on the facts that we knew.*

I want to end by quoting some words by Jared Diamond, a great writer and thinker. In his book *Collapse*, about how societies chose to fail or survive, he says, '*The monumental ruins left behind by past societies hold a romantic fascination for all of us ... We marvel at them when as children we first learn about them through pictures ... We feel drawn to their often spectacular and haunting beauty and also to the mysteries they pose ... Lurking behind this romantic mystery is the nagging thought: might such a fate eventually befall our own wealthy society? Will tourists someday stare mystified at the rusting hulks of New York skyscrapers, much as we stare at the jungle-overgrown ruins of Mayan cities?*'

Indiscriminate use of the earth's resources will, I think, come to be seen as profoundly wrong as slavery. We need to learn to *tread lightly* on the earth, and from that will flow a change in perception that will affect our lifestyles, how we influence our communities and the natural world, and how, ultimately, we influence our governments. It's a tough journey, but like all journeys, it begins with small, simple steps that you can begin taking this very minute.

A MYTHOLOGY FOR OUR TIME

Elaine Brook

Elaine, Director of the Gaia Partnership, lives in the Golden Valley near Hereford

What a wonderful thought that just by wishing, one could instantly eradicate the shadows of pollution, radiation, chemical, biological and nuclear weapons, not to mention the industrial chaos that pours greenhouse gases into the air and has already set the oceans spilling over the first low-lying islands ...

But what then? Just suppose we suddenly found ourselves in a world basking in freedom from these man-made burdens. Consider for a moment what would happen after those first heady moments or months had worn off, and the world began to go back to business as usual. How many of us remember the surge of enthusiasm for a safe environment after the fear of Chernobyl's radioactive rain? Or the outpouring of emotion and generosity following the worldwide screening of the Band Aid concert and its harrowing images of starving children? And how many of us remember how short-lived these emotional responses were?

These collective responses from whole populations mirror our own individual responses to try for something better. The spirit is willing, but ... the demands of family, a busy life, the need to earn a living, service the overdraft, and if we're lucky, have time for just a little personal space in between all this ... How many of us recognise where all those sincere New Year's resolutions usually go?

Even in a freshly 'purified' environment, if the values, desires and priorities of individuals and societies remained the same as they are now, we would gradually re-create the same problems all over again. So in the absence of a magic wand to remove man-made material problems, it might be interesting to look into our inner universe to see if there are changes within our reach that, if multiplied through whole populations, might gradually create outer manifestations that could change the world.

The Buddha (and many other wise and inspired teachers) pointed out that all human unhappiness is the result of desires and aversions taking over our lives. We exhaust ourselves trying to 'fix' life into a state of equilibrium where it will deliver what we want and exclude what we don't want. While a certain amount of this process is necessary to maintain basic food and shelter, most of us live in a world bombarded with messages that the key to happiness is the rapid acquisition of this or that product, relationship, experience, ability, appearance—and so on. Small wonder everyone is so busy! And then the very busyness becomes addictive; it becomes equated with success and status, and it prevents us from slowing down enough to question whether all these 'things' really do make us happy.

Why do so many people make fundamental life changes after recovering from a life-threatening illness? I have listened to so many similar stories about how having the time to stop, think, and feel brought insights into what really mattered, what felt important and valuable. All the doubts and questions that busyness kept well clamped down inside suddenly had time and space to surface, and then once addressed, became less frightening as the possibilities for change came into focus. A whole range of fixed assumptions about the way things need to be suddenly lose their reified status and, consequently, their hold over us.

The Dalai Lama expressed the teachings of the Buddha as 'a deep understanding of the interconnectedness of everything, and the practice of non-harming, or helping others, that comes from that understanding'.

Once we recognise on an intuitive as well as intellectual level that we are essentially all a part of each other in a mysterious and complex web of relationships, then concepts such as 'love' and 'compassion' take on a new meaning. No longer am 'I' a separate individual over here feeling sympathy and compassion for 'you' over there; we are manifestations of an interconnected universe and my sense of empathy and concern is as spontaneous as my own sense of self-preservation.

There are layers of subtlety in this, but even if we only look at the material level, we enter the world of Deep Ecology which recognises the intrinsic value of all life and all species for their own sake, not just their obvious usefulness to humans. The complex relationship of myself, the trees that give me oxygen to breathe through their photosynthesis, the soil bacteria and fungi without which the tree cannot draw nourishment from the soil, the weeds in my garden which nourish the bacteria, and the insects which pollinate the weeds—and which, if I am foolish, I may try to kill because they eat my lettuces—all are part of a pattern of life which extends outwards until it connects with everything else. Recognising this interconnectedness is the antidote to feeling a separate, alienated individual caught up in the cycle of acquisitiveness and avoidance that our society reinforces at every opportunity.

More and more individuals are reaching this understanding for themselves, whether it is from the teachings of ancient traditions or from the new holistic sciences—or even from a flash of intuition while gazing at the sun setting over the sea. But how do these individuals link up to give and receive support from each other instead of struggling against the tide of a society in a lemming-like stampede of speed and greed?

This is where mythology can have a powerful role, once reclaimed from the disused and disrespected recesses of our collective psyche. These days, 'mythology' is usually dismissed as a mere synonym for 'untruth'—but this is missing the point. The point of mythology is not whether or not it is true, in an empirical sense, but whether or not it *works*—in other words, does it contain a symbolic or archetypal truth about a process or principle? Mythology is a process by which a collectively held view, with its associated stories, images, songs and rituals, enables whole populations to act in a synergistic way. This process then reinforces the collective story and the patterns of behaviour become self-sustaining. If this sounds suspiciously like the start of an anthropological exploration of indigenous tribes in the darkest rainforest, think again, as the essence continues under other guises. In our world of computers and fast cars we have handed control of our collective stories to the corporate media with hardly a thought for the agendas behind the persuasive new messages.

Here is one example: our whole economy (and the politics it controls) is based on the myth that money actually exists, and is in short supply. We therefore have to compete to get some of it in order to survive. Most of us have to borrow from banks even if only for our house mortgage, and therefore we need regular work in order to service the loan. Therefore, anything that creates jobs is essential, even if it destroys whole ecosystems or puts other competing communities (perhaps in other countries) out of work or even out of their homes. 'Economic growth' is essential to keep it all going, even though the planet is of a finite size. While everyone continues to behave as if this story is true, the ensuing process continues to function in a self-replicating way—until the ability of the planet to support it is exhausted.

Now, just suppose enough people opted out of this story and subscribed to a different communal story of their own. These people decide not to participate in the tribal rituals of shopping and showing off their possessions, and they decide to reject the shared songs and stories of the advertising industry. Suppose they teach each other that money doesn't exist the way we thought it did, but that actually private banks create it out of nothing, lend it to people like us, and charge us interest on these loans of nothingness. Suppose they point out that banks have far too much money because they are allowed to do this, and consequently far too much power; power to own huge chunks of transnational corporations, power over labour markets, pensions, national currencies and democratic governments.

Clearly, if enough people simply opted out it would bring the system down and reveal the myth of money for the untruth it is, but the resulting social chaos would not be the kind of goal that idealists and inspired individuals would want to aim for. It is dangerous to debunk any current mythology without replacing it with something else; something we hope will bring about a more sane, healing kind of process than the one we wish to abandon. In order to function, a myth has to have qualities which strike a chord in the hearts of most people, qualities that resonate with a deep, intuitive longing that feels like coming home. Stories resonate not only with individuals, but also with the needs of the time we are in. So before we rush off, each to compose our own, individual mythology story in the hope that everyone else can share in its inspiration, maybe we should look at stories that are already spreading and growing and have already started to inspire and move people.

There are a few of these, but one I would like to explore here is the Gaia story. The Gaia hypothesis is a scientific theory put forward by James Lovelock when he was working as a research scientist for NASA. He named it after Gaia, the Goddess of Earth. So already we have a synthesis of science and poetry, an emerging legend which can satisfy the intellect as well as nourish our longing for beauty and the expression of the spirit. Gaia theory tells us that all the living beings on the planet, as well as the movements of the winds and ocean currents, affect each other and work together in harmony in the same way as all the cells in our body. If we disturb the balance in our own body or that of Gaia, the result will be sickness or even death. This communal story enables us to care for our planetary life-support system as spontaneously and naturally as we care for our own physical health. It enables whole communities to engage in mutually supportive patterns of behaviour to nourish self, family, friends and the wider community of unknown beings that make up the rest of our shared body of Earth.

It is my hope that if we are able to change our individual and collective stories, our contemporary mythology, to a more compassionate and holistic vision, this inspiration will spread to our immediate family and friends, and by following interconnected relationships it will eventually bring about a change in society as a whole. Becoming involved in the Gaia story inevitably leads to changes in the way we relate to each other, and the way we live in relation to the earth on which we depend for life. This process *is* the 'magic wand' which will gradually and naturally deconstruct the human-made problems we face today.

SEEING THE WORLD AS A CIRCLE

Healing the Planet through Natural Building

Katy Bryce

Katy runs a business with her husband in Cornwall creating beautiful and sustainable shelter made out of cob

We live in interesting times. The last 150 years, since the Industrial Revolution began and the technological age took root, have brought rapid, dramatic changes to the world we inhabit. Some of these changes could be said to have brought about vast improvements in the general conditions of most people's lives. On the other hand, some of these changes have brought about a false sense of progress and two main outcomes have arisen. First, the ecology of the planet is suffering badly. Although it is a naturally self-adjusting mechanism and is designed to accommodate waste and pollution, the changes that we have brought about have happened too quickly for it to adjust, and our levels of pollution and waste have become too much and too toxic for it to cope. We are at a crossroads.

We can go two ways—either we can stumble blindly on into the future and hope that something works itself out, or we can stop now and start to make conscious changes on a personal level. We can become aware and conscious of the small and large decisions we make on a daily basis. As a natural builder, building predominantly out of earth, I believe that one of the most fundamental decisions we can make is what sort of a house we live in—what sort of materials it is made out of, whether they are local, renewable, non-toxic, require little energy to produce, and whether the overall design of the house requires little energy to heat and cool. Can it make use of the free energy of the sun and deal efficiently with wastes? Can it encourage communities to come together and build? Can it help to take some of the burden off our already stretched planet?

The second outcome that has arisen out of these dramatic and rapid changes has been our estrangement from the natural world. For without this estrangement, how could we have so easily and flippantly used and abused it so much? Without our need to rely on the natural world for our survival, for food, for shelter, there seems to have emerged a separation between wildlife, 'wilderness areas', and the 'civilized' world—shopping complexes and cityscapes. This is sad, not just because the natural world is suffering at the hands of our insensitivity (which will cause us suffering in the future as it fights back), but because we too are suffering, through our estrangement from what is in fact a part of us, the whole of us. A rich and rewarding symbiotic relationship—you give me some rocks and mud to build my house, and I'll do my best to honour and steward the land on which I am building.

To help us move forward, we can take a glimpse back to a period before the Industrial Revolution—the last era in history when many people lived through this intimate, reciprocal relationship with the natural world. Or we can look at the tribes and communities throughout the world where industrialisation has not reached. We can study and learn from their buildings and dwellings, the ways they feed themselves and their relationships with the land by which they are supported.

A unifying characteristic of these pre-industrial societies is their sense of holism, and their understanding that everything is linked, that all actions have an impact on all parts of the system, and that the whole is more important than the sum of its parts.

To these traditional societies, progress is not seen, as it is in our societies, as a linear concept, moving along a straight line from the past, into the present and into the future, at each stage inventing newer and more sophisticated things, so that we feel that we are better off today than we were yesterday. Rather, time is seen as a circle—ever-linked to the eternal cycles of nature—the moon, the seasons, the spin of the earth around the sun, and the cycle of life and death.

I believe that if we can again view the world from a circular and not a linear perspective, we can begin to reconnect with the natural world and be inspired to act in ways that are healing and life-enhancing for the planet. As a natural builder who creates dwellings and structures out of natural materials, I also believe we can enhance our world by starting to participate in the creation of the buildings we inhabit.

On both metaphorical and practical levels, building with natural materials is about circles and cyclical time. Through the process of natural building one is encouraged to re-connect to this wholesome, everlasting form, to come full circle back to those ideas and techniques of the past that really worked, such as walls built out of earth and roofs made out of thatch. Natural building materials such as cob and stone are imbued with renewable cycles, as they are being constantly made by the planet and can be eternally re-used; thatch and sustainably harvested wood will decompose safely when they have reached the end of their life, back into the earth whence they came, and be transformed into something new to nourish the garden. If we use natural lime mortars and plasters instead of cement, we become engaged in their cycle as they move from the ground as limestone and are processed into a material that can be plastered onto walls, at which point it reacts with the air and effectively turns back into limestone. Lime can also be removed from a building, re-mixed, and re-used again.

When siting and designing a structure that is made out of natural materials and aims to have a light footprint on the planet during its lifetime, one should become aware of the daily and monthly cycles of the sun so that the building can be oriented accordingly and the inhabitants can benefit from the light and heat it provides, and so that it will be comfortable and joyous to live in and experience through all the seasons. The building schedule of a building made out of natural materials such as earth must respect cyclical, seasonal rhythms, and should be carried out during the best weather months—starting in spring and finishing in autumn.

There is a cycle too, present in the actual construction of a natural building made out of earth and other natural materials. In an ideal situation the materials present naturally on the site can be efficiently rearranged so that little waste is generated, costs are kept down, and transport of outside materials onto the site is kept to a minimum. For example, the turf from the potential building site can be removed, stored and later used to lay on top of a roof structure for a 'green' roof. The topsoil can be used to create flower or vegetable beds, and the subsoil, which has been removed to make way for the below-ground foundations, if suitable, can be mixed with straw and aggregate to make cob to build the walls. You may also need to prune some surrounding trees to allow more sunlight in, and these can be utilised in the roof structure. It is up to you how far you want to go.

Natural buildings may need more maintenance than a standard, modern house; yearly lime washing for example. This is a positive thing as it can again reconnect us to the natural seasonal cycles of nature.

Most importantly, although an earth building can be moulded and formed into whatever shape you desire, it is best, and at its strongest, when built in the round—efficient because no heat can get lost in corners, and cosy as it encircles you in an eternal embrace.

Ultimately, building with natural materials is a way we can literally get back in 'touch' with nature. Building with earth is about getting your hands dirty, touching the stuff, feeling its stickiness, its grittiness, its pliability and plasticity. To build with earth, it is necessary to wake up

41

your senses, to learn to recognise and understand its suitability for building; not through rigorous, scientific tests (although these can be done), but through learning what it should look, smell and taste like.

Building with natural materials fosters a rejection of global homogenisation, monoculture, mass-manufacturing, top-down solutions, and high-tech approaches. This age-old technique can be used in a truly fresh way to encourage regionality, the local, the specific, the appropriate, the low tech, the simple. It can be connected to a larger movement that is going on in the world right now, that embraces home-grown and locally specific entities such as indigenous music, local, organic and seasonal foods, and the resurgence of younger generations wanting to relearn their local dialect and languages.

To come back to the beginning is to talk not just about circles, but more specifically, about the spiral. For really, it is not exactly the beginning that we want to come back to, but a different point on the same cyclical journey. For a spiral always returns to itself, but never at exactly the same place. Spirals never repeat themselves; they remind us that life is movement and that nothing is ever the same—repetition is neither sought nor valued, and cob is all of these. Straight lines, on the other hand, measure, they are static and they separate and divide. Natural building is none of these. It is transforming, flexible, forgiving, empowering, practical, democratic, simple, inherently linked to the natural world, accessible, sustainable, renewable, beautiful and highly relevant to these interesting times we live in.

'A story that makes sense is one that stirs the senses from their slumber, one that opens the eyes and ears to their real surroundings, tuning the tongue to the actual tastes in the air and sending chills of recognition along the surface of the skin. To make sense is to release the body from the constraints imposed by outworn ways of speaking, and hence to renew and rejuvenate one's felt awareness of the world. It is to make the senses wake up to where they are.' (*The Spell of the Sensuous*, David Abram, [1998], p. 265)

THE VILLAGE DEBATE

Monique Caddy

*Monique, originally from the Netherlands, is a playright who lives in
Dorset and works with the mentally disabled*

*Barbara and Howard stand outside the village hall. They observe the
other villagers entering the hall.*

Howard:	This is going to be interesting.
Barbara:	How many have gone in from a population of two hundred odd?
Howard:	Not counting the farmers?
Barbara:	They don't give a damn!
Howard:	Farmer Drake does. He's always collecting newspapers.
Barbara:	To shred them for his pigs.
Howard:	That's unkind.
Barbara:	Well …
Howard:	I know, I know.
Barbara:	How long have we petitioned for a green box and recycling centre? We may be a small village but …

*Farmer Drake makes his way to the village hall. Howard and Barbara
look at each other, astonished.*

Barbara:	How about that!
Howard:	Well, well.
Farmer Drake:	Evenin' all, 'ow's turnout?
Howard:	Not bad. Good to see you.
Farmer Drake:	Need to do our bit don't we? Shouldn't 'ave to drive to town to recycle! 'Bout time we 'ad it 'ere!
Barbara:	Hear, hear. Most people can't be bothered to take their empties all that way.

Farmer Drake nods and enters the village hall. Howard turns to Barbara.

Howard:	Shall we?

*They enter the hall, where a quarter of the village are seated. Howard
looks around in appreciation.*

43

Howard:	Not bad. Not bad at all.

They sit down next to Farmer Drake.

Farmer Drake:	Who's speaker, then?
Barbara:	Councillor Cassidy.
Farmer Drake:	That pompous git?

Councillor Cassidy harrumphs, rises from his seat, stands on the podium and taps the microphone.

Cassidy:	Good evening all.

The microphone screeches and a few people screw their faces and cover their ears in agony. A teenager runs to the stage to adjust the sound level.

Cassidy:	Thank you dear boy.

Red faced, the boy returns to his seat.

Cassidy:	Well now. It is an honour to stand here this evening to discuss what matters most for the village. (Harrumphs)
Farmer Drake:	'Ere we go.
Cassidy:	As you know, the Third World needs us. I would like to talk about what upsets me the most. Something dear to my family …
Farmer Drake:	Stone me, 'E's off.
Cassidy:	… Mugabe, his vote rigging and his atrocities. Something needs to be done about him, don't you know! I would like to propose a vote …
Barbara:	Nothing like cleaning up our back yard.

Farmer Drake rises from his seat.

Farmer Drake:	God 'elp us! I'm off.

Farmer Drake walks away, watched aghast by Howard.

Cassidy:	… And this proposal would help my family …
Howard:	One moment, please!

Annoyed, Councillor Cassidy looks at Howard.

Cassidy:	Excuse me?

Howard rises from his seat.

Howard:	We are here to discuss recycling, not your family! Have

	you looked around recently? … No, I didn't think so. The landfill site is full of plastic bottles and other rubbish that will never rot. Glass everywhere! We must recycle! For the good of the Earth. In the rest of Europe everything is re-used.
Cassidy:	I am afraid that …
Howard:	Yes! So am I! Did you know that only yesterday a German friend was shocked to see my daughter throw her batteries in a bin! *In a bin!!* My friend informed me that in Germany one would get a hefty fine doing that! Mr Cassidy, I propose …
Cassidy:	You will do no such thing! I am the only one …
Howard:	I propose that this village sets an example and recycles *everything* as part of a sustainable earth policy. And by everything, I mean *everything*.
Villagers:	Hear, hear!
Howard:	I propose to you, Councillor that you provide us with recycling bins. Colour coded. For ordinary papers, for tins and glass, for used batteries and computer parts, for vegetable peelings and for clothing!
Cassidy:	Clothing? My dear man, have you gone mad! This proposal is outrageous …
Howard:	No, Mr Cassidy! *Your* proposal is outrageous! We want to do the proper thing and recycle, recycle, recycle! *Everything!*
Cassidy:	I … I … I …
Howard:	*Everything!* This country is backward! This village is in the dark ages! You should be fighting for *us*! Give *us* what we want instead of what *you* want! This planet is all that we have! If we want our grandchildren to swim in a clean sea, or play in safe fields, we must make the world *clean*! The only way to make the earth clean is by recycling everything instead of throwing it away!
Cassidy:	That's preposterous! I will not tolerate …
Villagers:	Out! Out! Out!
Cassidy:	I am your spokesperson …
Villager:	Get rid of him! He's not getting my vote again!
Villagers:	Nor mine! Not mine!
Villager:	Get Howard up there!

The villagers angrily push Cassidy off the stage and triumphantly put Howard on the stage. Farmer Drake returns.

Farmer Drake: Now, that's what I call a proper village debate.

In Heaven, God, after watching the debate, pushes the clouds back together.

God: Better leave them to it. They haven't learned a thing in the last two thousand years. Always bickering and arguing over the smallest of things without the least action required ... Men!!

AWAKENING TO OUR CONNECTEDNESS

Helen de Castres

Helen, originally from Australia, is a healer and sculptor now living on Dartmoor

For me it's about connection—connection first of all with myself—my soft body full of vibrant life, the open vulnerable child inside me, the love shining in my heart, and as well, the frightened person who just wants to hide from all the pain, the one who would rather be asleep and doesn't want to awaken to anything, much less to saving the world! She too is such a gift, she helps me when I'm judging and angry, she whispers in my ear, suggests time to drink wine, blob out and act for a while as if none of it matters.

It's about connection with others, dear friends who share this precious life; humans, animals, insects, plants, trees, rocks, elements and of course the beloved Earth herself. It's about connection with what I eat and wear, knowing where it comes from and at what cost to the Earth and other beings. It's about a conscious connection with my lifestyle, my car, my power supply, knowing how much of the Earth's resources I am using. It's how I care for my home and garden and the companions who share it; cat friends, birds, squirrels, badgers, moles, bees, butterflies and other insects. And of course the plants and trees. I honour those I need to remove; the ground elder which thrives but kills other plants; remembering to give solace as I weed it out, so grateful that I actually have a garden.

There are many choices I make as I act from connection; buying organic and fair-trade food and clothing; locally grown when possible and compassionately farmed. Recently, a strong connection with cows, as mothers, as Goddess, has encouraged me to choose less dairy produce, to slowly *wean*. One night I dreamed my breasts were being sucked by a machine, my babies taken from the warmth and safety of my body—how can I look into those soft brown eyes of the mother and drink her baby's milk? And so I recycle, repair, re-use, buy green energy and environmentally friendly house paint, use my car sparingly, garden organically, make compost; and when I don't, I forgive myself as soon as possible. Why add more guilt and shame to the load already carried in this disconnected world?

With friends, I have created a shrine in my garden to remind me to be grateful for the blessings my garden brings, to be tender and cherish all life, including my own (something I once didn't do).

It's about being with the many children in my life, sharing wonder and play and tender moments. They help me to stay with the wild and joyous present, they help me to be courageous, to want a peaceful and abundant, verdant green world for them to grow and thrive in—and to stand up for that world. It's about touching special moments with people; death and birth, celebrating union and the cycle of the seasons, dancing the wild flame of life, grieving through pain, terror, sadness; creating rituals for peace, love and continuing life. It's about being still, being with silence, and listening with all my senses.

And then there's my work, connecting with my clients, the awesomeness of their journeys, the ever-unfolding awakening and re-membering and the sense of being a part of the larger collective awakening; our diversity, our oneness, the moment-to-moment letting go of identification and coming into the present, being part of the pulse of life, being one body, one heart. It's the clay beneath my hands as I make my pots and sculptures, connect with the flesh and body of my precious mother, the Earth that caresses and touches my heart, supports my life. It's about connecting with my ancient indigenous roots, with my ancestors who squatted by fires, created sacred objects and pots to cook in; it's about feeling their wisdom, their knowledge about how to live and honour all life—life as prayer, as celebration—art as prayer. It's about reading newspapers, books, watching films and staying present with myself when I am touched, appalled, filled with empathy and a sense of kinship with others often far away; their stories, pain, love, victories, their rage and hurt. It's about not closing off, knowing they are me, that we are One.

It's connecting with rainforests that are being destroyed and the people who depend on them, as well as the brave people who dare to protect them; the animals who are being tormented, abused and slaughtered, as well as the people who care for them and speak and act for their freedom and well-being. It's feeling kinship with the women and girls who are sexually mutilated, raped, violated, dishonoured; the men and boys who struggle to save their homes and lands, and are sometimes tortured, beaten and killed for love of their place.

And what of those who seem to perpetuate the violence, who hold control and use their power to dominate because they are lost in fear and separated from the pulse of life and love? I want to hold a link with who they truly are, remembering that I too become lost in fear and sometimes make attempts to control. I need to have compassion for *all* of it, to recognize the pull to polarise and negate, and to resist by staying connected and aware.

I am inspired more and more deeply by all those who feel connection and take action from that place of wisdom and the truth—who choose not to be polarised; those who are involved in mediation, non-violent direct action, education about our Earth and our bonds with all life, peace activists, those who move with courage and commitment and stand up for love.

I too write letters, gather signatures, appeal for justice and compassion, make sculptures dedicated to connection, sell them to support projects touched by love; I endeavour to touch hearts, inspire, be true, help create stronger communities, talk in council, vision together, weave and dance into being our dreams. I pray, I listen to the wind, the rustle of leaves. I hear the voice of the great trees, the Ancient Elders, the laughing children, the wailing of those who are frightened and lost; I listen to the calling in my own heart and stroke the frightened creature who would stop me by remembering times of betrayal and crucifixion. I call on the courage of those who have gone first, so that I too will stand up for this Beautiful Planet, our home, where we are, all of us, cell by cell, one body—Gaia. I pray for the support of her powerful spirit, and that I, in each moment, can be true to my vision of connectedness. I invite you to join me if you haven't already taken this step. This is my way to Save the World! Blessed Be.

HOMES, SWEET HOMES

Jilly Cooper

Jilly is a well-known writer living near Stroud, Gloucestershire

A favourite quotation is from Jean Anouilh, in which one of his heroines says, 'How can I possibly be happy when there's a single stray dog in the world?' In an ideal world I would dream of all animals, but especially dogs, cats and racehorses, spending their lives in good homes where people could appreciate their lovely natures and they could have the happiness they deserve.

I'm particularly worried about greyhounds, often living in shocking conditions, who gallop their hearts out on the track and are jettisoned when they are of no more use, or sent to Spain to be raced to total exhaustion. Often then, the Spaniards take them into the woods and string half a dozen of them up and take bets on which greyhound will die first and which last. It's called the 'typewriter game' because the poor greyhounds' feet tap on the ground as they hang. Just writing that makes me weep with anguish and rage!

The greyhound industry makes so much money out of these brave creatures, they could at least put something back by ensuring they are either put down humanely or found wonderful homes.

Also, I have just written a novel where the hero is a boy in care, and in the end, does really well with his life after appalling hardships. One way I would improve the world would be to ensure that children in care are looked after at seventeen. when they are literally thrown out of their care homes and have to fend for themselves without any idea how to do so, having lived in institutions most of their lives. They have no *real* home to go to like other teenagers do, no one to talk to about their worries and achievements, and no one to give them financial support if they run out of money.

I know the government has schemes to improve this, and there is a mentor scheme to encourage children in care to go to these people and talk to them, but this is not the same as a halfway house where they could crash out at weekends and go and get the odd free meal.

I've always wanted to invent a halfway house in which married couples whose relationships are breaking down and who are not quite sure whether their marriage is over could just go and stay somewhere with the children, perhaps for three or four months, and decide whether they really do want the marriage to end or whether it's possible to save it.

So often I talk to divorced people who say the whole thing happened so quickly, and it was only after they'd left dramatically in the night, throwing the children into a car, that they realised a couple of months later that they'd made a terrible mistake and were too proud to get together again. In this halfway house they would just be able to relax and sleep and have someone occasionally to look after their children so they could do some proper thinking and have time for reflecting.

In the same way, I would like yet another form of halfway house to be provided for children coming out of care, when, as I've said, for a few years they need a refuge they could go back to and people there they could talk to. It is a dismaying statistic that only one per cent of children in care go on to university and equally sad that at least twenty-five per cent of the adult homeless were once children in care. And only because there was nobody to look after them.

Finally, I'd like to abolish all snares everywhere because they are a horrendously cruel way of maiming animals who either escape by leaving a leg behind and developing gangrene, or are forced to just lie and wait, suffering terribly from starvation and thirst until they die a hideous death.

A WORLD WHERE ANIMALS LIVE IN PEACE

Sarah Dawes

Sarah is a 14-year-old schoolgirl living in Surrey

I think animal cruelty is a sin and a stupid, childish way of trying to put your past behind you, and when I say that I don't mean fox or game hunting, I mean such things as the dumping of kittens in rubbish bags, leaving dogs on the motorway and reptiles unwanted in abandoned flats; all of these are what I'm talking about, all these depressing things that will make you think twice. It's not necessarily you but all those other people out there carelessly walking around looking for a quick way and lazy way of getting rid of things.

All they have to do is go to the nearest RSPCA and give the animal in— they're not going to pressurise you with questions because it's not you they are worried about; it's the safety and care of the animal. Isn't that just an easier way of doing it? Surely you must agree; who wouldn't? It's ridiculous!!!

The other day I heard two stories, one about an elephant, the other about a dog. This dog had been left in a flat—I believe it had been left with seven bowls of food, one for Monday, one for Tuesday and so on. Unaware of this decision, the dog had scoffed the whole seven bowls on the first day and obviously, by the time the owners had come back, the dog was—you guessed it ... dead! Long gone, poor thing, but not poor owners; who in this world would expect a dog to know when to eat each meal? No offence to dogs, they are pretty intelligent, though unfortunately not that intelligent. What a waste of a life, a total waste and all because of the stupidity of two of us humans not yet advanced to actually *use* their brain!

Anyway, the other story was about this poor defenceless elephant that had its trunk sliced off; now just think, its trunk had been chopped away from its body and it was just left to die. Now, ladies and maybe gentlemen, ask yourself, isn't that just sick? What sick-minded beast would do that? Unless we act, no one will ever know, no one would be able to stop it happening again and wouldn't that be disastrous?

If I could change this problem or if I had a magic wand or a single wish,

I would wish for there to be a world where animals could live in peace and harmony, without neglect and harm; a world where only true animal lovers could go and live. No poachers or killers, only those who understand and have feelings and respect for other creatures that roam the earth. I doubt if that would ever happen but there's no reason at all to stop wishing.

THE LOSS OF A WORLD

Polly Devlin

Polly is a writer and conservationist who has an OBE for services to literature. She has homes in Somerset and London

We live in an ark that is sinking. It is only a matter of time until thousands of our precious species of plants and animals that make this earth a paradise have disappeared into the galactic cold. When these things die they go for good. Man cannot re-constitute them. They are extinct. For me, the word 'extinct' is another word for mass murder. These beasts and birds go into a dark night from which there is no returning, a dark night into which we will surely follow. Some biologists think we are losing one or two species a day. Per day. The problem is worst in the tropics, where human populations are increasing (although when these countries start using plastic the way western civilisations do the human population will go into reverse. The sperm count of young males is down by 25%, and biologists think it is caused by the increased use of plastics). In what is called the Third World, they face overwhelming economic problems, and conservation is hardly high on their list of priorities. For us to urge these nations to spend time and money on saving species at risk must appear to them as a form of neo-imperialism, certainly a luxury they can't afford. But we can and we don't. Watch shoppers leave a supermarket; they all carry plastic bags containing food—some of it can be called food—wrapped in plastic. And the methods used to produce some of that food are unspeakable.

I've always been passionate about birds, have watched them in Ireland, England, Hungary, France and India. But our birds are in big trouble. The terrible statistics show how fast we are turning into a birdless Britain. The numbers of the common sparrow have declined by half since 1989, the lapwing by 70%. Skylarks have declined by half over the past twenty years. The decline in the numbers of the sparrow, the bullfinch, the corn bunting, the coal tit and the tree sparrow is linked to farming practices. The alders are dying; the hazel blackthorn, elderberry and hawthorn are not flowering as they used to and the blackthorn has stopped producing sloes in the same quantities. The hazel produces dry husks instead of nuts; and perhaps worst of all, an oak disease is now threatening the very essence of England—its great symbol, the oak tree. These natural things are dying and so are we. But the difference is that we are doing the killing and we are also killing the future. Every extinction foreshadows our own.

I listen to farmers and the Countryside Alliance prate about their love for and protection of the English countryside and I want to hammer them upside down in hard soil. One hundred and thirty seven British bird species are on the danger list because of farming practices. On my own land I sow spring cereal, restore dew ponds, cut tramways for owls, leave high hedges, plant trees—none of it too difficult, all without subsidy, but too difficult apparently for farmers subsidised to the hilt by your money and mine and fuel at 35p per litre. In the last fifty years 98% (are you taking this on board?—98% of our wildflower meadows have disappeared.

In the meadows at home here are some of the species I walk through: creeping bent, crested dog's tail, sweet vernal grasses, Timothy, reedgrass, field horsetail, fleabane, meadow vetchling, devil's bit scabious, sneeze-wort, bird's foot trefoil, hairy sedge, dyer's greenweed, red clover, pepper saxifrage, tormentil, cocksfoot, creeping thistle, dwarf thistle, spear thistle, ribwort plantain, betony, *self heal*, black knapweed, ox-eye daisy.

Our fields lie like multi-coloured medieval tapestries. They are striped, flecked, spangled and eyed like a peacock, every colour under the sun, a mille-fleur revelation which makes one understand that the great tapestries of the Middle Ages, the lady with the unicorn, were not an artist's dazzling inspiration of the celestial fields but an accurate representation of what he saw around him. Once not very long ago they were ordinary fields of England. Now they are so rare that they are listed as Sites of Special Scientific Interest. Those charming bright green fields you see from the windows of your car or train or house are plastic ground-sheets, livid barren deserts of rye-grass and silage grass, thin specious stuff hardly supporting insect and bird life.

Altogether, 75% of our heath lands and 96% of our lowland peat bogs have been destroyed. I could go on quoting statistics but they make such depressing reading; try living in the countryside to get really depressed. Effluent discharge and agricultural run off are killing aquatic life and in many parts of England it is rare to see a lake with clear water and a diversity of plants and animals. Some of you reading this may think you do not contribute to this litany of destruction and death of species. We all do. Do you use peat in your garden? We have wonderful peat lands and bogs in the British Isles but they are constantly under threat and until recently have been exploited as commodities for digging and extracting and burning and selling.

Recently, the mouse-eared bat has become extinct in England. Many other species of bat are on the verge of extinction. They are an integral part of our ecology, neither pests nor rodents, and are necessary for the cycle which eventually keeps us alive. They only eat insects, but because of increased use of pesticides by farmers and the loss of rich meadows and marsh and peat lands, they have lost their food source. You, reading this, who wants the cheapest food and makes no protest about farming methods, are contributing to your own decline. Don't think about why your eggs are so cheap—if you visited some of the factories for hens it would break your heart; but it wouldn't break the bank to pay a bit more so that hens could have a more organic life.

We all know about the corncrake; its harsh cracking call that was so much a part of rural life has all but disappeared. The problem is that it's a migratory bird, so you can't just re-introduce it; it's migratory instincts are set on the area where it was born. It answers the imperative of its migratory and navigational urge. If a farmer, greedy for a rood of land, another shilling to his income, mows in such a way and at such a time that its legs are chopped off as it stays frantically with its young, then that's the price he is prepared to pay. Never mind that we're paying him to the hilt in subsidies.

We could help. Those plastic bags you pick up in every shop are lethal. All plastic is. Sea turtles die slowly entangled in curtains of plastic fish net. Seal and sea pigs, their snouts clamped shut by plastic rings from a six-pack, suffocate slowly; herring gulls starve to death, their necks encircled by such rings. Sea lions become entangled in plastic line and die, trying desperately to wriggle free.

Many sea animals die because of ingesting plastic gloves. On land, countless small mammals die in carelessly discarded glass bottles and beer cans; once in, they can't climb back up their smooth sides. Twenty-nine little corpses were found in one glass bottle in an English wood …

I believe, gloomily, that there is a more radical stopper to all our efforts to save wildlife. Living things lose heart. Literally. In one sense, when the heart of their community goes, in another, when the odds are too long and they give up. This is what I think is happening to us. The heart of a community is not an easy thing to pinpoint. I'll give you two examples. One is the story of the passenger pigeon. It was a native of North America—from Canada to the Gulf of Mexico. There were billions of them, and the male was slate blue with a russet breast and white abdomen. The young were fed on milk produced by both male and female. At the beginning of the nineteenth century, when they were migrating, the days were darkened; sometimes the sky was black for mile upon mile as the birds arrived for nesting. People spoke of flocks one hundred miles wide. For the settlers in America the birds were an invaluable source of food. They were hunted by bands of professional shooters, they were used as bait in trap shooting. Even in the 1880s after relentless butchery they still numbered millions. Then quite suddenly they died. They needed enormous flocks to create the conditions for continued life. The last passenger pigeon, a bird called Martha, died in Cincinnati Zoo in 1914.

The second story is more recent and is happening now. Many amphibians and reptiles are simply sliding off the scale. In the USA, where research is more advanced, biologists have found that ponds that once echoed thunderously to sounds of bullfrogs are silent. Millions of toads have always hatched in a place called Lost Lake. In all the years that Lost Lake has been monitored there was never more than 5% mortality. Then in 1990, 50% of two million eggs didn't hatch. Last year only a few thousand hatched. In Australia, biologists have not seen a certain species—the gastric brooding frog, which raises its young in its stomach (remind you of anyone?)—since 1980. Frogs are vanishing from Denmark, Nova Scotia, Peru, Panama, Switzerland, the United Kingdom and India. Amphibians are among the oldest creatures on Earth. They evolved more than 350 million years ago. If they are dying off, we're in heavy trouble. They really are the canaries of our environment. They have dual habitats, so they get the worst of both worlds—contaminated earth and polluted water. Their skin is as vulnerable to ultra-violet rays as ours—or more so. And everything is so connected to everything else.

Before the war, white storks sat on the rooftops in many German towns. They don't any more. They fed mainly on frogs.

You know, I am sure, the analogy; one rivet falls out of the aeroplane, it keeps on flying, ten fall out and it keeps on flying, twenty fall out—it keeps on flying, one more drops out and the plane crashes. We've lost a lot of rivets lately.

Biologists say they don't know what is happening—they're a conservative bunch and they need a lot of time and data to talk definitively. Well, they don't have the time and I can tell them why. Look to the passenger pigeon. In fact, I'm amazed that more species don't just give up. Fish in rivers and oceans must live in terror. They communicate with each other as all living creatures do and the tom-toms signalling danger between their shoals must tell them that everywhere they turn lies destruction. I'm sure that falling stocks aren't just to do with over-fishing. They are to do with losing heart, being frightened to death; but fish fingers and fish and chips are the cheapest of meals and fish restaurants have never been so popular as they are now.

And now many more countries are joining the European Union and the same collapse of bird numbers may well happen to many bird species in those places. Fertilisers, land improvement (oh, weasel words) will mean loss of irrecoverable habitats within a few years. Already, alas, English consortia are organised to buy the bird-rich plains of Hungary and no doubt wring it dry as they have done so well in England.

It was a storyline in *The Archers*; as far as I know no one protested. Certainly in the programme there was never any discussion about why it might not be a good idea to ruin Hungary, having so effectively ruined England. I wrote to the producer of *The Archers* but didn't even get the courtesy of a reply.

A blink ago on the evolutionary scale, the yellow bittern became extinct in the British Isles. In another blink it will be us. 'The lark, the corncrake and the grouse/Will bring good luck to any house' ran an old Borders song. The good luck is going fast unless we have a mind to stop it. You can support the many organisations that are trying to halt the decline in our species. You can pay a bit more for your food, support fair-trading organisations, write to MPs about farming practices. You can stop using plastic bags, be careful about your rubbish, stop using the car so much, pressure the authorities to provide better public transport. You can do all sorts of things, but most of you won't. That will be ultimate betrayal of our beautiful planet. That good men and women did nothing.

NUCLEAR ABOLITION

A Possible Dream?

Kate Dewes

Kate lives in Christchurch, New Zealand, where she is an anti-nuclear campaigner and advisor to the government and the UN on disarmament issues

> *Each time a person stands for an ideal, or acts to improve the lot of others, or strikes out against injustice, he or she sends forth a tiny ripple of hope. And crossing each other from a million different centers of energy and daring, those ripples build a current that can sweep down the mightiest walls of oppression and resistance. Few are willing to brave the disapproval of their fellows, the censure of their colleagues, the wrath of their society. Moral courage is a rarer commodity than bravery in battle or great intelligence. Yet it is the one essential vital quality for those who seek to change a world that yields most painfully to change.* (Robert F. Kennedy, 1966)

How many of us have had the privilege of experiencing those 'tiny ripples of hope' which have given us the energy and courage to try to help to improve our world a little? How many of us have risked societal and family censure, ostracism and government intimidation for daring to challenge the status quo by demanding change for the sake of the future of the planet? For many of us, it is the knowledge that millions of others are striving to uphold similar ideals in their local communities that empowers us to continue pursuing seemingly impossible dreams.

Let me share a dream which came true when 'millions of centres of light' converged to take the nuclear weapon states to the World Court to challenge the legality of the threat and use of nuclear weapons. This initiative, known as the World Court Project, grew out of a little local peace group based in Christchurch, Aotearoa/New Zealand.

When my eldest daughter Jess was born in 1979, the global nuclear arms race had amassed a stockpile of 53,000 nuclear weapons capable of killing her at least 24 times over. Despite many attempts at nuclear disarmament by peace groups and governments worldwide, humanity seemed powerless to prevent a nuclear holocaust. There was little hope that she would live to see the nuclear stranglehold on her future eased, let alone lifted. Inspired by opposition to French tests in the South Pacific and the attempts to declare the Southern Hemisphere a nuclear-free zone, some friends and I formed little peace groups which successfully campaigned to declare Christchurch nuclear-free in 1982. By the time Jess started school in 1984, women had encircled Greenham Common and the Pentagon, millions had marched all over the world, and small Pacific islands, including New Zealand, were declared nuclear-free.

In 1986 Harold Evans, a retired magistrate who had been a member of our local Christchurch peace group since Jess was a baby, initiated a campaign to ask the World Court (also known as the International Court of Justice) to give an advisory opinion on the legal status of nuclear weapons. The dream was to mobilise enough citizen and government support worldwide to persuade governments to sponsor resolutions requesting an opinion through the World Health Assembly and the United Nations General Assembly.

Emulating the non-hierarchical, cooperative, participatory model that our peace movement had developed in the successful campaign to secure New Zealand's nuclear-free legislation, we plunged into making the dream a reality. When we had been declaring our homes, farms, offices, cars, bikes, universities and city councils nuclear-free, part of our vision had been that once New Zealand and the South Pacific were nuclear-free, the rest of the world would gradually follow suit. A small group of naïve, committed 'Kiwis', bolstered by our government's courageous stand against the nuclear bullies, pursued what many dismissed as impossible. Armed with the courage of our convictions that the threat, let alone use, of nuclear weapons was illegal and immoral, we designed a flow diagram to challenge the legal status of nuclear weapons—and followed it!

Despite having no email, no salaries and meagre funding, we mobilised an international coalition of individuals and groups who succeeded in building a wave of support behind what became known as the World Court Project. A coalition of groups led by doctors, lawyers and peace people used their networks and personal contacts to secure the endorsement of hundreds of prominent people, including former Prime Ministers, judges, bishops, politicians, Nobel Laureates, and over 700 citizen groups from many countries. Nearly four million ordinary citizens worldwide signed individual Declarations of Public Conscience requesting the court to give its opinion, which were later presented to the United Nations and the World Court along with over 11,000 signatures from judges and lawyers.

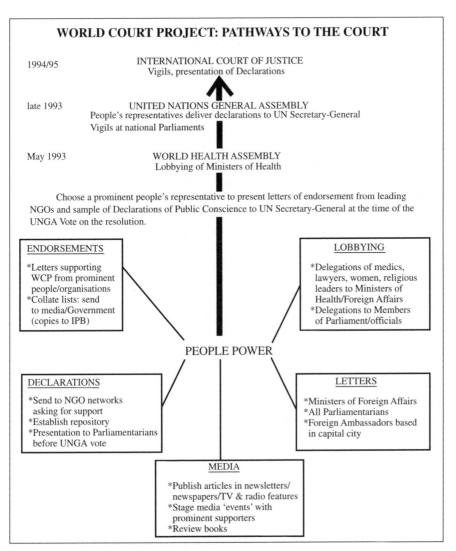

WORLD COURT PROJECT: PATHWAYS TO THE COURT

1994/95   INTERNATIONAL COURT OF JUSTICE
Vigils, presentation of Declarations

late 1993   UNITED NATIONS GENERAL ASSEMBLY
People's representatives deliver declarations to UN Secretary-General
Vigils at national Parliaments

May 1993   WORLD HEALTH ASSEMBLY
Lobbying of Ministers of Health

Choose a prominent people's representative to present letters of endorsement from leading NGOs and sample of Declarations of Public Conscience to UN Secretary-General at the time of the UNGA Vote on the resolution.

ENDORSEMENTS

*Letters supporting
 WCP from prominent
 people/organisations
*Collate lists: send
 to media/Government
 (copies to IPB)

LOBBYING

*Delegations of medics,
 lawyers, women, religious
 leaders to Ministers of
 Health/Foreign Affairs
*Delegations to Members
 of Parliament/officials

PEOPLE POWER

DECLARATIONS

*Send to NGO networks
 asking for support
*Establish repository
*Presentation to Parliamentarians
 before UNGA vote

LETTERS

*Ministers of Foreign Affairs
*All Parliamentarians
*Foreign Ambassadors based
 in capital city

MEDIA

*Publish articles in newsletters/
 newspapers/TV & radio features
*Stage media 'events' with
 prominent supporters
*Review books

Helped by letters of introduction from former New Zealand Prime Minister David Lange and the Minister of Disarmament, doors opened for talks with a range of UN ambassadors and diplomats, including the Chair of the 110-strong Non-Aligned Movement countries. They warned us that we would need a coalition of at least 50 countries to withstand the bullying of the nuclear-weapon states. As the movement grew, some brave states such as Ukraine, Belarus, Kazakhstan and New Zealand even broke ranks with their former nuclear allies. Nuclear-capable India was convinced by strong legal arguments to submit that nuclear weapons were illegal.

We encouraged participation by women at all levels of the project. At times, it was the eloquently heartfelt interventions, sharing of stories and challenges by women and indigenous peoples that helped shift hearts and minds of key individuals within the World Health Assembly, the UN General Assembly and at the World Court. Because women are often perceived as the nurturers of present and future generations, and they usually adopt a 'power with' rather than 'power over' model, their passionate and urgent messages about the threats to global security were often heeded by beleaguered decision makers.

On 8 July 1996, after deliberating on submissions from 43 states and the World Health Organisation, 14 World Court judges found that 'a threat or use of nuclear weapons would generally be contrary to the rules of international law applicable in armed conflict, and in particular the principles and rules of humanitarian law'. They also concluded that 'there exists an obligation to pursue in good faith and bring to a conclusion negotiations leading to nuclear disarmament in all its aspects under strict and effective international control'.

As a teenager, Jess, together with her sisters, heard this historic news from the Hague with 80-year-old Harold Evans at her home in Christchurch. They were exuberant. At last their futures and those of their grandchildren seemed more secure. Nuclear abolition was in sight.

Governments that had voted for nuclear disarmament for decades were inspired to work together to use their anti-nuclear majority in the United Nations. In December 1996, a resolution was adopted calling for a Nuclear Weapons Convention similar to the binding, enforceable treaty banning chemical weapons. Bolstered by the strength of international public opinion and the World Court decision, some nuclear allied states (such as Norway and Canada) reviewed their positions.

During the 1995 World Court oral proceedings, Australia announced the establishment of the Canberra Commission on the Elimination of Nuclear Weapons as a response to international outrage at the resumption of French nuclear testing. This prestigious 17-member committee included former military chiefs, political leaders, diplomats, scientists and doctors. In their report published in August 1996, a month after the World Court opinion, they criticised current nuclear policy and provided a plan for abolition: *'The first requirement for the five nuclear weapon states is to commit themselves unequivocally to the elimination of nuclear weapons and agree to start work immediately on the practical steps and negotiations required for its achievement.'*

A few months later, a member of the Commission, General Lee Butler (former Commander-in-Chief of US Strategic Command in charge of all American nuclear forces from 1992 to 1994) and 60 other generals and admirals from 17 countries issued a statement calling for an immediate reduction in nuclear stockpiles and taking all nuclear weapons off alert.

In early 1997, the European Parliament noted the importance of the World Court's decision and called for negotiations to begin leading to the conclusion of a Nuclear Weapons Convention. A US public opinion poll showed 87% support for such a treaty. The World Court project network expanded into *Abolition 2000,* with an 'abolition caucus' established on the Internet allowing participation by peace groups and individuals from all over the world.

Activists and lawyers began to take their governments to their own courts in an effort to apply the World Court decision. In Belgium, Germany, France, the United Kingdom and the United States, courageous teams broke into nuclear bases in order to be arrested and argue in court that they were upholding the law. In some cases they were acquitted! (See the website www.tridentploughshares.org) As with the campaigns to ban slavery and landmines, these initiatives are tapping into a deep and growing awareness that they are on the right side of morality, common sense, the law and public opinion.

Nevertheless, it is sobering to remember that there are still over 30,000 nuclear weapons worldwide, and the United States now wants to use nuclear 'bunker buster' weapons pre-emptively against extremists armed with weapons of mass destruction. On the other hand, in her short lifetime, Jess has witnessed most of the southern hemisphere declared nuclear-free, a Comprehensive Nuclear Test Ban signed, a successful Chemical Weapons Convention, and the World Court opinion. As an intern in 1999 with the Oxford Research Group thinktank and then the Lawyers' Committee on Nuclear Policy in New York, she saw at first hand how her government was taking a leading role on peace and disarmament in the United Nations. Her younger sister Annie is now working with Alyn Ware, another Kiwi pioneer of the World Court Project, in promoting a Nuclear Weapons Convention, establishing the Parliamentary Network for Nuclear Disarmament (www.pnnd.org), and supporting the Middle Powers Initiative (www.middlepowers.org) and Mayors for Peace (www.pcf.city.hiroshima.jp/mayors/). Recently she addressed a 3,000-strong Youth Rally at the sixtieth anniversary commemorations in Hiroshima and Nagasaki and is helping to establish Wellington as a Peace City.

All my daughters are fortunate to have been, and to continue to be, part of making the dream of nuclear abolition a possibility. My undimmed hope is that we will achieve this in my lifetime, and that one day I will hold a grandchild born into a nuclear-weapon-free world.

(See www.disarmsecure.org for more information about the World Court Project and other nuclear abolition initiatives.)

WHAT AILS THE HUMAN SPECIES?

Tania Dolley

Tania is a counselling eco-psychologist living in Wales

When asked to write about what I would do to make the world a better place, my first thought was, 'Wow, that's a tall order – where to begin?' As I contemplated the challenge of putting on paper many thoughts and feelings on a range of issues, I alighted on a few closest to my heart. Among the multiplicity of complex crises in our world, one that I feel urgently needs addressing concerns the wilful and relentless destruction perpetrated on the Earth and the consequences of this for all species, including ourselves. What is it about 'homo not-so-sapiens', particularly in industrial societies, that leads us to think and behave in ways which are environmentally – and potentially self-destructive?

It seems we have somehow got caught up in systems which disconnect us from natural sources of nourishment and simple ways of being and living. The effects of this disconnection can perhaps be felt in our hurried lifestyles, our belief in what it means to be wealthy, and in our separation from community and from our natural roots. As I thought about what action I would take, I realised that a central theme is time – or rather, lack of it: the lack of time just to be or to seriously pursue concerns that fire me.

Time and Being both tend to get lost in a society that places little value on these intrinsic necessities of wellbeing. Lacking time in this ever faster-paced world, too busy trying to survive and meet the demands and pressures of work, family and household finances, we have little time to engage with other things that really matter. To express my voice or make any contribution towards 'saving the world', however humble, I need to have enough 'spare' time to respond to issues beyond these immediate demands. Time is needed in order to read and be informed, to take appropriate action, to make connections with other people and groups and to participate in campaigns or in the democratic process, such as expressing my views to MPs. To connect with my own being to any depth also requires time. At the end of a two week holiday for example, a sense of restoration, energy and inner connection re-emerges – only for these precious new shoots to be drowned again in the deluge of daily demands upon return to the work routine. I struggle to keep my nose above water as too many tasks clamour for the crumbs of time available. Yet having time to *be* feels all the more important at a moment when the Earth, perhaps even our future survival as a species, needs our full authenticity, power and creativity to respond to the challenges that face us.

During my youth I travelled and lived in Asian societies where a different relationship to time exists, and discovered the great richness and depth this brings. One gift in having time to *be* is the freedom to discover and follow one's rhythm and inner process in ways that hectic daily schedules and modern time pressures do not allow. While occasional short retreats reaffirm the great need for and benefit of this quality time, I find the contrast with a Western lifestyle stark. Our economic system would appear to value neither this need nor time in itself, but only the thirty-five to fifty hours or more hours of our life utilised each week in work and productivity. Using up our time in production and consumption whilst ignoring the damaging effects of this on ourselves, others and the planet, we can end up denying part of our very being. Becoming strangers to ourselves, we seek surrogate sources of self, often by consuming commodities to fill an 'empty hole' inside but which can never truly 'feed' our deeper emotional needs and spiritual hungers.

The effects of these unfulfilled needs and hungers appear widespread. Statistics on mental health indicate that, along with the fast-growing percentage of the adult population suffering from depression, anxiety and other mental health disorders, an alarming number of children are now also prescribed anti-depressant medication. No doubt several factors give rise to these conditions, but reports rarely seem to enquire into why it might be that so many are suffering from psychological dis-ease. What is it about our society and lifestyles that may be generating such widespread unhappiness? Studies show that despite increased material wealth over the last fifty years, beyond a certain threshold allowing fulfilment of basic needs, we appear to be, in fact, no happier. This must surely call into question how we are currently living; once this threshold is attained, what do we really want for our lives? What values, priorities, and quality of life do we want to foster and create for ourselves and future generations? Do we really want to be working so flat-out to make ends meet or buy all the products and amenities we believe are an essential part of modern life, that we have no inner space or time to connect more deeply with ourselves, with family, friends and with nature?

I would like to see a reassessment of the value-basis of our society and economic system. Why do we, in the West at least, apparently value the creation of material 'wealth' above all else? While work may be a source of satisfaction, our compliance with the work ethic and spending the lion's share of our life's precious time and energy on the work treadmill, raises further questions. For what exactly are we creating prosperity? What, in fact, is real 'wealth'? We appear to have reversed Thoreau's maxim, 'that man is the richest whose pleasures are the cheapest'. We have come to expect high levels of material privilege, yet five Earths would be needed to provide enough resources for all six billion-plus of us to attain the same standard of living as the average American. But for whose gain have we been led to believe that it is only through constant consumption of goods and material products that we can be happy and acceptable? The advertising and marketing industries, for example, seek to cultivate feelings of inadequacy, deprivation and unfulfilment; as an advertising chief executive said over forty years ago, 'it's our job to make women unhappy with what they have'[1]. If their success lies in convincing us that our lives will not be happy unless we purchase their products, then to what extent might this consumption reflect manipulated insecurities and desires that 'products' can never fulfil? Since when, in short, was our purpose to serve the market, rather than the other way around?

A consequence of the prevalent unthinking behaviour towards our precious planet is the destabilisation of the global climate. Among increasingly frequent weather-disasters, we have recently seen chaos wrought in New Orleans by Hurricane Katrina. It seems somewhat ironic that it is the oil-refining area of a nation whose government refuses to participate in international efforts to reduce CO_2 emissions that is bearing the brunt (in this instance) of nature's likely response to global warming. Yet I have so far heard scant comment in news reports relating this to climate change. Notwithstanding natural cycles which contribute to extreme weather events, I wonder if this seeming unwillingness to make connections reflects a reluctance to face the uncomfortable truth that we may be reaping the results of our unsustainable lifestyles.

One of the psychological dimensions at play resembles the syndrome of addiction. Many of us seem unable or unwilling to moderate our high levels of consumption of energy and material goods. Like addicts in denial of the detrimental effects of their addiction, resistance to facing the destructive nature of excessive consumption to planet and self appears prevalent. Worst-case prospects of a runaway greenhouse effect – which we would be powerless to mitigate – and the consequent fate of life on Earth, fills me with dread. The overwhelming implications of the climate threat, including what we may have to change in our lifestyles in order to survive, may be too frightening or unpalatable to contemplate. Who truly wants to acknowledge that every time we jump in our car or fly off on holiday we add to this predicament confronting us all? Preoccupied with our daily stresses and commitments, we tend to avoid the issue in what looks like a cultural denial of what we do not want to face. At the 1992 Rio Earth Summit, George Bush Senior perhaps spoke not only for US citizens when he responded to suggestions that a major cause of the environmental crisis was industrial nations' huge demand for consumer goods by tersely claiming, 'the American way of life is not up for negotiation'. This apparently intransigent assumption of an unlimited 'right to consume' also reveals a collective addiction to over-consumption, dependent as it is on dwindling fossil fuels, that leaves four-fifths of the world's population below Western standards of poverty and deprived (as yet) of this 'right' to degrade the common global resources and ecosystems upon which all life on earth depends.

We surely have the capacity to produce solutions to these self-generated dangers. In resolving addiction and other psychological problems, one of the premises of therapy and healing is 'naming the unnameable'. This involves facing that which is avoided, suppressed or denied, and being willing to sit with uncomfortable and difficult feelings that may arise. Only once we can fully acknowledge a problem as it is, can we begin to address it. If I had a magic wand, it would bring about a 'consciousness revolution' to facilitate the shift in awareness and attitudes needed to embrace these global challenges, create sustainable and more equitable lifestyles for all who share this planet. It would help us recognise that somehow we seem to be colluding with an unhealthy system that threatens to carry us, lemming-like, over a cliff. It would broaden the scope for people to meet and express feelings about wider social and environmental issues, maybe with community-supported public discussion, to help generate a groundswell of shared concern and healing reconnection that could initiate a sea change in attitude, perspective and behaviour towards the way we live on this Earth.

My magic wand would also create a social and economic system that aspires to support and fulfil human needs and values; one that recognises the benefits of time: to think, to feel, to contemplate, to read, to meditate, to create, to connect with others and with nature, to listen to our deeper whispers and intuitions, to nourish the soul and spirit, to 'follow our bliss'! These are simple yet profound sources of nourishment and fulfilment that we seem to have forgotten. This approach would enable people to cover basic needs without having to work full-time and more, just to survive. That would indeed seem to require magic. . . Yet this may be similar to the early days of capitalism when employees would not work more than two or three days a week, since this was enough to make ends meet and free time was their priority – until bosses realised that the only way to make people work full-time was to halve their wages. Having time to *be* could also allow opportunities to connect more deeply with nature[2] – if we can experience in an embodied, felt-sense way our inter-connectedness with the Earth, we may be less likely to harm it.

Finally, if I could wave a magic wand, we humans would comprehend our interdependence with each other and the web of life, and engage deeper wisdom, psychological understanding and healing processes in addressing multifarious social and environmental challenges; at least we would begin to cooperate in a concerted and willing endeavour towards that end. Maybe the difficulties we face will serve as a kind of global wake-up call to jolt our seemingly adolescent species towards greater awareness and maturity. A spiritual revolution and enlightenment of humanity, perhaps?

Notes

1. Seager (1993) Earth Follies: Coming to feminist terms with the global environmental crisis. New York: Routledge, p.120
2. Reports indicate that one in seven children never plays in the countryside and that a generation of children have lost touch with nature (Woodland Trust, 2005).

WOMEN AS TEACHERS OF LOVE

Sister Dorah

Sister Dorah, a nun originally from the Solomon Islands, now lives in a convent in Surrey

What a good thing it would be if all the women throughout the world took on the responsibility of teaching their children how to love one another, to be honest, to care for both human beings and creatures, to live in peace, harmony and unity with each other. We should teach children how to be like this because it is *right*.

I think guiding children in this way is the most important thing in the whole world. If all women everywhere would bring up their children to be familiar with these qualities, I'm sure we would all wind up living in a better world. This is how everything could start to become reconnected. For it to work, this kind of teaching should be given when a child is small and continue until it is grown up.

In my view we must encourage all women everywhere to speak up and take their role as teachers more seriously and try harder, beginning with their own children in their own homes, towns, countries.

Here are the qualities we need to make a better world:

- *Love for each other, no matter what colour or race*
- *Respect for each other*
- *A desire to live in peace, harmony and unity*
- *Honesty*
- *Obedience*
- *A sense of caring*

Try this and see what happens. You will find it all makes a very big difference.

THE POWER OF FEMALE INFLUENCE

Bunty Dowell

Bunty, a Quaker, recently lost her husband and moved back to Coventry

Why? Why? Why? Now that the female has taken such action in the world's affairs in so many different ways—particularly in designing and running organisations—why isn't a greater impact being made on saving our planet and helping it continue? Are we perhaps *still* too intent on furthering our individual likes and so-called needs?

There is destruction all around us, and yet we continue to accept things which we have too many of anyway, even we who could have a tremendous influence on a different way of life.

How then do we make this change?

The answer is surely in *action* rather than words, and to do that, one has to be heard *by example*—show others the way. We have been accustomed to the majority's way—jumping in and out of cars, sometimes very *big* cars. Pride-making tins. Having and eating all things at all times in and out of season and nearly always resulting in masses and masses of space on container ships, together with aircraft carrying tons and tons and *more* tons of boxes filled with *things*. Things we'd mostly be better off without. And these ships and planes are all running on fuel which is most surely pouring destroyers of our ozone layer into the atmosphere.

We in this country make many weapons and sell them to practically any country that will buy them. Even though weapons of mass destruction will *never, never*, ever bring peace!

The big problem is that *change* is a long, long process, and I wonder how and if we can stop something now, when it has got to such a state, even though it's the thing we should concentrate on. How can we do it???

I can only go back to my sentence which stated: *by example*. To begin with, I shall feel lucky if even my close friends will see that this is really worth it and make the effort!

EQUALITY OF INCOME

Margaret Drabble

Margaret is a writer/sociologist with homes in London and Porlock Weir

> The grass is softer to my tread
> Because it rests unnumbered feet;
> Sweeter to me the wild rose red
> Because she makes the whole world sweet

This is the verse of a hymn we used to sing at school. I have never forgotten it. It may not be great poetry, but it expresses a fine attitude. I would like to save the world by reducing inequality, and giving us all a greater share in the world's pleasures. It is my hope and belief that pleasures shared are pleasures increased, and that we all have a capacity for greater happiness. The uneven spread of happiness is a constant misery to me, and, I'm sure, to many.

I would like to press a button that would radically redistribute the world's wealth. Thirty or forty years ago, I believed that this redistribution was going to take place, gradually and inevitably and peacefully, as democracy spread and technology improved. A form of benevolent egalitarianism would triumph—not a levelling down, but a levelling up. I would look at a map of Africa and believe in my lifetime all would be well in that troubled continent. There would be no *Heart of Darkness*. I thought that aid and development would abolish poverty in vast areas of the globe.

I was hopelessly wide of the mark. Not only has Africa plunged further and further into poverty, disease and warfare, but the gap between the rich and the poor in the affluent West is widening, not closing. We now seem to accept that selfishness, not common purpose and common interest, is the driving force of human nature. We seem to have lost any conception of a fairer world. In April 1988, at the aggressive height of the Thatcher revolution, I gave a lecture to the Progressive League, later published as a Fabian pamphlet, in which I argued what I call the 'Case For Equality'. In this lecture, I noted that the very word 'egalitarian' had, by a kind of relentless slippage, become a dirty word in politics. Hardly anybody defended egalitarianism then, as very few defend socialism now. I think I then blamed the worship of market economics and the triumphalism of unmediated capitalism for this shift away from a sense of justice as fairness and fair distribution, but now I see that even a New Labour government cannot commit itself to a programme of open redistribution. When the Chancellor of the Exchequer redistributes from the rich to the poor, he has to do so by stealth.

In America, the richest country in the world, the gap between rich and poor is ever widening, and the spectacle of private affluence and public squalor shows little sign of vanishing. Even in America, there are wage slaves, with an ever-diminishing share of the national cake. True, America is a democratic society in which, in theory, the careers are open to the talents, but the real income of the poor has been dropping and the numbers of the poor increasing, despite a thriving economy, despite the political success of Colin Powell and the ever-rising curve of the income of Bill Gates. A larger cake does not mean more for the poor, it means less. And globally, this trend continues to accelerate. We are moving into a world of the mobile, international, state-free rich, and the static, powerless poor. The best that the poor of the so-called developing world can hope for these days is an ill-paid job in appalling conditions to produce tourist facilities or sportswear or other luxury items for the markets of the West.

A world in which a minority of the world's population enjoys a living standard so much higher than the wildest dreams of the majority is neither fair nor stable. How can it be stable, when those dreams are displayed on satellite television to the poorest of the poor? No wonder resentment breeds, and take strange and violent shapes.

On September 11, 2001, the extent of that resentment became shockingly apparent. The twin towers of Trade trembled and fell, and the world trembled at the biblical spectacle. I see no hope of a better or more peaceful world until those that have reach some real accommodation with those who have not, and stop using them as a kind of disposable slave labour. There has been much heart-searching in the West about the causes of terrorism, and I am not alone in suggesting that global inequality has something to do with it. I think Tony Blair agrees with me. But he'll have to express himself very simply if he wants to get through to Mr Bush. There is a terrifying lack of imagination in some of the statements that have come out of these recent events. One of the most shocking was from an American military apologist for the conditions in which the prisoners of the Afghan War were—and as I write, still are—being held in

Guantanamo Bay in Cuba. He said, 'It's like the Hilton Hotel there, compared to what these guys have been used to.' Anyone who can't see how inflammatory that remark is should try working for a year and keeping a family on local wages in a hotel kitchen in a developing county. And those who work in hotel kitchens are some of the lucky ones.

So my solution to the world's problems is really very simple. Let us introduce a global minimum wage. I am very happy to have my own income reduced to a global level that would permit this. Think of the joy of going to bed at night knowing that nowhere in the world are people dying of poverty and hunger. Think of the delight of a world without envy and fear. I agree to pay up with pleasure. I will gain, not lose, from this new world order.

Ignore the cynics who say this would remove incentive and invention and progress. Let's give it a try. Ignore those who tell us it would make the human race stagnate. On the contrary, it might release untold energy. Ignore those who tell us that the poor are used to being poor, and wouldn't really know how to cope with being a little less poor. Give the poor a choice, and let them find out for themselves. Ignore those who say it's not practical. The way we live now isn't practical either.

We've already invented a way of destroying ourselves at the push of a button. Is it beyond the wit of man and woman to invent a machine with a button for redistribution, instead of a button for destruction?

SAVING THE WORLD

Ann Drysdale

Ann is a writer who has published both poetry and prose, and worked as a journalist for the Yorkshire Evening Post

I am thinking about it. A cup of tea at my elbow and a deadline in my back like a gangster's gun. Why did I let myself in for this? Save the world indeed!

Whose world? My world? It seems a little arrogant to save that at the possible expense of anyone else's and I have lived long enough to know that there are as many worlds as there are minds to construct them. Where shall I look for guidance?

Jesus of Nazareth had a few good ideas till the tentmaker from Tarsus started fiddling with them and the various churches, exclusive, seditious and militant, teased them out into heresies and obsessions. The Lord Krishna, on the battlefield of Kurukshetra, went into the minutiae of man's duty to the universe, but answered Arjun's most perceptive questions with a quick flash of his divine self and the subtext 'Because I say so'.

The Dalai Lama has written of 'Kindness, Clarity and Insight'. The order intrigues me. Kindness comes first. What is kindness? In the medieval codes of chivalry it was one of the distinguishing features of a true knight. In our western mysticism it is one of the seven contrary virtues, direct opposites of the deadly sins. In that context it is the other face of envy. The work of envy in the world is evident and needs no sad catalogue.

I am a poet, of a sort. My work is quoted as satire; I am accused of wit. My hero, Samuel Johnson, wrote prose that could scorch a man at fifty paces. Yet it was he who wrote, 'Kindness is in our power, even when fondness is not.' It is having that choice that makes us human, that marks us out from the rest of the animal kingdom. It is the exercise of it that gives us what Yeats called 'these great responsibilities'. Accepting those responsibilities, albeit with pursed lips and an irritated sigh, and using kindness as a yardstick in their execution might be as good a place to start as any.

WALKING OUT OF THE SHADOWS

A Call To Power

Sally Eaves

Sally is a teacher at the Small School, works with the Wholesome Food Association, and lives in Devon

When I sit in my mind and watch the earth from that high place that sees all, a sort of sickening lurch grabs me in the pit of my stomach. How *can* they be doing this? Why can't They see? … It is always 'They'. When I come out of the high place into the present moment, it's quite simply, 'What am *I* doing? It's down to me.'

The interconnectedness of the whole of our present existence on planet earth is inescapable. When the pursuit of power, profit and financial well-being and the betterment of our own individual lives is the major driving force, only a radical rethink of our human consciousness can hope to unravel the Gordian Knot. I have chosen to look at three out of many issues.

First, it's the Bigger and Better, *Travel Further To Have More Choice* decisions of government, business … and ourselves: industry, schools, hospitals, supermarkets. Despite all the present awareness of global warming, the immense machine continues on its unstoppable trajectory, with no regard for a need to change *now*, not in ten years' time. We all find ourselves trapped in a web of endless journeys which feels as if it is not of our making.

Second, there's the War Machine with its many layers of intra-personal fears translated onto the world stage, political machinations to guarantee future fuel supplies, and no doubt personal gain for individuals and industry. This is where the 'How can They be doing this?' turns into an ear-splitting scream of horror, dismay and powerless guilt. How *can* They be destroying human lives on this scale and polluting land which They do not love with a farmer's heart?

Finally, the Consumption Machine, where we in the West and North live like emperors of old with infinite, overwhelming choice; so stuffed with consumer trash that we can no longer move in our houses and are filling distant rubbish dumps and landfill to overflowing, like we fill our supermarket trolleys which groan with the excesses of infinite credit

83

while glossing over mountains of food rotting just out of sight off the supermarket shelves or in our own personal dustbins.

All this is so truly sick it is unbearable. We are behaving like a species with such profoundly flawed genes that it would be better if we were exterminated. Our minds have been developed at the expense of the free and feeling heart. We are held in the grid lines of social and work structures largely devised by human brains and they are running roughshod over our organic and natural selves.

What have we to offer as women? As those who give birth and are still mercifully connected to moon cycles, we have a better chance of reconnecting to our hearts and to our earthbound selves. As a single working woman, I personally was blissfully disconnected from the powerlessness of women across the world and through the ages. When I became a mother, it hit me like a blow on the head and I went under, hanging onto material securities in a world which had no caring structures to support the parenting I was programmed to do. I colluded with the system, glad enough of the security of a roof over my head and food on the table, even more glad when once again I had a regular pay packet.

So, don't we all end up like that, women and men, just doing what is next on the list, accepting the status quo, quietly despairing about what They are doing on the other side of the world or in places of power to which we have no access? We make few private adjustments: buying fair-trade (if we can get it), eating organically (when it is not too expensive), cutting down on car journeys (when we can).

Heaven help us! The world is cracking at the seams; glaciers melting, polar bears drowning, winds howling, and we are still travelling 120 miles every week to work; the government is still planning to close smaller hospitals, and my own local authority is rebuilding a 2,000-strong school to serve a 30-mile-wide radius, busing children hundreds of miles a week.

So, women throughout the whole world, it is time to take your power. We in the West and North hardly know what it is to be powerless compared with those who doggedly serve and love, where starvation, droughts, floods and war rob them of the basic means. It is down to those of us who have the material freedom to make choices, to start saying loud and clear what we know in our hearts to be true. *Enough is enough.*

It has never been right to close our hearts to the suffering of others, to treat the Earth and her beauty, her resources, like an inexhaustible Goddess whose only role is to service our needs. We are behaving like infantile children, using Her with careless unconsciousness and trampling on the powerless like ants on our roads.

It has to stop. Now. It won't stop unless we as individuals make radical changes in our own lives. Not just little adjustments, but major restructuring. It won't stop unless we force our governments to do the same. It won't stop unless those whose hearts are still alive enough allow themselves to see that our planet is falling apart, physically and morally, and to weep for the destruction we as a species have caused.

Our hearts must break and scream so loudly that the resonance will shatter the prison walls which defend us from our neighbour's pain. The change has to be at this heart level, because unless we can all openly weep for the mistakes we have made and allowed others to make on our behalf, we cannot reach that sea of mutual forgiveness and openness which will be the current that unites us. For centuries we have been practising the importance of the individual, the boundaries of the family or tribe, the sanctity of the nation-state. At this point in earth's history, if we don't work *together* with our neighbours; if we don't open ourselves to people of every class and colour; if we don't care as much for the destinies of those on the other side of the planet whose lands are already sinking under the oceans, being washed away by floods or burning in the heat of the sun—then we as a species have scant hope of survival other than as bedraggled remnants, no wiser than before, lucky enough to scrabble for a living and start the whole charade all over again.

We must work together across national and personal divides to save not only our material beautiful sparkling planet, but also the soul of humankind, which for so long has lived in competition and strife. Disaster and catastrophe I believe are now inevitable. We as women must take our role as *equal* leaders ushering in a new age of compassion built on the wreckage and grieving we have all created. Please let us use this hard path of learning to make profound changes in the human psyche, to create a world where Matter and Spirit live in balance and where the *I* and the *We* dance together into the spiral of eternity.

TOO MANY, TOO MUCH

Morag Edwards

Morag, born in Scotland, now lives in Somerset, where she does voluntary work for the RSPCA and performs in her local panto

If I could wave a magic wand to make the world a better place, I'd do something about capitalism and greed and the fact that it's being spread around too fast by far too many people. *People.* There are far, far too many of us!! That's the biggest handicap we have to confront. Scientists are wasting money on attempting to extend our lifespan. (It could be useful to remember that all other species which suffer from over-population eventually destroy themselves.)

Who wants to live to 150 with all the problems age brings? (I do wonder why we have IVF treatment when there are already so many humans and plenty of kids waiting to be adopted. IVF treatment should be scrapped.) On the other hand, we'll need all those young things to look after us; take us to the lavatory and mop our chins as we dribble into our soup.

Building more houses, Mr Prescott, is *not* the answer, though maybe a few more terraced old people's homes might be a good idea. Of course, we could always implement a major cull every September for both the over-60s and the under-10s, and do it alphabetically just to make it fair. If your name begins with 'A', you're stuffed.

Forget the diet, cancel the pension payment, and make the most of the time you have left, like watching England beat Australia at cricket. If we carry on as we are, we'll end up with still more cars, more roads, more rubbish (talking of which, does anyone pick up litter other than me?), more pavement, more noise, more landfills, longer queues, harder benches, more crowded classrooms, shorter sausages (there won't be enough food to go around or oil to transport what there is; the whole house of cards will crumble) ...

This silly capitalist system relies on growth, but doesn't take into account that growth ultimately means more pollution, more, more, more of everything. For decades, scientists have been warning us about lowering our CO_2 emissions, but far from cutting them back, perpetual growth means they are increasing, and when you put countries with huge populations such as China and India (China, incidentally, is building hundreds of coal-powered power stations) into the equation, it wouldn't be advisable to build or buy property on the flood plains—which each successive government and new batch of COs seem to think is a good idea. (Perhaps this is Prescott's subversive plan to eliminate the poorer classes; if the cull doesn't get you, the floods will.)

Surely if we don't come up with a system that sets limits to population growth *and* emphasises environmental factors which harmonise with nature (unlike the capitalist system, which seems to disregard them), we'll *all* wind up on the flood plain, metaphorically speaking. I mean, don't those bigwigs at the top have children? What sort of future do they think *they'll* inherit?

My goodness, there are more than six *billion* of us and we are growing at the rate of roughly a million a day. How can the earth ultimately cope with those kinds of numbers? I'd wave my magic wand over and over and simply quietly and gently *eliminate* a lot of them so things would become more manageable. And maybe then we'd have an easier time figuring out how to create an educational system that really worked and taught people what they most needed to know—like $2 + 2 = 4$, then 1,000, then 10,000, a million, ten million and on and on. One thing we *do* know (or should) is that if unstable countries are helped to become stable (through literacy programmes, self-sufficiency work programmes, etc.), birth rates decrease, and this would ultimately help increase stability in the world.

I'd also limit the population by stopping Family Allowance. If you want kids you should be able to pay for them and be responsible for them on your own. (After all, if you want a dog or a horse you have to pay for it.) I'd even go so far as to say each couple should be required to have a *licence to breed*. I'd install some sort of tax system too—every couple would have to submit to a kind of environmental tax (or levy) on their kid. Actually, why not extend that to every human; if you live, you have to pay for the privilege. But if you have no money, the taxpayer would have to come to your rescue, and maybe that way eventually the Moneygrubbing System would learn to become responsible. (As a boost to population decrease, I think I'd also put typhoid in the water. Well, it's a thought.)

In any case, too many people means too many consumers, and all those consumers want a house, a car, a TV, a computer, electricity, fuel, toys, clothes, gadgets, microwaves, washing machines, hair dryers and on and on. This capitalist system relies on *growth*—a permanent state of growth, and we simply can't have that on a planet built on finite resources. When you go watch a football match at the stadium, when all the seats are taken, no more tickets are sold. That's one way of dealing with what's finite; stop offering seats in the stadium of Planet Earth.

Another way to help bring the population down: I might open a shop and start serving botulism sandwiches. Why not? Fewer people would mean less pollution, less money spent on industry and agriculture, no need to build new roads and houses. We could get back to the corner shop and make Tesco shrink (and I'd start serving wholemeal sandwiches filled with cheese and home-grown lettuce and tomato, skip the botulism). There'd be fewer planes, fewer old car tyres (what happens to them in the end, anyway?), freely flowing sewers, no traffic jams. We wouldn't have to disappear under concrete. There'd be smaller classes in schools, the NHS could cope. It would relieve the huge strain on city centres, government, county councils, the police force. Everything could become smaller too: malls, car parks, halls, housing estates. We could get rid of lots of superfluous ugliness and start afresh with a less greedy mindset. (Maybe eventually we could live in dolls' houses—that would really conserve space!)

The quarry at the back of my house could be gotten rid of. There'd be more land for my chickens to run around on. I wouldn't have to keep driving past those tatty council estates. There'd be far less strain on natural resources (whose are they, may I ask? Why do we assume they all belong to us?) There are simply too many of us taking too much from the environment. We take too many fish, use too many trees, foul too much water, squander too many animals, extract too many goodies from the earth. We don't use things, then put them back and recycle them the way all other living things do. Whatever happened to our mental wiring???

I feel so strongly about this that I'd eliminate everyone who takes more than one annual holiday abroad (maybe I'd eliminate the long-distance fliers altogether). And when they do take off, they'd have to go by bike or train. Ditto with anyone who uses plastic bags (or *anything* plastic), anything that pollutes. I'd just tap them with my magic wand, and *poof,* they'd permanently disappear. With fewer people, we could slow down, make time for each other, work less hard, learn to tell stories, and maybe for a change, we'd realise how damn lucky we are to be here at all.

MY POINT OF VIEW ON HOW TO SAVE THE PLANET

Martha Ekins

Martha, who was 12 when she wrote this, is a schoolgirl living in Dartmoor, and is a leader in her neighbourhood

If I was given a wish that I could change the environment I live in, it would be to stop any aircraft flying in the sky above us. This would change the smells we inhale every day, smells which damage our health as well as the health of plants and animals around us. The noise planes make is awful; it runs through your head and right out the other side. When you take off on planes, your ears pop. People say it is good to chew something, but does that really help? Altogether, it would save time, money and the health of everything if we didn't have those big machines to get around in.

My second wish would be to stop people from making mobile phones, televisions, computers, PlayStations and other unnecessary electrical appliances. This is because so many children have been harmed by what some of these machines can do to their brains. For example, mobile phones can seriously damage your hearing because of the sound waves put into your body whilst you are using the phone. Also, too many children, instead of playing outside, are choosing to stay in all day watching television and playing on computers and PlayStations because they think it's cool and good fun! Your friend might think it's cool and fun to stay inside all day and do these things, but don't go with your friend's point of view, stick with your own.

My final wish would be to stop people and machinery from chopping down trees in the rainforest and other forests in the world. I think this is why so many animals are becoming extinct, homeless, or dying—because of what people and machinery are doing to their territory.

Some animals are rare, but even so, people don't care what will happen to them. Some people kill animals just for parts of their body, like their head, hooves and skins. Other people do it for money and fun. Animals are beautiful creatures and when you see a certain type, it can be very exciting. If we were actually good to animals, all kinds of people would be able to have the pleasure of seeing them living as they were meant to.

Together we can help save the world and make it a better place for plants, animals and humans to live in!

MORE YIN; LESS YANG

Scilla Elworthy

Scilla is a peace and social activist who lives near Oxford

Women saving the planet? Hummm … I'm not so sure that women themselves are the issue. The issue seems to me to be a disastrous imbalance in the world between yin and yang.

You know the famous symbol for yin/yang?

Well today, in the reality of the 21st century, it looks more like an overwhelm of yang:

It makes me want to scream when I see what we're doing to our planet by this excess of yang – the masculine principle. Yang does many things well, but when out of balance it makes a deadly and terrible mess. For example:

- In our passion to make money we have destroyed three-quarters of the earth's forests and polluted much of the fresh water, rather than caring for the earth.
- We spend $800 billion on armaments every year, yet do not provide the food and water needed by half the world's people.

- In our passion for energy and speed we have fundamentally altered the climate of the planet.
- We listen obsessively to strangers in the media, yet cannot listen to our children, our family, our neighbours.
- We want a quick fix, we believe technology will sort out all our problems; we don't take time to develop and use wisdom.
- We use force to fight terror, rather than understand its causes and break the cycle of violence.

But it's not too late. For over forty years I've been working to restore the balance, and I'm just amazed at how—quite suddenly—people are now waking up and taking action. *And* having a good time doing it.

So, what can people do to restore balance?

1. We can take care of a piece of the earth: find a bit of land to restore to natural health. In most cities you can rent an allotment for a few pounds a year, and it's fun to see your seeds coming up. And even more fun to eat your own gorgeous organic pesticide-free lettuce. If you prefer water, find a river to clean up. There are plenty around full of plastic bottles, and kids love to help. Or help to re-plant a forest.
2. We can refuse to pay that part of our taxes spent on arms. Brave pensioners are going to jail for this (find out how it works on www.conscienceonline.org.uk).
3. We can cut our use of fuel, especially air travel, in half every year. If everyone did this, the fuel/energy shortage would be history.
4. We can seek out those we disagree with, understand their point of view, step into their shoes. Listening, and a deep willingness to understand the situation of the other is a vital ingredient in breaking any cycle of violence, however domestic. It is difficult to do, and requires all the yin traits of quietness, attention, patience and courage.
5. We can use any of a multitude of ways available now to develop wisdom (visit www.wisdomuniversity.org or www.integralinstitute.org or www.transcend.org).
6. We can break the cycle of violence. Peace Direct is offering all sorts of ways that people can do something for peace, and they have a book—*War Prevention Works*—with fifty stories about what people have already done (see www.peacedirect.org).

I could go on explaining other ways to break a cycle of violence, but you will have many ideas of your own. I must add that, in all the practical suggestions I can think of, I do believe that men are needed just as much as women.

Plus we have a secret ingredient, an extremely powerful ally. Nature, as we have seen in recent years, is awesomely powerful. Nature naturally re-balances itself. So we can work with nature, rather than fighting her.

So, what we need to do, urgently, is to re-balance yin and yang. We need to do this in the world, and we need to do it in ourselves. The ancient Chinese goddess of compassion, Kwan Yin, illustrates this balance more beautifully for me. In her quiet, calm, serene way—and in her bare feet—she is riding on the back of a fierce dragon in a storm. In China the dragon is a symbol not of menace but of power and force—in other words yang. The two together, in balance, make their way through a ferocious storm. This storm can be no fiercer than the storms our world faces now.

SO YOU WANT TO BE A POWERFUL WOMAN?

Liz Evans

Liz is ex-manager of Happy Landings animal rescue centre in Somerset

There's nothing like a powerful woman, and Karen's threatening me right now, so I must write. I am to be your conscience for animals. I have worked in animal welfare for over fifteen years and I manage an animal rescue shelter—therefore I am supposed to be qualified.

What aspect of animal welfare should I hit you with? There are so many. But let's go with Women and Animals—now that should conjure up some ideas, but probably not the ones that a man may think of!

Let's look at your purchasing power—let's hit 'em where it hurts. From the young teenage girl who visits the cosmetics counter very regularly, to the woman who buys for the family—oh my! What purchasing power we have. What influence we have. We can deny companies their sales and their income if we want to. We can make statements with what we do or do not buy—very often on behalf of many people—our families. We can do it individually, every single day. Can you imagine the power of even 50,000 women, the effect that would have? How, then, do we use this power?

Hands up all those who are reading this who have pets now. Hands up all those who have had a pet at some stage of their life. Most of us. And yet how many of us think 'animals' when we go shopping? Very few, I suspect. We go for the cheapest food because we are pressurised into buying economically rather than with morality; we go for cosmetics to keep us 'young and beautiful' … check on testing? … probably not. Who looks to see where it has come from? … very few. Yet we have such power that we don't use … we stand in the corner, wringing our pretty little hands and saying, 'Oh, what can we do about it?'

Working in animal welfare means, from time to time, we get batches of bunnies from breeding farms that were destined for the laboratory to have chemicals dropped into eyes with lids that are pinned back to see what effect they have. Bits of skin cut out to drop more chemicals into to check the reaction … oh, I could go on but I fancy you wouldn't have the stomach for it. So what is the choice? There's loads. Yes, by all means buy

97

things to keep you 'young and beautiful', but how difficult is it to find out if it or any of its ingredients are tested on animals? You look on the back—if it *doesn't* say anything about animals, it has been tested, if not in this country, far worse—abroad. Look for supermarket products; you can check right the way back to individual ingredients. The cheapest toothpaste in Tesco is not tested on animals, so you can still have pearly white teeth. How difficult is that? *You* are responsible for animal testing these days—*you* have the choice.

Then we come to meat. I am a most reluctant vegetarian. I like meat, I can eat meat, but I must know where it has come from. I took a year out of animal welfare and went to work for a transport company delivering refrigerated and frozen foods; much of that was meat. The screams of 'it must be with the buyer by 10 a.m. this morning' had nothing to do with the buyer needing the product—it meant it was out of date if it arrived much later! 'Don't tell the buyer where it has come from, he thinks it's British'—that means it's been imported with British labels on it! Oh yes, it happens.

Do you have any idea where your meat comes from? What conditions those animals endured before ending up in a sanitised packet in front of you? Probably not. If it's cheap chicken it could have come from the Far East, enduring conditions you wouldn't put a dead chicken through. Do you care? But you say 'love' animals. Shouldn't that 'love' include responsibility and some sort of morality? Every time you buy something that causes an animal to suffer—face the fact—*you* have the choice. *You* have the power.

Learn your labels—your pizza was packed in the UK—big deal, it probably died abroad, or worse, was transported, terrified and suffering to the UK—to die. Why bother? Your meat pie is likely to have bits in it that would make you heave if you knew what part of the animal it came from—and you can put that in your mouth and swallow it?

I am in my fifties (alas), so can remember the small farmer who knew his animals, who cared for his animals, whose remit was not to earn a fortune but to earn a living. After the war, successive governments encouraged farmers to produce more and more food, but in doing so, they produced sheep who can suffer and be in pain from foot rot for their entire lives without it being treated since the treatment costs more than the sheep itself; pigs that breed in spaces that mean they cannot even turn round; turkeys for your Christmas that are so top heavy with meat for you that their legs often give out before they are slaughtered—Merry Christmas. And chickens. 'Oh, I got such a bargain in the supermarket today—the chickens were £1 each.' Fed antibiotics daily to keep them from dying before they get to be sanitised packets; forced to think day is night and night is day—to eat more and put on more weight so you get a better 'bargain'. 'I only buy it for the dog'—you might, but it perpetuates the market.

Eggies are good for you—but if you saw the battery or the barn hen, the conditions your eggies are laid in, you wouldn't put them near your mouth. But there is choice: free range eggs, free range chickens, organic meat, non-animal-tested cosmetics and cleaning products, etc. I am not saying that everyone wants to be vegan or even vegetarian, we should go without leather shoes or not buy wavy crisps manufactured by the biggest tester on animals in the United Kingdom; but I am saying, you want to be powerful women? You can be. You want to change things? *You* have the choice. *You* have the power. Whether you use it is another matter.

A NEW MYTHOLOGY

Josie Felce

Josie is a social activist, a storyteller in schools, plays the folk harp, and lives near Stroud, Gloucestershire

I love men passionately and have a keen appetite for sex, but find I am still unable to live comfortably with a man. It has turned into a lifetime's quest to find a compatible mate. I ask myself, '*What is the difference between a man and a woman?*'

I have started with the obvious: his sex organs are on the outside and hers are on the inside. He ploughs, furrows, goes hunting, shoots arrows and reaches out into the world to find meaning and satisfaction. As for a woman, she considers how she feels, and consults the cycle of her womb before relating to the outside world. She intuitively knows seasons (as her womb does), when it is time to be passionate, when to care for her family and when to retreat and nurture her inner body. And from this inner rhythm comes a great glow which can be both seen and felt. Men cannot resist it!

At a summer camp this year, I saw and heard an Aboriginal storyteller named Francis Firebrace. He had painted a picture of the sun goddess as she rode the skies, lighting the masculine moon that followed her. I was amazed. All the pictures and stories I had heard were about the *male* sun god casting his light on the *feminine* moon. I was brought up with the idea that men had the power and energy, and women were the followers. What would happen if I changed this around? Woman rubs her fertile belly, knows it is time for passion, and beckons her man. If she is on cue, she gives birth and everyone rejoices in the new life. She does this even when she has enough real children; she births ideas, projects, home redecoration, grandmothering, paintings, writing, dances and anything else she feels passionate about. She shines out! Man loves her in this mode; if she is skilful, she can turn his head from hunting expeditions and wild projects far away into focusing his energy as she desires. She is the sun and he is the moon.

How would this affect the solving of our day-to-day problems? With this new mythology, we view things from the cradle of creation, all the way down through the birth channel. If processed food makes us ill, then we won't produce it any more or try to sell it on to others—because we care for all the family of humanity, not just our bank balances.

If too many cars have caused a jamming-up of motorways, and air pollution around schools has brought on asthma in our children, then we must try to use other forms of transport. We don't need to continue high-powered selling of more and more petrol cars, to the point where no one can move or breathe. If laws are no longer useful in serving the well-being of all, then they can be changed. If the media is abusing our sense of horror and drama, then we need to report in a more harmonious, balanced way—so that we can live joyfully, with hope in our hearts. If one nation has offended another, powerful and useful negotiations can take place. Nations do not need to go to war; doing so will only kill off the children we have borne and lovingly cared for.

As I write, some of these changes are happening. Children wait at a 'walking bus' stop to meet an adult who will walk with them to school, rather than be driven all the way into the school playground, the vehicle clogging up the road and spewing out noxious exhaust fumes to be breathed in by the parents' own children. Car-sharing clubs are being set up in the city nearest to me, Bristol, and probably in many other cities too. There is talk of enough wealth being enough: downshifting materialism. Perhaps this is just pragmatic; an obvious solution to the problem.

To really change the world effectively, I think we need the new mythology of cherishing humanity, understanding its need to grow in a wholesome way, a multidimensional way, the way in which a mother nurtures her children. This is the feminine dawning as the sun on a new day, reflected by a masculine moon ready to glow with a new light.

> If women dropped bombs,
>   they would be full of flowers, balms
>   and healing herbs.
> If women went to war,
>   they would go to hear their sisters' pain
>   and tell their own.
> If women moved boundary lines,
>   they would negotiate changes in child care
>   and community centers.
> If women were arms manufacturers,
>   they would fit them for free to mutilated
>   children.

If you love a woman,
　　Can you hear her deep longing
　　to sing this song of love?

COME HOME TO EAT

Molly Fisk

Molly is a poet and writing teacher living in Northern California

Some holy person—I can't remember if it's the Dalai Lama or Thich Nhat Han—recommends a spiritual practice of tracing what you use back to its source, whether it's a piece of clothing, a type of food, your toothbrush, your car tyres, or your Sunday *New York Times*. I've always loved the idea of this, but have never done a darn thing about it. However, I live in a town where the phrases 'local food production' and 'peak oil' are suddenly mantras, resonating even in my distracted middle-class brain. As I was eating dinner last night, I looked at the zucchini—cooked in a little olive oil and a lot of garlic—and suddenly wondered where it had come from.

In the summertime I successfully grow tomatoes and zucchini in my garden. I buy the rest of my vegetables from the farmer's market. Those are grown within about a 40-mile radius. In winter, I know enough not to purchase grocery-store tomatoes because they taste like styrofoam cooler lids, but I still buy zucchini. I'm ashamed to say it didn't occur to me until very recently that if I wasn't growing zucchini in *my* garden, there was a good chance nobody *else* around here was either, and what I was buying in the store might come from some place quite far away.

The zucchini from Trader Joe's says 'grown in Mexico' right on the package, and that's where my local grocery gets theirs too, both the regular and the organic. No one could tell me *where* in Mexico, so I don't know how long the truck ride for these zukes is: 400 miles, or 1,400. Do they even come by truck? Maybe planes loaded with zucchini fly into Sacramento Airport. Either way, that's a lot of fossil fuel used up to make dinner. I'm starting to see why *peak oil* and *local food* appear in the same sentence.

If a person is not going to buy zucchini in March, what should he or she eat instead? Broccoli? Cabbage? Those are cold-weather crops, and grown in Texas, says my grocer. Carrots right now are either from Bakersfield or Washington State. I'm going to need a road atlas pretty soon, and some mileage tables, I can tell. How do I even begin to eat locally? Set up grow-lights in my basement? Freeze enough in summer to last me all year? And then what's the price of the electricity for either of those methods? It can't be as much as one plane trip from Mexico, or can it?

I hate math problems. I know I can get eggs nearby, and organic milk from the Strauss Creamery in Marshall, three hours away. Ditto organic beef from Niman Ranch, although I'm sure there's some closer and cheaper. I can bake my own bread, although I don't know where the nearest flour mill is. But what do I do about vegetables? Store turnips in a root cellar? I hate turnips.

As you can see, I'm in a muddle. Luckily, this week there's a conference in town called *Come Home to Eat* that can answer these questions. I'll be there. I'm trying to do my part to save the planet, even if it means learning to eat turnips. And who knows? Maybe they can tell me if there's a source closer than Burlington, Vermont for Ben & Jerry's ice cream.

RADICAL KINDNESS

Mandy-Louise Fletcher

Mandy-Louise, originally from Hampshire, now lives in Devon. She has a degree in world religions and teaches meditation.

Problem

The other day I heard my eight-year-old niece playing with a hand-held computer game, chanting 'kill him, kill him', and wondered how that will help this child grow up into a well-rounded adult. What impact is this going to have when she grows into womanhood? How will she know what compassion is? How are all the children around the world going to view each other when they see through the jaundiced eyes of the media? After eighteen years of looking at each other in the news in black and white, how are these young people supposed to have a balanced view of other people and nations? How will they relate to their sexuality? (As a way to manipulate, or to be held as sacred or a mystery?) If they are not treated with kindness and respect in our society, how will they learn the meaning of respect and kindness? If parents and society as a whole don't think about and take responsibility for what a child is absorbing, mentally, emotionally and spiritually, then we'll continue to land up with the mess we're in now.

In 2004 we watched the tsunami with horror on our television screens, dead bodies and all. But I suggest that this constant exposure to seeing such things in graphic detail is unnecessary and damaging. It anaesthetises us to suffering, rather than helping us understand it. We are no longer appalled when we see a dead person on our screen; such sights have become normal. Many years ago women were considered to be gentle creatures who needed protecting. I'm not saying I agree with this, but I think there should be global standards of decency beyond which no one should venture. This would be for our good mental health and well-being. It's not something that should be imposed by government; it will occur organically as we citizens of the planet demand it.

We are the ones who want change to be brought about. We are the ones who are raging against the dying of the light, the death of our humanity, our being-ness as humans, which is all that separates us from the animals.

The aggressive, self-centredness at the heart of the media, this disregard for each other in pursuit of money, has to lie at the heart of the problems in our society. As sensible people we can see that. As sensible people we talk about these things—-and feel impotent. Maybe it is only through the movement of women that things can change. Women tend to have kinder hearts than men.

Our media plays a huge role in this. I believe it's the glue which holds the world together or forces it apart and as such, has a huge responsibility. We're at a point where indiscriminate sex and violence on TV are normal. When we challenge the media moguls they say such things are germane to the plot. What we all need to ask is, what are stories like this doing on TV in the first place? Films are just as bad. The action thriller has gone way beyond what is decent. Horror movies are truly horrific, yet people attentively absorb every moment of them. Any sensible individual will recognise that this has to affect our brains, and therefore the way we behave in society. Anything that promotes horrific violence should never be made public. Why deify violence? By doing so we wind up with a society that is increasingly violent and feels that violence is justified.

In the same way, computer games are an increasing threat to society. I would argue that the violent ones shouldn't be allowed and certainly not be accessible to children. Would you feed your child poisoned food that made them aggressive and uncaring? Why give them mental food that will do the same thing?

Lately in England we've had a spate of children killing other children, and even attacking and killing adults. Bob Geldof talked about children in Africa who were made to kill each other. We can't say, 'Oh, it's in another country, and they're not the same as us.' We *are* the same. We may live differently, but ultimately we are all human beings who need love, kindness and understanding.

We are accepting all of this, being complicit in its action, allowing our children's minds to be poisoned. We're allowing our minds to be anaesthetised to violence, to unkindness. We like to *think* of ourselves as kind people, but are we? As we step past the homeless, the beggars, as our ozone layer shrinks, as wars rage, as we ignore our neighbour's plight, as we vie for getting our own way regardless of the other fellow, we think, 'Well, it's not me, so it doesn't matter and anyway, I didn't start it.' Or, 'How can I do any thing about it? The problem is far too great for me to have any effect.'

Solution

The solution has to be to look at our common humanity and see what is needed to hold it together. The main thing we all desire in life is for people to be kind and to respect us. This is why we have a certain set of friends—because we know they will be kind to us. This is why we go to certain places on holiday. We seek out the places where the natives are friendly, where we feel it is safe to rest, relax and recuperate. When we are ill we don't expect our nurse or carer to be unpleasant. To live a happy and complete life, we need a strong dose of kindness. Otherwise, just like a dog that is cruelly treated, we become aggressive and go on to create an aggressive society.

Therefore, I would like to offer *radical kindness* as a solution to today's ills. I believe a lack of kindness has caused all our problems and is also what can cure them. We need to start the ball rolling by asking for and expecting a more caring attitude. We need to spread the word to everyone we know so that eventually all people everywhere will take responsibility for how they behave toward each other and will make kindness of paramount importance. I think the story about butterflies that flap their wings very gently in one country and send out enough energy to create a hurricane somewhere else has a bearing on this.

Radical kindness should include not only how we treat others but how we treat ourselves and, very importantly, how we treat all the creatures of the planet and of course, the planet itself. We have to rid ourselves of the idea that we are separate from each other and our environment, and treat every person we meet and every action we take with this question uppermost in our minds: '*What is the kindest way of acting in this situation?*'

When Gandhi worked to liberate his nation from British rule, he employed the force of nonviolence. In a similar way, we need to use radical kindness at every twist and turn of our lives and insist that it is adopted wherever we go. If we give up being self-serving and think of the whole, not just the self, eventually the world will become the kind of place we'd like to bring our children up in. Radical kindness could result in a cooperative world where poverty, despair, global warming, wars, disease and unkindness are a thing of the past.

Let innocence and harmlessness return and peace be restored to earth. Happiness is what we all desire, kindness is what we need. Radical kindness everywhere is what's required. Self-interest has to be left outside the door of politics and the media. Why send young men to prison when we know that national service would help them? Our armies need to be employed in rebuilding the world, not destroying it. Why allow our politicians to wage war on people, when all it ever results in is more harm, more suffering?

Let's ditch our self-interest, let's think of the whole. Let's think about what makes people happy. War doesn't make people happy; therefore we should end war. Recreational drugs make people happy temporarily but give them severe problems later, so there should be no more of them. Allowing children to soak up violence through the media is almost as bad as actual violence, so again, this should be the end of the matter. We need to create a zero tolerance for things that are obviously unkind.

We need to *insist* on kindness. Ask yourself before every action you take: *'What is the kindest way to act in this situation?'* Before you wander off leaving your children in front of the television, check what they're going to watch. If it's really awful, turn it off and write to the company that thinks such things are fit for our youth. Before you take out the garbage (have you recycled?), before you make a decision at work (how does this affect other people?), before you lambaste your neighbour about the noise they're making (how can I put this across in a friendlier way?), before you etc., etc. ... *bring back the milk of human kindness*. Let's restructure our world. Let us not shirk from our responsibility for doing this. Do it today, do it now. Let radical kindness rule so that our hearts can open to the world, so that all people everywhere may live in a state of peace and kindness.

SOMETHING SACRED

Holding The Earth In Our Hands

Rose Flint

Rose, who lives in Wiltshire, is a poet, artist and art therapist, and teaches creative writing

I once read about an ancient baby's rattle that a Native American tribe used. It was marked with stars—real constellations—and the moon, the sun and the earth, so that from infancy the child was taught the wonder of the universe to which we all belong. Perhaps the nearest the modern world has ever got to something approaching this concept is the first photograph of earth taken from space, that wonderful picture showing earth as a beautiful blue-green jewel, shining in the dark unknown that surrounds us. When it was first published, many people were profoundly touched; we found awe, reverence even. And we could never be innocent of that image again, we can not unlearn the knowledge it gives us: earth is precious, and at this point in time it is all we have.

Set this beside our maps and models, distorted into mathematics by Mercator, boundaried by economics, histories and war. Here, the named shapes of continents, countries and seas seem only to be formed of geology, geography and politics, nothing more. In our belief in god-given dominion we have staked out world-as-utility, a ball of useful elements in the quarrelsome playground of humanity. We have twisted the body of earth into a useful perspective, stretching and snipping at land masses and oceans until we have lost our sense of proportion, not understanding the true vastness of Africa or the smallness of our own northern islands. Nor do we have much of a concept of how everything fits together, how it is as a unit, how it is all related. Even when we travel to far-flung places, still we take with us our baggage of life experience, our needs and wants which we expect to be met: hot water for our baths in the Himalayas, Internet cafés in the heart of Africa, cable TV. Even though the web gives us the ability to fly across any distance in the space of a heartbeat, we remain insulated from the world, insensate; the world does not touch us with its climates and terrains and peoples, its sheer physicality.

Looking at earth from space we see rivers tracking continents, like veins flowing through flesh. We see mountains rising like articulated bones, a living skeleton of rock; we can see the deserts and savannahs as tight-stretched skin, the forests as green hair flowing under the comb of winds. We can see the marvel of earth's place in the universe, the mathematics of solstice and equinox become the music of a patterned dance, each turn and twist as elegant as ballet, the chorus of stars illuminating the whole theatre of space. As our gaze zooms in, we become aware of the intricacies of eco-systems, of the fit and rightness of variety that can be seen in the most minute of natural plans. Yet wonder and astonishment that this is so—that we live in a world that is a miracle of beauty and design—is not our birthright.

I was once asked to run a 'green' writing workshop in a secondary school in Milton Keynes. Two things I remember clearly: one was that the council had produced a map of a 'Green Path' through the area. This followed the route of destroyed villages and fields but contained no mention of either flora or fauna which could be encountered in the green lanes and track ways. I also remember that when I asked the sixth formers to tell me what the word 'environment' meant, I was surprised to discover that it was connected only to street signage and furnishings or to litter in the park. More recently, working with younger secondary school children on the theme of 'Future', I found that most of them were afraid of what the future would hold for them, citing war and crime as the most dominant features of life. Very few had any understanding of environmental issues, or how they themselves could be affected by, for instance, global warming. They knew nothing about rainforests or oceans and cared little about what happened on the other side of the world. But they expressed a vague formless fear of what the future might hold and believed themselves powerless to make choices which would affect it. Over many years of working with schoolchildren of all ages, from pre-primary to university level, it is very clear to me that knowledge of the natural world in which we live is diminishing very fast. Most children—both rural and urban—cannot name even the commonest birds or trees, they are separated from the cycle of life that produces food, and cut off from their most ancient playgrounds, the teaching-grounds of rough woods, fields, patches of wasteland. If they are not even part of what is 'local', how then can they understand the holism of the earth?

I would advocate the teaching of 'Earth' from infancy. Something more than life-sciences or nature walks. Reverence perhaps? The pagan idea of the earth and all the life it holds as *inspirited*. I'd keep a place for the teaching of economics and politics, but I'd start with creation stories, with the faces of ancestors, with the names of the birds in the back garden and where they go in the winter. I would offer the earth as it used to be, as Gaia, as Mother Earth; sentient, strong and vulnerable, capable of bliss and fury; world as Goddess, creative-destructive. I would offer earth back to us through our imaginations, not through the systems and numbers of science or religion, but through our deepest understanding of metaphor and narrative—and love.

If we love the earth—we cannot harm it. To love it would mean *knowing* earth; closely, lovingly, caring and nurturing. We would have to understand our own individual relationship with earth, what she gives us and later, what we can give back. One simple act of imagination changes so much: earth gives us life, as a mother she nurtures us. And as we grow into responsibility, we attend to her needs.

> *The Earth is our Mother*
> *she will take care of us,*
> *the Earth is our Mother*
> *we will take care of her.*
> *(Native American chant)*

If we think of living on the body of Mother Earth, it changes our perspective of how important we are in the scheme of things. She only has to shake herself in anger and we could all fly off like fleas, whatever our race or creed—but she will feed us for ever, shelter us, care for us. How beautiful is the form of this mother who is made of mountains and creatures and atoms, intricate and strange with mysteries beyond our knowing, familiar with the sounds and scents of home. She is our back yard and garden, our field and our living room; she is our health and our heart. We could reclaim her as the spiritual pulse that could beat within each individual, each nation, flow beyond any man-made barrier of power or fear. Imagine a globe marked with sacred masses of lands and oceans. Made of the most precious elements, a blue-green jewel lit from within with the light of life. It is small enough to hold in a child's hand. It is a gift. We could tell them: *This is the Great Mother of us all, the earth that holds us all in her hands of stone and fire, as we hold her in our flesh and bone. As you hold her, your hands holding her future: as she holds yours. Earth is a goddess who changes as we do. She is the manifestation of your dreams. Dream her well.*

We live in a world-wide culture that swings between religious fanaticism and a cynical scathing negation of humanity's capacity for spiritual thought. We have let go so many of the ties that controlled our behaviour that we have sanctioned a dry selfishness that eats us up from the heart. I believe the earth is sacred, that all life is sacred. I would ask that we teach our children to honour, respect and care for this sacred earth and its peoples, its lands and creatures; to love the whole interconnected web of life that gives us life and our future. If we do not, this beautiful blue jewel will die and all our futures will become a handful of dust blowing in the timeless uncaring solar system.

The Source

They have taken the soft birds from under her breasts
cut the blue roots out of her veins.
They stood inconsequentially talking of meat and money
while they peeled away the skin of her arms
where the tongues of deer and bear were recorded.
They dusted their poisons into her spaces, let her bees
fall out in a firestorm. They cut back her hair
and singed her scalp so nothing will grow there now
no green horses, no lianas, no lizards, no babies.
They drank the water out of her eyes, dammed
the silver water table in concrete so she stares blankly

but the tears still come.

No one can quench the source of the river under the river
and myths and dreams and healing still flow out of it.
We know she lives. She is the voice of the newborn
and the Ancestor, the gaze of the last white tiger
and the flower that breaks through the road.
She is the red thread of life in all of us;
she is tomorrow and we cry for her: *Mother, free us*.

(Rose Flint, 2003)

THE IMPORTANCE OF ACTION AND THE PHILOSOPHY OF SLOW

Helen Gee

Helen, a writer and environmentalist living in Tasmania, is a founding member of the Wilderness Society in Australia

I have worked as an environmentalist for three decades: at the grassroots level of wilderness preservation on an island which still has large tracts of old-growth forests and wild rivers and where you can walk for three weeks without seeing another human being. I have experienced strong personal rewards for my campaign work along the lines of 'save the forests, save the rivers ...'. Enough has been saved to reinforce my continued efforts, and those of my wonderful friends here, to protect biodiversity. Our determination to stand firm for free speech and to protect the rights of rare and threatened species is a message we would shout to the world! Twenty of us are being sued by a giant logging corporation for simply caring about our island state. Our democratic right to free speech and protest is on the line. But if we don't stand up, our rights will be lost. There's simply no choice!

Forty-seven members of the British House of Commons have condemned the action by the Australian woodchip company, saying it is an attack on civil liberties and freedom of speech. Legitimate public protest must not be stifled, they have said. They have noted that 80% of the Australian people want the old-growth forests of Tasmania to be fully protected and have urged Gunns to withdraw its lawsuit. A number of Japanese paper companies have now stopped buying woodchips from Tasmania and the MPs congratulated one company, Mitsubishi. When parliament resumes in autumn, the full House will have a chance to condemn the prosecution of the Gunns 20. It is this solidarity that keeps activists going, and when so many women get burned out with all the competing calls on their energies, recognition *is* important.

It is little wonder this island was the birthplace of global green politics and remains pivotal in world environmental politics. Strong and sustained actions failed to save Lake Pedder from being flooded by a power development scheme in 1972 but were the catalyst for ongoing opposition to dam building and woodchipping. Peaceful activists in Tasmania have regularly chained themselves to bulldozers, to gates, to woodchip-loading towers and company office hardware. They climb trees and hold rallies, funerals and wakes outside Houses of Parliament, they blockade rivers, roads and forest machinery, plant trees and paint white crosses on stumps, erect tripods over bridges and regularly go to court. They know that if the law is wrong, the proper place for a citizen who objects may be in jail.

We conservationists are developing alternative strategies and ecologically sustainable alternatives to massive clearfelling practices. The One Tree Project is inspirational. *One Tree* initially aimed to high-light the true value of the forests by exhibiting the produce that can be created from just one tree destined for nothing more than a pile of woodchips. One mill-rejected tree with a forestry value of just $100 was transformed into over fifty finely crafted products, which were exhibited around the country and auctioned on the Internet. The money raised secured the rights to selectively harvest an area previously designated for clearfelling, under an internationally accredited timber certification. A growing number of inspired timber workers and craftspeople are now demonstrating the true worth of value-adding timber, a plus for employment *and* the natural environment.

These are empowered, questioning young people in the main, with passion and ideas. They are the most creative of their generation, organising consumer boycotts and art exhibitions, taking their message around the island by bicycle (*Forest Cycle*), engineering extraordinary general meetings of company shareholders. However, the brightest minds of a generation are often still relegated to the role of 'protesters', marginalised and demonised by the timid local media.

So, how do I cope with my desperation when, despite massive public opposition to the logging, power remains firmly in the hands of the corporate bosses and a self-regulating forest corporation removed by law from public scrutiny? Do I despair? Multinational logging corporations hold the labour unions and the politicians in an unholy alliance through the power of political donations, the promise of *jobs, jobs, jobs* and their own self-serving version of forest science. The spin-doctors have co-opted the *clean, green and clever* language of the environmentalists, exploited its advertising advantage, and the gullible economic rationalists fall into line! How can David overpower Goliath?

How do I cope with the fact that every day Gunns Ltd, with its monopoly of the resource, successfully loads a ship, and it's costing Tasmania, and Tasmanians and future Tasmanians? The natural capital squandered has not been, and is never, calculated. *The terrible loss of biodiversity is not ever calculated!* And Gunns Ltd reports a record net profit.

I have spoken with students, foresters and politicians on three continents, who, on the basis of hard evidence, all regard our forest practices in Tasmania as Third World. Of course I feel ashamed and realise afresh we really haven't got a lot of time left—in 2003 the rapacious industry exported another five billion tonnes of our precious forests, over one-fifth of it entailing the destruction of ancient eco-systems. A planned new pulp mill will potentially take another three billion tonnes.

And finally, how *does* one cope with the desperation? I try new angles involving artists and musicians, and take delight in the widening circle of support. I say, 'If we don't want a pulp mill we won't have a pulp mill!'

Working for something so worthwhile, being a voice for these magnificent forests, is a joyful and extraordinary experience, one to share. I have been tremendously uplifted and enriched by the teamwork of a growing band of forest activists, some of the best people on this planet! And I feel I owe it to my children to fight on, regardless of the outcome. It is important to me to bear witness, to stay hopeful, intuitive and to believe in magic! However, even more important to me is the spiritual nourishment I receive from these very same forests we are fighting to save. Here, in these last wild areas on earth, delicious moments of stillness keep us focused and sane; they pave the way for mysteries to unfold and remind us the universe is on our side. All one has to do is take one step at a time—each step empowers the next! People living one hundred years from now will thank us for caring. Turning the tide is so very urgent; we have less forest every morning when we wake up than ever before in history.

At last alarm bells are ringing around the globe and the work of an array of international writers and artists has put Tasmania in the spotlight. There is the sense of being on a great wave that is unstoppable, and the tide having turned, it's about to break on a brave new shore where we do consider future generations, where a living tree has a future. Today's global issues are more complex than the forestry issue, of course, requiring comprehensive institutional and cultural change to address problems such as resource depletion, nuclear-power proliferation, and climate change. It is harder to see the results. However, I have an incurable optimism largely because of two significant gatherings I was fortunate enough to be able to attend.

The first Global Greens conference was held in Australia in 2001, and was hugely inspiring. I saw the strength of the global network for change as 800 people shared their experiences and visions and launched the Global Greens Charter, a blueprint for planetary survival. And the Greens are gathering support very solidly now in many, many countries.

And I attended the Restore the Earth conference at Findhorn in Scotland in 2002. I met so many wonderful people actually making a difference through their positive actions in eco-villages around the globe, working to build Slow and Sustainable Cities, Gaviotas in Colombia and Auroville in India being two shining examples. I met a professor who has spearheaded the restoration of the war-ravaged forests of Vietnam. I met Aubrey Meyer, co-founder of the Global Commons Institute, who presented 'Contraction and Convergence', which has rapidly become the most widely supported framework for averting serious climate change. I met the editor of *Positive News* and many more people living their dreams by *doing*.

The essence of Earth Restoration is seeing everything as sacred. Attending the conference filled me with hope and affirmation that we can together make a powerful difference, that our positive transnational links transcend governments and carry with them the power to transform social and political structures. In short, a world consciousness for earth restoration and sustainability is with all of us who choose the path of action; action defeats pessimism, depression and fear. At a personal level we are all responsible for the earth and can downsize, slow up and live sustainably. *Affluenza* is the disease of wealth, wastefulness and over-consumption propelling so many global problems. The Slow Food Movement supports sustainable farming and local produce. The foundation of the Slow Movement generally is vital, because we are what we eat. The health we promote is a first base. You have to feel good before you can promote green space, local heritage and preservation of nature. You have to be healthy to be taken seriously as an example. Women are, from time immemorial, the nurturers and as never before they must become strong, united and resilient to lead society; not from a position of power in the patriarchal sense of the word, but by powerful example. I am filled with hope when I see so many fine inspirational women and the work they are doing for change.

Finally, it's enough to bear witness, to stand for the values I have spoken of. Then, whatever the outcome for this little planet, we have given of ourselves and we can be at peace.

THE SILENT ARK

Juliet Gellatley

Juliet is the founder of VIVA! (Vegetarians' International Voice for Animals), and lives in Bristol

We think we're so smart, but we kid ourselves about the extent of our knowledge, pretending we have reached a peak of understanding, arrived at through superior intellect. The truth is much more prosaic and much less complacent. The earth has existed for nearly five billion years, during which time various life forms have developed and evolved. One common thread runs through this extraordinary phenomenon and that is the ability of individual species to live within their environment—both part of it and dependent upon it. In evolutionary terms, human beings have been here for little more than a twinkling of light. But already we have begun to tear and break the individual strands which go to make up this fine web of existence.

We destroy without knowing the long-term effects of our actions, and even when we do know, we *continue* to destroy because *today* is much more important than tomorrow. Thus every supposed environmental agreement, whether to limit fishing or reduce logging, is quickly ignored in the scramble to make money. When it comes to a choice between preservation and destruction, if the short-term interests of multinational corporations are involved, it is invariably the latter which triumphs.

As a species, we have set ourselves up as the arbiters of the globe in an act of such breathtaking arrogance that it usurps the role of gods and creates a monstrous imbalance in the natural order. There is hardly a species we will not exterminate if their interests and ours collide. By so cavalierly playing with the fate of other animals, we are risking our own. It seems we are incapable of understanding that every living creature has its part to play in maintaining the glorious fabric of our world. None of the animals we slaughter, or even those we demonise as vermin, pose any threat to the survival of our planet. *It is not they who threaten its existence, but us.*

When the slaughterer's hand grabs the muzzle of a lamb to stifle its bleating and applies the knife to its throat, there is no compassion. And without compassion there is little hope for any of us. What is a first step

119

toward embracing compassion? Vegetarianism is one of the few individual acts you can perform that has an immediate impact. It is a political act and a clear expression of a belief in a different way of doing things, a different kind of world, a better world.

I was 15 years old when I decided to become a vegetarian. It wasn't the outcome of argument or debate, or the process of intellectual investigation. It was because of a *look*. A student friend was working on an agricultural project and I went along for the ride. The veil of silence which surrounded animal production at that time, and even now, had not prepared me for what I saw. We were in the pig-breeding shed where there were rows of sow stalls, and separate, slightly larger pens set aside from the rest, each of which contained a huge boar. The one nearest to me stood motionless, his massive head hanging low towards the barren floor. As I came level with him, he raised his head and dragged himself slowly toward me on lame legs. With deliberation, he looked straight at me, staring directly into my eyes.

What I saw in those sad, intelligent, penetrating eyes was a plea, a question to which I had no answer: '*Why are you doing this to me?*' Without embarrassment or shame I burst into tears, silent sobs shaking my body, and I repeated over and over: '*I'm sorry, I'm so sorry ...*'

It was an emotional response, but that emotion has not diminished with time, though my age back then put me in that group which is described as 'vulnerable', 'impressionable' or even 'over-emotional'. You may call it *emotion,* I call it *compassion.* That pig experience and other newly discovered information made me believe all I had to do to stop people from eating meat was to tell them the truth.

WAS THIS THE CASE? HAS THE TRUTH BEEN SUFFICIENT?

The world's problems are discussed by suited men whose vocabulary is lacking such words as *vision* and *compassion, care* and *concern, honesty* and *trust.* All the great concepts which have engaged philosophers through the ages have been reduced to profit and loss. We set the greatest store by the things of least value. And with all the monumental challenges of the world we face, our leaders can think no further than the next election. So they continue to exploit anything which might provide some short-term advantage—humans, other animals, the world's resources. They have the resources and knowledge to end hunger throughout the world, but *reduce* their aid budget instead. They ensure that the gulf between rich and poor widens at home, profess concern for the raging poverty abroad and do nothing about either. There is no longer any serious dialogue about important issues, only excuses and clichés and cynicism.

Governments will not change their policies, because to do so would threaten the control and resources which maintain them in power. Fortunately, we, as individuals, *can* take action.

Meat consumption is obviously not the only reason for world hunger, but it is high up there in the major league. It is also a practice which we don't need permission to do something about. We can wield an immediate influence today, simply by changing our diet. By not eating meat or fish, vegetarians reduce the need to import food from poor countries. A vegetarian diet also throws down a challenge to the established order and breaks the cycle whereby people go hungry, while ever-increasing numbers of appallingly treated animals are fed huge amounts of food (grown on land that could be used to feed humans *directly* instead) in a hopelessly inefficient system.

Vegetarians, and even more so vegans, use far fewer of the world's resources of food, land and energy, and offer the only feasible and sustainable example for the future. Unless there is a positive global move toward this way of living, the expanding world population will be condemned to disease and suffering on an unimaginable scale. In a desperate search for protein, all the living creatures on the globe will be hunted and killed. The wonderful diversity of living things, the last of a species, the most beautiful of creations, will mean nothing more than a mouthful of food to get a family through another day. And we will wring our hands and ask how on earth it happened.

So *now* could be the start of a great movement for change. Certainly, such a simple and effective choice has rarely confronted people. By changing your diet, you can take the first step in allowing the planet to breathe again, allowing the healing process to start. There is nothing else under your control that can immediately ease the destruction of the environment and begin to correct the impoverishment of the world's poor. There is nothing else that can so effectively improve your own health and there is certainly nothing else that will have such an influence on ending the barbarous existence to which so many countless millions of animals are subjected.

Compassion is one of the greatest human traits and it has been diminished to the point of frailty. If our children are to grow and prosper, then we must reassert it and we must be aware that it is incompatible with our present society. Changing the world has to start with first changing ourselves, and then the system under which we live.

THE VOICE OF COMMUNITY

Reverend Beth Glover

Beth is an Anglican priest on the Wirral, and a trained 'deed' nurse

Quietly each day I go about my work. Each morning I wake not knowing quite what the day holds for me, who I will meet and in what circumstances.

I am a priest in the northwest of England and the 'cure of souls' in my parish consists of around 13,000 people in three distinct geographical areas.

Woven through these three places, whether it is the Village, which is a conservation area, a large council estate now 70% privately owned, or a modern suburban estate, runs a cord which binds people together. But it is a cord which binds people not always together in care and support, but sometimes to their own private despair, hardly ever vocalised but emotionally destructive.

So many people I meet have such low self-esteem, such lack of confidence in themselves or in society, that it leaves them raw and vulnerable. Even in just one week I can touch so much pain and despair.

Take, for example, the woman suffering from depression to the point that she is suicidal. She has so much to live for, a lovely marriage of only two years, her own home and the hope of children. But she herself has no hope; instead she feels despair and weakness and failure. She is spiralling downward and is reaching out for help.

Or the young single mum, in dreadful debt because money is so easy to come by. She has no thought for the future; each day is a struggle, and she can't work because she can't afford child care on what she earns. She is trying to survive and is lonely and isolated.

I listen to the parents who have lost their young teenage son, only 14; a suicide because of bullying. I see a wasted life, angry parents and a bewildered sibling, an unrepentant school and I speak to the bullies themselves. What misery drove that young boy to hang himself in his bedroom? Their community seems paralysed, unable to find the right words, and has withdrawn from the family.

I sit with the lonely old man, almost blind, almost forgotten; his voice completely unheard, living in a room that dates straight back to the 1940s with a kitchen and bathroom to match. When I visit, it takes him a long time to get used to the sound of his own voice. He can go weeks without speaking. His neighbours do not know his name.

I visit the once beautifully groomed woman now left in a nursing home, wheeled in and wheeled out of a 'common' room day in and day out … 'Waiting for God,' she would say. Her children take it in turns, once a month, to visit. They bring photos of grandchildren and talk proudly of their achievements.

Most of us do not see these people. Instead, they visit us through the media sometimes and give rise to our disparaging comments on the side effects of medication for depression or young women with no sense of moral responsibility; we argue that no one needs to get pregnant these days and we should just withdraw the benefits; we blame the parents of the bullies and feel we should isolate them from society; and we accept the out-of-sight-out-of-mind mentality which stops us giving older people a dignity and quality of life.

We rightly give so much of our money to the tragedies and disasters overseas, but basic needs of vulnerable people in our own community are not being addressed.

And this is increasing. As our society becomes increasingly insular, where computers reign supreme, our children are too frightened to play outside, when our youngsters suffer from asthma because our homes are too clean and the number of suicides is rising, especially in the male 18–24 bracket, what 'cure' is there for the souls in my parish?

I believe in a compassionate, caring God whose essence is Love. I believe in a man who came to this earth 2,000 years ago, God in the flesh, Jesus. He roamed the local countryside, caring, teaching, healing and restoring all he touched to their community, whole and loved by God. Each one of us is capable of being God to those we meet. It is instilled in us by God himself to love. We do not need to go to church to be God's agent for good in our community.

We need to set up networks, create a soul space within our communities, a heartbeat that sustains a flow of active care and love, where we seek out the lonely, the isolated and those in despair. A place where people are never bullied as they so often are, in any way, shape or form, and where we see and acknowledge the spiritual side in everyone, including ourselves. A place where we stand up passionately for those older people whose rights have been eroded. People are living longer now and retirement can mean another 15–20 years of active live. Retirement is not a precursor to dying any more. We could really make a difference, if we wanted to. What is stopping us from returning to communities which cared for each other, even when they had next to nothing themselves?

What stops us? Time, energy, commitment? Our lives are too structured, busy, and self-oriented. There is precious little time for looking to the needs of others when we feel that we too are being eroded by all that is around us. But in all of our lives there are seasons and there comes a time when we can step back from our own lives and see what is happening to the community in which we live. Perhaps that is when we can offer the skills and gifts and experience we have acquired for the well-being of others. Where communities have developed a heart and soul, there is a growth in trust and compassion and dependency and love. There is a new sense of freedom of mind and of belonging.

I believe we cannot just think and not act, and the time is now, before we become isolated and fragmented so much that caring for each other is not an option.

A STORY OF LIFE AND LOVE

As It Was And As It Can Be

Aruna Gnanadason

Aruna was born in India and currently works with the World Council of Churches in Geneva

Once upon a time, there was a thing called PATRIARCHY. It was a destructive spirit. It flowed over the earth and polluted all it touched. It infiltrated the lives of all creatures and all institutions. All it encountered became victims of its influence and the earth moved in the path of violence, war, poverty, exploitation and the death of creation. It was out of a patriarchal mindset that the industrial development paradigm had its roots, and soon became the 'development' paradigm for the whole world to follow. It was the cause of much of the poverty in the world and of inequalities within and between nations. PATRIARCHY was the source of the desire to explore, to pillage, to colonise, to destroy ancient cultures, peoples, their ways of life, their knowledge. It was the origin of contradictions and grave inequalities within all cultures—the justification for various culturally specific forms of violence. It was PATRIARCHY that was at the root of racism that has ensured that ethnic origins and colour have determined human relationships and social constructs. One of the most effective institutions in PATRIARCHY's grasp was the family, which, rather than being a space of comfort and refuge, soon became another source of control of the powerless within it. The manipulation of human sexuality was another of PATRIARCHY's methods of domination—giving the space for new forms of violence, particularly the violence of homophobia. The destruction that PATRIARCHY had set going is yet to be resolved in so many ways.

Then there was a creature called MAN. He was a beautiful creature. He became PATRIARCHY's tool to maintain power. He fell deep into its clutches. It took his muscular body and turned it into a source of physical power, abuse and violence. It took his mind and programmed it to be objective and rational. From man was taken away his capacity for expressing feelings and emotions and his ability to be nurturing. PATRIARCHY put into man's head the notion that being 'scientific' implied the right to dominate and exploit all that is voiceless—the resources of this earth. It tutored him into believing that the market, profit and competition, even if it meant unfair trade practices, are the things that 'real' men need to be preoccupied with—social welfare, care for the marginalised and re-structuring of economies so as to make them more humane are issues that he should not be bothered with. He learned how to use the gun and to produce weapons of war and nuclear power for warfare too. Man soon came to believe that he must keep on discovering new and sophisticated ways to dominate and control all of creation, all other creatures and all other men.

There was also another creature, called WOMAN. She too was a beautiful creature. She was a victim of PATRIARCHY and the primary victim of man. She was put on a pedestal and called the 'queen of the home', and attempts were made to manipulate her; her femininity was defined for her, and what was 'acceptable' behaviour for a woman was dictated to her. Always powerless, always marginalised—she watched with bewilderment and then with more and more anger, the violence done to her body and soul and the violence done to the earth. Man, as an object for his use and abuse, mistreated her soft and tender body that was programmed into being a baby-making machine. Her sexuality appropriated, she became a thing prostituted, trafficked and sold; or used as a military weapon; or raped and violated just anywhere—on the street, in a police station and even in the apparent security of the home. Her womb was colonised and denied her reproductive rights. The same technology that had rendered some women barren was used to manipulate her body to produce children artificially—the assumption being that it is her obligation to bear children—and until she did so she is incomplete.

PATRIARCHY had ensured that she had no power to make her own choices and sometimes made her believe that she was making conscious choices of her own! Her mind was taken away from her, her knowledge undermined, her wisdom denied. She came to believe that she was incapable of being 'scientific', and that she was an emotional creature whose feelings tended to overpower her. Her contributions were to agriculture and the care of the earth, to weaving or embroidering intricate patterns in complicated colour combinations, to the production of handicrafts that commanded the dexterity of her fingers and the back-breaking and tedious tasks related to house care and childcare. But these contributions had all been pushed into the periphery and were not counted as 'productive work' and therefore found no place in the reckoning of a country's wealth. PATRIARCHY safeguarded a male-dominated society by seeing that women, their aspirations and dreams, their wisdom and common sense were excluded from the discourse of politics, of economics, of understandings of human rights and of law. PATRIARCHY made every effort to destroy the creature woman's being and to stamp out her soul.

Then there was an institution called the CHURCH. PATRIARCHY took hold of this thing too. The Church claimed that it was born out of the womb of Jesus Christ, the great teacher and liberator God. However, he and all he taught about living in right relationships as human beings and between human beings and creation were ignored. Instead, the Church clothed itself in pomp and arrogance, in rituals and hierarchical systems of abusive power, in liturgy and symbols that were exclusive and triumphalistic. It wrapped itself around a comfortable theology that legitimised the power and privilege of a few people and legitimised grave inequalities. It centred its faith on the cruel and violent death of Christ on the cross, sanctioning violence against the powerless in society.

The creature woman was a victim of this institution, the Church, too. She was considered a thing polluted and polluting and was therefore kept out of participation in the sacramental aspects of the life of the Church. Her gifts of preaching, of teaching, of caring and of administering were trivialised and pushed to the periphery, while man appropriated for himself all power and authority. Even the Bible, that sacred book, which is the primary source of Christian faith, did not escape the influence of PATRIARCHY—it was written, translated, interpreted and taught from a particular vantage point that excluded women and all those on the margins of societies. The Church, which, if faithful to the liberator Christ, should have been in the vanguard of struggles for freedom and human dignity but had, in fact, strangled itself in institutional apathy. The Church, as an instrument of PATRIARCHY, had lost its ability to represent Christ.

However, there was one thing that PATRIARCHY was unable to control or stamp out—this is the beautiful FEMININE SPIRIT that flows over the land. She has been given many names in different cultures—in India, she is called Shakti. PATRIARCHY's regular attempts to destroy this energy source were of no avail, because she represents a kind of power that PATRIARCHY cannot fathom. This FEMININE SPIRIT is a creative spirit—she brings healing and health to all she encounters, all she touches. She is a loving spirit who affirms sacrificial love as her basis and not the sticky-sweet sentimental love that the Church often teaches. The FEMININE SPIRIT is passionate in her challenge to forces of death as she is compassionate in her attitude to all people and all creation. She spreads a holistic vision of life that all women and men can appropriate.

This positive creative spirit, a distinctive female culture that is life-centred and justice-affirming, can influence all women and men.

So there is hope for the world—the story can yet have a successful conclusion. It is the story of love as it was and as it can be. It all depends on us—you and me.

Moral of the Story: The many resistance struggles of women, their engagement in movements for justice, for peace and the care of the earth, all provide an opportunity for change, for a new Church, which will act with courage to appropriate the FEMININE SPIRIT and create a new world. Some evidence of her active presence in the world:

1. It is the new theological visions of women, emerging in every region of the world, that are symbolic of this presence of the FEMININE SPIRIT. The call is for the reconstruction of some central theological symbols—for example, the image of God and the significance of the Cross. In a global context, where violence and the use of force have become the norm, the violence that the Cross symbolises and the patriarchal image of an almighty, invincible Father God need to challenged and reconstructed. This becomes imperative if Christians are to play a reconciling and peace-creating role in a world torn apart by the abuse of power in its manifest forms.

2. The FEMININE SPIRIT calls on us to recognise that we belong together as women of the world. Women of the world are the South. However, this affirmation cannot be glibly made. We have to recognise the many attempts made to keep us apart—not least of all the unhappy fact that women have themselves been unable to hear each other and be empowered by each other. We have the possibility of the building of a global network of women. This of course has to be a conscious political decision that we as women make, a decision to recognise each other's cries, each other's words of courage and hope. It has to be a conscious political decision to create the space for the voiceless women of this world to be heard—women of colour, women of indigenous communities, women of the Third World and women of the East. It cannot be ignored that theirs has been an endless struggle for human dignity and sometimes even for survival—and out of their experiences of suffering, they have a word of hope to share.

3. The FEMININE SPIRIT calls for a radical shift in our lifestyles, in the way we have lived with creation and the way we have dealt with each other as human beings and as a community of women. She calls for sacrificial love—not only for the sake of the familiar, the known, but also

130

for the 'little ones' of the world, the unknown. She calls for courage, for commitment and determination that as women of the world we will not rest until every tear is wiped away and songs of laughter and joy fill the earth.

BABEL

Angela Goodman

Angela, an author and book illustrator, works for the Hospital Education Service as a teacher

People were building a tower to reach Heaven. God saw it and was disturbed. He imagined human hordes overrunning those streets paved with gold; drinking the milk and licking the honey; peering into all His Wondrous Works with their insatiable curiosity, that curiosity He had given them ... Stop. He had to stop imagining it. Because He was God. And whatever He imagined would come to pass.

But of course it wouldn't come to pass, because the tower, built on a bubble of vanity, would eventually tumble, bringing devastation to the earth and to humankind. It was an indisputable fact (perhaps the only indisputable fact, since even His Holy Existence was in dispute from time to time) that the tower could never reach Heaven. It was against the rules. He had devised strict procedure, in which entry visas were only allowed to those souls who had striven and suffered to live a perfect life. Bodies and any remnant of earthly matter were strictly forbidden.

Nevertheless, He tossed and turned on his cloud bed until Mrs God awoke. He had always preferred to keep Mrs God's existence quiet: Herself, the feminine half of Himself. It was bad enough with all those male priests on the celestial telephone to Him day and night, claiming a direct mandate from a Supreme, Male Being, without women doing it as well.

'For Heaven's sake, go to sleep!' urged She, for His unrest had separated them temporarily.

But still He worried, for six days and six nights. On the seventh day He was *supposed* to rest. It was tradition. But instead He paced the Universe, not noticing how the flying hem of His robe scattered and tumbled planets still under construction; brushing infant galaxies aside and retarding for a billion years the development of countless new species.

'You're upsetting the Universe!' grumbled His better half. At this point She was One with Him again, 'I don't know why you're so fussed. Why not send a flood?'

'Just done it,' sighed God, 'only a few of their generations ago. And I promised I'd never do it again. I can't take away their rainbows!'

'Plague of locusts?' suggested She soothingly.

'It's *not the time*. "To everything there is a season" ...'

'Oh my *God*, not that sickly song! Well, what about a teeny localised earthquake?'

'*We* don't *do* earthquakes. They are randomly generated—part of the fabric of the cooling planet. They just happen. I wish with all my heart they didn't.'

God rested His divine forehead sadly in His hands. He had not wanted to hurt mankind, but things had happened which might be called unforeseen (if He/She had not been God, who foresaw everything): the creation had taken on a life of its own. It was developing at a faster and faster rate.

It was all meant to be. Yet it was painful.

She had read His mind (unsurprising, since they were One). 'Perhaps we shouldn't have been so impatient to populate that little planet if it's not quite finished. What about those other things? The ones *He* designed?'

'Whirlwinds? Hurricanes? We loathe those too.'

'Yes,' Her voice whispered inside the limitless caverns of His Being: 'Don't worry. It won't come to anything. You'll see. Their lives are short. They'll soon get tired of it.'

But the humans didn't tire of the tower. They went on, until heavenly nights began to be disturbed with the sound of hammering, banging and sawing. They were getting nearer.

'This isn't the way it's supposed to be,' said God.

'It's all metaphorical,' reminded Mrs God, 'You know they won't literally get here! They're only doing what you do yourself: creating something beautiful and wonderful, striving for intellectual knowledge. You made them in Your Image.'

'*We* made them. In Our image,' God snapped, 'It wasn't an *Angela Goodman* immaculate conception, for god's sake!'

Some cherubs who had been dangling idly from a cornice fell off and fluttered away crying.

'Yes, but they're mortal. They want to be immortal, like Us. That's why they build their little creations—'

'—and whose fault is it that they're mortal?'

Neither wished to answer that eternal question. Clouds floated slowly by, and only the multitudinous roaring of the human voices could be heard, as He/She silently pondered the Great Deliberate Mistake. It was She who eventually spoke. 'We'll have to set up a meeting ...'

'Yes. I know. We'll suspend Time ...'

134

In the blink of an aeon, a man and woman appeared, treading gingerly over sharp stones in the purple-shadowed valley from which the tower rose. He was elderly, with a flowing white beard. She was small and plump. It was impossible in the deep shade to see what colour their skins were. Three leafless trees stood starkly silhouetted on the brow of a bare hill against the blood-streaked sky of an earth dawn. The sun, however, did not rise, because Time was suspended.

'Where has the forest gone, the green forest?'

'They've cut it down to build the tower. We made them Lords of the Earth, remember?'

A vast, ramshackle city of tents stretched for miles along the barren valley. There was a brownish haze in the air, of pollution caused by the activities of so many people crammed together.

'The lush fruit bushes? The wild animals? The dewdrop-bladed grass?'

'Plundered for food and never replaced. Our lovely earth. They've let it all go to ruin.'

They could see the tower rising through the haze, pale and lovely, into the clouds and beyond; it seemed for ever. It was embellished with intricate yet simple designs: replicas of all forms and living things on earth graced the sturdy walls; delicate arched windows spiralled around them to disappear into misty infinity ...

'It's beautiful.'

'Are you surprised?'

'But this is the first time I have seen through a man's eyes ...'

'... Ah, these bodies ...'

'... We need to practise living in them. For the plan to unfold ...'

'... The Plan ...'

All was still at the base of the tower. Blocks of stone stood in pyramids, waiting to be used, but Time had stopped, so the hollow-eyed masons, who had risen in the chill of dawn to begin their work, stood as statues. A thin child, whose task it was to bring water, knelt on the bank of a glass stream, with bucket stilled and diamond drops hanging in midair. In tents people lay motionless in sleep or stopped in the act of waking; someone who had been making bread stood by a fire of frozen flames, fingers stilled, deep in the dough.

God saw that many of these people were diseased. Many were menial workers drawn to the tent city by despair and starvation: all resources had been diverted to the building of the tower and human beings had ceased to tend the land, so the land was now barren.

Two people clothed in gold stood, heads bent over a large architectural

135

drawing, her hand on his shoulder, his face turned to hers, his lips parted to speak words which never came. The World had been silenced.

All except for a low dark building where a fire glowed and metal rang on metal. The Gods made their way towards it.

In the interior of the smithy, a great many polished objects gleamed on shelves. Among them, God noticed a small model of a guillotine.

'Those haven't been invented yet!'

'Nor that!' said She, admiring an engine block for a British Leyland Allegro.

'Yet?' echoed a voice curiously like their own, '"*Yet*"? Why speak of Time, which is only a prison You created for these little creatures to move in? We have suspended Time—*We* are in eternity!' The speaker stood in the glow of the fire with a hammer paused over the great dark anvil. Smoke seemed to rise from his hair; whites of teeth and eyes gleamed in a dark and handsome face.

'We haven't come to quibble!' said God in unison.

Smoke swirled momentarily and the dark beautiful features morphed into something softer. 'I never quibble!' laughed a woman's voice. She began to hammer again, 'I create!'

'Well, you've gone too far!' exclaimed Mrs God. 'It has to stop! Your disguises and your trickery! Your jokes, your inventions!'

'*My* disguises and inventions?' laughed the woman. 'In the Beginning was the Word ... the Word was made *flesh*! And was it not *You* who switched the spotlights on? "Let there be light"?'

The smoke rose again from the forge and the woman's form morphed again: this time into something horned. Her voice grew deep, 'Who named *Me* (I who had been part of You) Lucifer?' Her scaly claw pulled something white-hot from the anvil. It was a small golden tiger, which leapt away and disappeared. 'Did He who made the lamb make thee?' murmured Lucifer speculatively, coiling his now snake body around God's ankle.

God tried to ignore the snake. 'The human race is out of control ...'

'It's not the first or the last time.'

'You gave them free will.'

Lucifer, a woman again, smiled beatifically, smoothing her dress. 'Yes. Yes I did, didn't I? How Promethean of me. And how predictable of You Both to have left it out of the original design. What on earth could these creatures have achieved without it? Why do you so resent their attempts to overcome those clodhopping, faulty bodies you gave them?'

'That's not the problem. It's what they are doing to the home I gave them.'

136

Lucifer hammered until a golden calf was formed, 'Look at You both. Look at Me. You built flaws into the programme. Global template errors. You split them into male and female, rather than an indivisible whole. Just as You separated the light from the darkness. You made them mortal, made them multiply.'

'It was You who engineered that!'

'I, Lucifer, merely shed Light on their situation. "Let there be Light." What did you expect? You'd given them power, creativity and intellect which they were not allowed to use.'

'They couldn't handle it. This tower is a vain and pointless construction at the expense of the rest of creation. It is power without responsibility, creativity without purpose, intellect without Love. It is *You* without *Us*.'

'Yes, We are divided. Me, and Both of You.' Laying the golden calf on the anvil, Lucifer reached into the fire and drew out a pink cake with four lit candles. 'Oops! One too many!'

'The imbalance will be fatal. It will destroy Us All!'

'So what're You going to do about it, Big Shot? Another flood? But You already know a subtler solution; one much more dangerous than any of my divinely deadly designs.' Lucifer, now a grinning white-faced clown, plunged the golden calf into water where it hissed and spat. He lifted it out and set it on a shelf with a statue of Elvis Presley and a few other small idols. 'You talk about power and responsibility. You can only take away their power. Take away the Word.'

We know how the story ends. A few stone blocks lie half buried, fingered by the keening wind, in a bleak and remote valley. Mankind scattered and divided, unable to communicate, forever quarrelling, warring, killing.

We can't help it, can we?

We know how the story ends, over and over. Or do we? Yet what if all were reversed? The great paradoxes—dark and light, creation and destruction, male and female, good and evil—cannot exist without each other.

The apple from the Tree of Knowledge of Good and Evil was eaten so that we should know which was which.

Together, human beings have the power to create anything: a heartless tower, death, a slum, a bomb, a concentration camp, a war, universal destruction.

Or we can make a well for drinking water, a child, a hospital, a university, a peace, a better world.

PUT THE BEAUTY BACK INTO ART AND ARCHITECTURE

Clare Maryan Green

Clare, an artist working in architectural stained glass, lives in Somerset

Let's cut the nostalgia. The twentieth century has gone and I for one say good. Harking back to the Swinging Sixties and the flared-trousers Seventies really gets my goat. The most destructive architecutral 'movement' in history. Concrete—the new brick. High-rise everything with multi-storey car parks for pudding? Please!

And what of Art? A whole century of negation. I know it was awful. 1914–1918 and a generation of young men slaughtered or maimed. Just as society began to recover, 1939–1945. We cannot hope to understand, but we still carry the loss. Generations of knowledge—painters, carpenters, masons, glaziers, smiths of every kind, lost. Skills lost. Trades lost.

In their place we now seem to have idiot degree students with their nihilist 'socially aware' and babyish 'Art'. Postmodern? Modern electric? Does that mean something? Anyone in a trade becomes a 'craftsman'. The term 'crafty' used to mean thief. Now it means knitted yoghurt.

Can we turn the spotlight? There are some spectacular artists around, many who have been quietly working all their adult lives, and who love, and make lovely work. Before it's too late, can we put the beauty back into Art and Architecture?

THE VOICE OF THE PLANET

Jennifer Grierson

Jennifer is an artist and activist living in Lyme Regis

Years ago during meditation, I discovered that the words *silent* and *listen* are made up of the same letters.

I would implore everyone to take more time to be quiet so that they can listen to the earth, our home, so that they can *hear* the earth.

Those are the three steps: *BE QUIET. LISTEN. THEN HEAR.* If you put two ears together, side by side, you get a tuned-in, listening heart. There is a mysterious connection between the words *earth* and *heart*, since they are made up of the same letters and each contains the words *ear* and *hear*.

'The Listening Heart'

My deepening experience of this was during the two months I lived in a yurt—a great quietness and heart-listening came to me while I was all by myself in that field and under the trees—with no electricity!

By living in a heart-listening way, the Aboriginal people of Australia were able to hear the voice of the earth itself—by being tuned in to the

Schumann wave resonances, they developed about five hundred different languages based on the sounds of the actual *locality* of earth song. Those became the Songlines they learnt from the earth herself, and the native people follow these lines by *listening* to them. Their oral stories, each one related to a specific place, are known to be up to 175,000 years old—and have carried the great teachings of the Laws of Life ever since.

If we all listen, we will all be in resonance together and with one another, and with the earth. That will truly bring about creative Peace.

HOW LONG DO WE HAVE?

Sarah Gurteen

Sarah lives in Cambridgeshire and works for The Times *Book Service*

I love the outdoors and own two horses, which are my life. They make me realise every day how important they really are, important just by being horses. Bad day at work, or bad news, I tack my young mare up and lose myself with her, or give my old companion, who has seen me grow from a young girl into a woman, one huge hug, this wonderful creature that has seen so many tears and so many smiles.

There is nothing to compare with a winter morning when I am mounted on my horse watching her breath circling into the atmosphere, hearing nothing but birds, my own heartbeat and the hoof-falls of her feet on the hard ground.

I sit looking joyfully around me and ask myself: why are we all in such a rush? Too busy to appreciate what Mother Nature has to offer us, to realise how amazing She is, how She repairs the damage we do to Her. And too busy to stop and think: how long do we have until She can no longer be repaired?

I feel for those who have never taken a deep breath of fresh sea air or stood at the top of a cliff and looked far out to where the sky touches the sea … stood at the top of a hill and watched the tranquil valley below.

If I could change one thing in this world, it would be *us*. What I can't bear is that no matter what we love about the *real* world, if it makes money in the one humans have created, who gives a damn what Nature thinks? Humans believe money will always prevail and it's what makes the world go round, not Nature.

Therefore, I am not interested in anything the rich and famous have to say. They talk too much and do too little and whatever they take on is for their own pretentious needs. Their money alone could solve many things if it was applied in the right way, but the rich can't see past their materialistic lives, so their money goes to waste.

In the end, those who *care* will be the ones who make a difference; those who love horses and misty breath on winter mornings and the singing of birds. Those who care enough to honour Nature and know She is beyond price. That is what I would do for the earth; make people understand it is *priceless* so they will treat it like the most precious thing in the universe.

WHY GREEN CONSUMERS CAN SAVE THE WORLD

Julia Hailes

Julia is an environmental consultant and writer, co-author of the original Green Consumer Guide. *In 2007 she published its revised version,* The New Green Consumer Guide

Apparently, when I was a baby standing in my cot, my older brother painted me green. Perhaps the paint has never worn off. The issue that I feel most passionate about is the destruction of the rainforests. But when I started campaigning for them, I found there were lots of other important environmental issues to be concerned about.

Returning from a backpacking trip in Latin America (mostly), I started working with John Elkington at an organisation called Earth Life. I'm afraid it floundered soon after I started there, although I hasten to add that my joining had nothing to do with its demise. John and I went on to work in the back room of his house in Barnes. That's where we wrote the *Green Consumer Guide*, which was published in 1988 and went on to sell over a million copies worldwide. There were 11 print runs in the first 6 weeks.

Whilst the *Green Consumer Guide* was a phenomenon, I firmly believe that if we hadn't written it, someone else would have. The time was right. So what was happening in the late 1980s that raised public awareness of green issues? One thing was Chernobyl. Only a couple of years earlier, this nuclear disaster sent shock waves that spread even wider than the radiation that swept across continents.

Then there was the ozone layer. Even people who hadn't known such a thing existed had started to worry about the hole that had been found in it. And they were shocked to discover that this was a man-made problem on a global scale. The unlikely villains of the piece were aerosols. OK, not just aerosols but refrigeration, air conditioning, fire extinguishers and foam packaging too. The really brilliant thing is that consumer power played a pivotal role in pushing manufacturers to find alternative technologies and governments to set deadlines for phasing out ozone-destroying chemicals.

Almost 20 years on there's been another surge in green awareness. This time the issue of climate change has pretty well knocked all other environmental concerns out of the window. 2006 was extraordinary in terms of a global shift in thinking—if you weren't aware of climate change at the beginning of that year, you couldn't fail to be by the end of it.

There are still doubters but their numbers are dwindling. A key part of the debate is about what we can do and whether individual action can make a difference. My answer is that it most definitely can. You might think that the many small measures you can take are trivial. Things like turning off the blinking digital clocks on your electrical appliances, buying a more energy-efficient washing machine or taking the train rather than driving your car. On their own they *are* pretty insignificant, but if millions of people—or even billions—make these changes, the cumulative impact can be huge.

Even more important is the effect our choices have on business. Have you noticed how supermarkets are falling over themselves to establish their green credentials? Well, you can be pretty certain that they wouldn't be doing that if their customers weren't interested.

I haven't forgotten the role of government. But I'm amazed how many people see them as the only answer—or at least the main one. I don't. Politicians won't do anything if they don't think the voting public will support them.

Look at it this way. You cast your vote once every four or five years if you go to the polls. But as consumers and citizens we vote every day of our lives in terms of what we buy and how we live. If these votes show government that we want them to take green action, they'll respond—there's certainly little chance of them taking drastic measures *without* our support. After all, if we're not prepared to make changes to our lifestyles, why would we choose a government that will *force* us to do just that?

The really exciting thing is how much has changed from 20 years ago. Now there are plenty of green products to choose from. The problem is knowing which ones will truly make a difference. So in *The New Green Consumer Guide*, I've not only given people the facts but said what I think is the best option. As one of my reviews said, the book is 'wildly opinionated, rigorously researched but best of all explodes with surprises'.

In fact, some of my conclusions have led to challenges about whether I'm a real 'greenie'. One blog I found on the internet said they weren't sure that they wanted to take advice from someone who wasn't 'beyond reproach'. How ridiculous is that. I don't want to set myself up as a paragon of virtue that no one else can match. Much more important to me is to show that whether we're buying coffee or carpets, mobile phones or motor-bikes, lighting or lavatories, we as green consumers can make choices for or against the planet. After all, every little bit makes a difference. I'm sure that being painted green as a baby was the start of something that will be with me until I die. Actually, I wonder if I'm not getting more passionate about it all the time!

HOZHO

Alyson Hallett

Alyson is poet-in-residence and a writer/teacher at the Small School in Devon

These are things my grandmother taught me. She taught me to tell the truth no matter what the consequences. She taught me to bring meticulous attention to everything I do. She taught me to begin in the place I found myself: here, in my heart, in my body, in my home.

There was nothing easy about my grandmother's life. She raised seven children in a small terraced house, cooked all her own food and made the clothes they wore. She polished the brass strip at the front of her house, swept the pavement, talked to her neighbours. She knew them all by name and they knew her. She grew a fabulous bush of sweet-smelling daphne out the back and hung the washing she had washed by hand to dry on the line. My memories of seeing washing blowing in the wind in her back yard are some of the most treasured I have.

Most Saturdays we would sit and watch the wrestling together on tv in front of the gas fire. I remember Big Daddy and Giant Haystack, the enormous fear I felt as the huge men flung each other from corner to corner of the ring. She loved to see them fight, and during the adverts she'd make tea and fetch slices of cake she had baked that morning. Years after I had left home and moved away, she never failed to bake a special cake for my return. Chocolate cake with walnut halves on the top or cherry cake or sponges filled with jam and topped with icing. She was constantly busy but always managed to have time and although she rarely travelled anywhere, she was uncannily in touch with what was going on. She was like the still centre of a spinning wheel; always there, always caring, always challenging and questioning.

Human relationships came before anything else and she was never afraid to speak her mind. She was immensely caring and generous but never wavered from her own truth. This gave her a quality of incredible strength, one that I knew I could trust and rely upon. It was precisely her lack of confusion and ambivalence that made her presence so heartfelt and strong; she never complained, had few doubts about what she thought or felt and lived her life accordingly.

Nothing was ever wasted. A small amount of water was swilled around an empty milk bottle and all crumbs and crusts were put out for the birds. Worn-out clothes were constantly recycled and she continued to knit jumpers and socks until her eyesight failed. She adored the plants she grew, in particular the flowering cactus that she kept in the front room. Viewing it was part of the ritual of visiting her and through this I too learned to adore the incredible ability of a plant to push forth blooms of the most vivid and incredible colour.

My grandmother died in August 2001. As her body relinquished its hold on life, she took to her bed and was nursed by her remaining sons and daughters. It took two weeks for her to die and when the doctor called to visit, he was shocked to note that he had not seen her for over twenty years. She was ninety-three years old.

During the time of her passing she requested that none of her grandchildren visit her. Although this was a hard thing to live with, we respected it. Instead, I spent time supporting my father whilst he looked after her and every morning I meditated and held her in my heart. The time of her dying was one of the most illuminating in my life. I felt very close to her and was able to connect with her spiritually even though I was unable to see her in person. Every day I brought my awareness to the life she was leaving and to the part of me that would leave with her. I prepared myself for the letting go so that her journey from this world might be as painless and swift as possible. It was a sad and liberating time—I stayed with the pain I was feeling and through my prayers felt very close to her.

Hilda was a strong woman and she faced her death with immense dignity. I felt that these last two weeks were her final gift to us. It was an entirely natural death and she did it in her own way and in her own time, choosing to leave the world in much the same manner as she lived in it. She was a woman who knew herself well and lived according to this knowledge. This was one of the greatest things she ever taught me. Do justice to the truth of your own soul and let no one stand in your way.

I was sitting in a café by the sea when she died. The clouds opened for a moment and the sun shone through; small diamonds scattering across the water and a perfect line of light underlining the island of Steepholm. I remember being struck by the immense beauty of something so simple, so brief.

Two days later, I was possessed by the desire to climb a mountain. I hired a car, packed the tent and a few clothes and took off to Cader Idris in North Wales. I climbed it alone, consciously carrying the memory of my grandmother with me, letting the image of her gently nestle in my heart. I had never climbed a mountain before and I had certainly never intended to climb one alone. But there I was, going higher and higher, the whole of Wales stretching out around me. The topmost point was shrouded in cloud and I nearly lost my nerve. But some fellow climbers assured me I would be all right and so I moved through the mist and continued right to the top. There were mountain crows cawing and the wind was cold, but there was something about the spirit of the mountain that made me feel as close to my grandmother as I had when she was alive.

She was cremated the following week. I wrote a poem for her which I read at the funeral and that reading was the most special I have ever done. We had a good party afterwards and then visited her house one last time, walking through the rooms where the cactus had bloomed, where the gas fire had burned, out onto the yard where the daphne was growing and the washing had once blown. We said goodbye the way she would have wanted us to, with smiles in our hearts and few tears. All of us brave enough to witness her passing and welcome her death even though we knew the space she left behind would never be filled.

With this story I offer you an example of the way things have made and saved my world. Simple things that will never find their way into television programmes or accounts of the great and mighty. But for me, my grandmother was a woman who possessed life in great measure and who brought every drop of the essence of her being into reality. What more than this any of us hope to do I shall never know.

Hozho: What you strive for in this world is hozho (beauty, balance, harmony). How you live, how you treat one another, the way you cook, how you arrange your home, how you live in your surroundings—in the Dine (Navajo) way this would be art and religion ... your home and environment are your church, your place of prayers. (Taken from All Roads Are Good)

151

COMPASSION AND
INTERCONNECTEDNESS

Clare Hamon

Clare is a GP who chairs the Plymouth Global Justice Group

You are the only person who can discern your unique contribution to saving the world. The best I can do is to pose some questions and invite you to reflect on my own answers to them.

What do you mean by 'saving the world'?

'Saving' means preserving and rescuing, and 'the world' refers to Mother Earth and the people on the planet. The current levels of environmental degradation, poverty and injustice are unsustainable. There is plenty of evidence that we are consuming resources and producing waste products at dangerous levels. A quarter of the world's population lives in abject poverty. There are links between the two. Just as Fair Trade enables farmers to invest time and energy in sustainable practices, the current trading systems are driving a 'race to the bottom', in which the profit motive overrides workers' rights and protection of the environment. War is caused by competition over natural resources or the grievances of groups of people, and damages both to an obscene extent.

Some theologians would say that the world is perfect for the job for which it was designed: to facilitate the development of individual human souls. In my opinion, this attitude just traps us in a vicious spiral. I think we are being challenged to act more thoughtfully and vigorously, both personally and collectively, in defence of the natural world and of human rights.

Why do you want to save the world?

I love and respect Mother Earth because she gave me life, and I feel a sense of solidarity with the rest of the human race. The well-being of both is unconditionally important to me. I know I am being authentic in acting lovingly, and in this state I am happiest and most fulfilled. I can't rationalise these beliefs further: they are a matter of faith. I want our descendents to enjoy a decent environment and quality of life.

An Australian Aboriginal woman greeted every outsider who visited her tribe with the following words: 'If you have come to help, please leave now. But if you have come because you believe that somehow your own struggle is tied in with our struggle, then please stay.' I believe that real love can only be offered from a position of equal neediness and of respect. So if I do something 'for the world', I am really doing it for myself: the action is essential for my own personal integrity or growth.

A shaman once told me that the first of my many incarnations was on a faraway planet. I believe him, and feel that, as a guest here, I want to treat my hostess considerately.

What are the core principles of saving the world?

I think that there are four: acceptance of insecurity; individual everyday choices; interpersonal relationships; and collective action.

Our craving for security leads us to hoard goods and money, to act possessively in our relationships, and to accumulate weapons and defences. All of these are selfish. We may defend our behaviour as being necessary for achieving unselfish goals: but can the end ever justify the means? At some stage we have to accept that absolute security is never attainable, and that our individual selfishness is threatening our communal future.

Which of your everyday activities could you re-evaluate?

Every item I use and every journey I take has an impact on the planet and other people. In many cases, living more simply and consuming fewer goods and less energy also improves my own well-being. For example, swapping my car for a bicycle has made me physically fitter and more aware of changes in my health, such as an imminent head cold, and the endorphins that my brain releases during the exercise make me feel great.

Pervading our culture is the idea that we should always buy the cheapest option: instead I try to buy ethically. The best choice is an organic, fairly traded product marketed by an organisation with a clean record on a raft of ethical issues such as workers' rights, boycott calls, and links with the arms trade. There are excellent sources for this kind of information, such as the *Ethical Consumer* magazine.

My everyday activities also include the following: using public transport, harvesting the sun and the rain (with a solar water-heating system, and rainwater tanks which store filtered rain collected from my roof), recycling, growing vegetables and eating a vegetarian (mainly vegan) diet.

How are your personal relationships relevant to global problems?

Thomas Merton, a Catholic theologian, said, 'In the end, it is the reality of personal relationships which saves everything.' In my opinion, they are the best thing about being human. They nurture us and give us happiness, and are therefore the foundation for our effective action in the wider world. Furthermore, love and respect provide the best environment for fostering compassion, questioning our motives and actions, and finding effective ways of dis-illusioning ourselves and others. As Max Lerner said, 'When evil acts in the world, it always manages to find instruments who believe that what they do is not evil but honourable.' Rational argument will achieve nothing in this case without the kind of love which opens the heart and mind.

When a journalist hounded Mahatma Gandhi for a soundbite, he eventually said, 'My life is my message.' The main basis for my choices is my own personal integrity, but I am aware I am also a role model and a challenge to others. When people get to know me personally and understand more about my actions and motives, I am likely to be more effective.

What collective action can you take?

Over the past thirty years, my heart has led me to local groups and national organisations which have needed my wisdom, time, and/or money. Between them, they are concerned with the environment, international peace and justice, and groups of people in this country (such as users of the maternity services).

Currently, my greatest commitment is to a global justice group based in my city. We produce a local guide to fair trade and publicise global issues through events such as a fair-trade fashion show.

Isn't the task overwhelming?

It could easily become so. Therefore I ask myself, 'What does love inspire me to do today? How much of my energy should I devote to providing personal care to myself and the people around me, and how much should I expend on the wider issues?'

If you had to produce guidelines, what would they be?

Love unconditionally, deeply and widely, including yourself. Consume ethically. Hoard less. Voice your support and censure.

If I had to replace all of the above with only two words, I would choose *compassion* and *interconnectedness*.

Postscript

Satish Kumar entitled a recent book *You Are, Therefore I Am*. His main premise is that, in relating to another person, I can identify the differences between us and therefore my own qualities.

Love is one of the most misunderstood and exploited words in human language. My definition is *the desire for another's happiness and progress*, the latter being physical, intellectual, emotional and/or spiritual—whatever is the most appropriate for that person's development, *and a commitment to act to further that desire*.

Children and dependents need our long-term commitment in order to thrive. Relationships of equals are more complicated, and need a delicate balance of love, openness, security and commitment. Some of the tasks we want to achieve require stability, perhaps for the rest of our lives, whereas others require the freedom to explore and to move on if and when appropriate.

Are women and men fundamentally different? If we say that women are more compassionate, more peace-loving, or more connected to the earth, and a lot of men are going to carry on doing harm or doing nothing. I think that men *and* women need to feel that a positive gendered self-image incorporates all desirable attributes. For me, four of these are love, courage, creativity and wisdom. I can readily draw on feminine images of these qualities. The archetypal representation of love is that of a mother and child. The greatest bravery and ferocity throughout the animal kingdom is witnessed when a mother is defending her offspring. One of the most awesome examples of creativity is a woman's creation of new life. Wisdom is a feminine noun in the Old Testament, and the Holy Spirit (divine inspiration and divine immanence) has feminine connotations. These female affirmations encourage and empower me. It is up to men to create their own masculine images of these qualities.

Loving an enemy entails three activities: searching for the good and humanity in him or her; seeing wrongdoing as the result of alienation from his or her true self (through fear or misinformation, for example); and working at transforming or dissolving whatever has created the enmity.

THE WORLD IS FINE, IT'S US THAT ARE THE PROBLEM

Jean Hardy

Jean, who lives in Devon, is a university teacher, editor of Green Spirit *journal, writer and speaker*

I am asked what I would do to save the world. Well, I suppose my first response is—nothing. 'The world' is a wonderful, unbelievable place to me, one of its creatures. Over the whole period of human consciousness, people have been overcome when they consider its magnitude, order, colour, beauty, imaginative construction quite beyond our own human capacities. The more even western science advances, the more we see patterns at every level repeating and embroidering their artistry and never-ending forms—the snowdrop, the galaxy, the slug and the oak tree, bacteria and dinosaurs, fire and water. And everything is alive.

Our most immediate physical expenence of 'the world' is our own bodies, and the body of Gaia, the earth. We too, earth and person, are self-organising living beings, as Plato perceived centuries before Christ and as we see today as a strand in modern quantum science. And here, as given, all is more or less well. Even so, it's tough for many sentient creatures living on earth and has been over the millennia, as we live in what we have come to see as the complementary and opposite forces of creation and destruction, which have been present, as far as we now can tell, from the beginning of time. That means that we are born and die, two sides of the same coin; it means our bodies decay as do those of all creatures; and it can mean that life can be harsh, in the nature of things.

I don't think the question above means what can we do to save Gaia— because Gaia will save herself in the end. If this flea of the human race begins to really bite, she will get rid of us. If her systems are threatened, they will change and that change may mean the end of much life presently existing here, possibly including us. We cannot 'save the earth,' we haven't that power, but in the end, maybe we could save ourselves and the many other creatures we are presently destroying in the sixth biggest extinction which, to our knowledge, has happened so far here. It is estimated that by the end of the twenty-first century, if we get through to that point, half the present species now existing will be made extinct because of human action. There is no doubt that the rest of life on earth would express a huge sigh of relief if we disappeared pronto. Sometimes, at my worst moments about the state of humankind, that seems to me the optimum scenario.

But that disappearance would save everything but the human race, and, even when I am most depressed, sad and angry about the unconscious way we live here, I can see there is a lot worth saving in the human race, much courage, love, appreciation of beauty, gardens, art, music. What I would most want us to do to save us is what I have been doing, consciously and unconsciously, all my life: that is, first, to try to pin down the root causes of our violence, unhappiness and greed, which I believe fundamentally lie in the myths we learn to tell ourselves about our position here, often related to the harsh experience many humans suffer especially in early childhood; and second, to work with others on a new story, using, of course, some of the old stories to inform the search for something truer, gentler, more comprehensive and open. This is not just an intellectual search, it is one about a changed experience for many people—particularly for vulnerable babies and children. I believe it is our experience as babies and children that begins to shape how we live, whether fundamentally in fear or in love.

Consciousness and matter may have emerged together in the universe, and are one. When we are thinking about changing things, it is our own consciousness that is the issue.

We need to feel at home here on this earth, within our own being, body and soul; within our societies, families and relationships, on earth and in the Cosmos. Feeling at home implies a profound relationship, an I–Thou relationship and a deep spiritual trust. This is what is lacking in most of our present stories and in much present experience. The stories we now have can be entirely secular, very ego-based and about personal 'advancement' and being 'happy ever after'; or they can be about an all-powerful God whom we 'worship'; or they can be despairing, as in the view that life is essentially about suffering and the best thing we can do to get off 'the wheel'; and they can be entirely centred in the human being, anthropocentric, ignoring everything else that lives, which completely skews our present understanding. Our modern sense of the creative spirit of which we are a part is not yet big or little enough, not subtle or personal enough, not humorous or awed enough, not comfortable or inspired enough; and mostly in modern society the sense of the spirit is totally lacking, so life seems one-dimensional, flat and pointless.

So what can I do? I can write. I can think and reflect, as I've never

158

stopped doing. I can use all my opportunities to become more and more coherent and articulate about the myths we live by, the experience we have as human beings, the search in which we have to awaken, to turn our unconsciousness into conscious and spiritual living and create alternatives to the often destructive way we live here, as forcefully and lovingly as I can, in word and deed. We can only try to do these things, as we are all affected by the forces within and without. That, I feel, is my life's work, and has been since I was a child.

OUR PATH TO SURVIVAL

Maddy Harland

Maddy, lives in Hampshire and is editor of Permaculture *magazine*

I recently met Joanna Macy, the American deep ecologist and activist. She has campaigned on various vital issues from the Sixties onwards in reactionary America: nuclear disarmament, the Vietnam War, the conservation of rainforests and indiscriminate logging of old-growth forests ... and now, in the autumn of her life, she has started campaigning for political, economic and scientific accountability for climate change and peak oil.

At one point in the evening, she spoke about her friend and fellow founder of the deep ecology movement, John Seed. She described him as standing in front of a hostile crowd of loggers with bulldozers in an Australian rainforest, determined to prevent logging. Suddenly, he had an epiphany. He realised that he was not just one small individual protester. He was the rainforest. He was the life-force of this beautiful, biodiverse and irreplaceable sanctuary and he was the intimate web of life that flowed through the landscape.

The rainforest took the shape of his body; it flowed through him, within him, throughout him. There was no question of not standing there and facing the angry crowds and the bulldozers and he did it with equanimity, in a state of peace, realisation and love. And he was literally immoveable. He could 'think like a mountain' and that force transformed his physical body as well as the power of his intentions. He later wrote, 'There and then I was gripped with an intense, profound realisation of the depth of the bonds that connect us to the Earth, how deep are our feelings for these connections. I knew then that I was no longer acting on behalf of myself or my human ideas, but on behalf of the Earth ... on behalf of my larger self, that I was literally part of the rainforest defending herself.'

This to me is the key to our transformation as human beings and the essence of deep ecology: to realise our oneness with the web of life—not just as an intellectual understanding of systems science or applied ecology—but as knowledge, consciousness ... This is real power. There is no force on earth greater than this consciousness. It is beyond the personal, not driven by the personality, but fired by a deeper connection with the Self. Our personal philosophies will define this Self according to our beliefs, but whatever we call it, when we have this consciousness we become a part of universality, which can be characterised by peace and harmlessness. Joanna's story made a deep impression on me. I saw how we can face the challenges of this century and maintain our enthusiasm, our humour and our love of life without denying the realities around us. Above all, we can be powerful yet at peace.

We live in a time of terrible violence. During the 2005 G8 meeting I watched balaclava-wearing so-called eco-activists smashing police windscreens. I wondered how many peaceful protesters were there, attempting to put their message across, largely ignored by the press and blockaded into camps by the police. It must have been tough being sandwiched between police and a violent anarchic element. It is not that I am beyond anger myself. I can understand rage at our leaders who have forced our national involvement in the Iraq War with its proliferation of low-grade uranium weapons and other atrocities. I can be angry at the 'system' that manipulates aid, demanding conditional procurement, and wields subsidies like weapons, blocking fair trade and a decent price for commodities.

I can feel impotently angry about our dysfunctional culture whose values seem so selfish and skewed. And though I could never condone terrorism, I can understand how we have arrived at the door of suicide bombing in Britain. The escalation of British aggression in the Middle East has invited this awful symptom of impotent rage. I cannot begin to imagine the horror of being bombed and crawling out of the underground, nor the terrible grief of losing a friend or relative. My heart goes out to those who are bereaved. I have compassion for the British Muslim community and how they feel accountable as a whole and vulnerable to racial attacks. I also feel compassion for those who feel driven to commit suicide so horrifically.

Yet these events can bring clarity. We have no choice but to deconstruct this culture which threatens the ecosystems on the planet and our survival and we cannot deconstruct it with violence and rage. That will only fuel the current paradigm. We have to painstakingly deconstruct whilst holding a vision of a peaceful future, when the basis for our civilisation is founded on harmlessness; harmlessness to each other, harmlessness to the ecosystems, harmlessness to the planet. We have so many of the tools and technologies that can enable us to live more ecologically, more justly, sharing resources with both the North and the South, but until we develop

162

a more ecological and spiritual worldview we will continue to exploit each other and the earth.

The means of developing this worldview is through a shift in consciousness that will make our interdependence on the earth and each other an unassailable reality. John Seed's understanding of his complete identification with his greater self, the web of life, is the potential realisation of each one of us. Once we glimpse it, however fleetingly, we begin a journey in consciousness that makes clear the path of transition humanity must take to survive. The necessity of us all making this transition will only become clearer as global events escalate.

TRESPASSING IN PARADISE

Tanya Hawkes

Tanya, from Gloucestershire, now works at the Centre for Alternative Technology in Wales

'More than 400 million women worldwide are illiterate, but not one of them is Cuban.'

(Lonely Planet)

My first great love affair was with a country. Seven years later, I still lie awake at night, longing for that initial rush. A two-week fling. You're supposed to get over them, aren't you? Everything was the opposite of my usual life while I was in Cuba. It felt strange at first, uneasy. The lizard that lived by my bed for one thing. But it was more than that; there was just less. Less of everything. Less busy, no advertising, less shopping and fewer *things*. It took me well into the first week to realise that less really is more.

So by the time I got to their house I didn't feel sorry for them anymore for having less than me. I had brought along some clothes, some soap and shampoo, but I couldn't give them to Arelys's family. The shampoo bottle looked gaudy against Arelys's shining hair. She didn't look like a woman in need of extra beauty products. She wanted to know everything. Not so much about where I lived, but about me. What did I do? What did I think? She was like a child who still has a thirst for knowledge; who hasn't had it peer-pressured away by distractions like boys, products, magazines, clothes, sex, food and cigarettes. She took me back to a place in myself that I had forgotten. A time when time didn't mean very much. How old was I in that era? Eight or nine perhaps. When climbing trees was more exciting than coming in to eat tea, talking in friends' bedrooms went on for hours with no added stimulation. When riding a bicycle up and down my road felt like the best thing ever. It all came back to me and I felt stupid for changing.

'On the one hand, the girls' press educates them about girlness and what little girls should want and how they should look, but even more fundamentally and more pervasively it teaches little girls that they do not exist until they acquire. Theirs is not to make but to buy.'

(Germaine Greer, *The Whole Woman*)

I arrived at Ciego de Avile with great ceremony. A bici-taxi cyclist had persuaded me to give him a dollar to take me through the dusty market streets to the address I showed him. They all laughed at me when I arrived—*a whole dollar!* They couldn't believe it. They told the cyclist off and he bowed his head and sped off again. The family was waiting for me, but Arelys pushed past them all to get to me. Her mother and sister were sighing and rolling their eyes at her while she showed me all round the house, where I would sleep, how I could tune in to the radio. The grandmother came out to look at me. *Would I like a drink?*

—*I'll have a coffee, if you have any.* Arelys translated in Spanish to her grandmother who, by the way, could not stop laughing at me.

—*Why is she laughing?*

—*It is a man's drink,* said Arelys. —*Her husband always drank coffee. He would say, 'I am going to the kitchen to kiss the Black Lady.' You are reminding my grandmother of him.*

Their house had four rooms: a living room, a long bedroom (beds separated by screens and thick mosquito nets), a dining room and a kitchen. A long, semi-outdoor passage joined all the rooms. The back yard housed some ducks, a pig and a small dog called Tracy. We spent a long, humid afternoon talking and picking over the rice, while everyone watched me drink my coffee.

We went to market the next day. Picking out plantains and tomatoes, and drinking sugar-beet juice so thick it coated my teeth for the entire day. People stared at me and asked Arelys questions. She didn't stop talking, to me, to passersby, to stall holders, to anyone who would listen.

—*Was there a food shortage?*

—*Yes. Bread is rationed. We can't grow too much wheat here. We have lots of rice and vegetables though.*

—*Are they organic?*

No one was sure.

—*Are they sprayed with pesticides or chemicals?*

They all laughed. —*Why would they be?*

There were no pesticides or insecticides. There was nowhere to make them. No power for the factories that would produce them.

—*Meat. Was there much?*

—*Some. Cattle and pigs mainly.*

—Vegetables?
—Cheap markets; we grow our own at the end of the street.

'Anyone who thinks shopping is fun has only to study the body language and facial expressions of women in the supermarket or the department store. What you will read there is not gratified desire but stress. Believe it.'

(Germaine Greer, *The Whole Woman*)

We spent much of the night, Arelys and I, walking, talking about our countries. We passed a sexy young man with Arabian features and green eyes. He was leaning on a lovingly maintained Buick. We went to her friend's flat and rigged up a radio. Arelys had learned how to do this. Wires and antennae were everywhere. We discussed music for hours and I promised to send them many tapes. When we went home to Arely's house, we watched the Pope on their telly. He was talking to Fidel Castro in front of thousands of people and the family wanted to know what I thought. Was I a Catholic? What did I think of the Pope? They patiently waited for my replies while Arelys translated.

When it was time to go, back to my hotel, then back to England, I cried. I got lost and boarded the wrong bus. Eventually, with a bit of Spanish and a phrase book, I managed to tell someone, a man. He was a teacher and a taxi driver. Taxi driving earned him more dollars, he said. He took me over a hundred miles across Cuba for twenty dollars. Through Camaguey, with its dust and pot holes. Past real cowboys with spurs on their heels, and away from a different, simpler life.

'Government vehicles in Cuba are legally required to pick up hitchhikers, and officials with yellow clipboards stand at large crossings directing people onto the lorries. Hitchers call the thumbs up *hacar bottella,* which literally means, "to make a bottle with the thumb".'

Lonely Planet website

When I was back in the buzz of London and feeling blue, my friends all returned from Thailand talking about drugs, cheap designer clothes and fake ID cards. I felt alone so I chased a dream of sustainability for a while, saving the world by refusing to own any part of it. Urban housing co-ops offered a haven for a time, while I fought fights for rights and ran around in ever-decreasing circles.

167

I yearned for Cuba, a place where goods are repaired, not sent to landfill sites. For a while, I liked to think that one day, in my country, there would be fewer cars. Except for some antiques. That there would be legal requirements for large vehicles to pick up hitchhikers. That there would be a guaranteed high level of education for all. That there would be no advertising as my children walk down the street or watch television. That there might be space to stop the insistent march of consumer duty.

When I stepped off the water-powered cliff railway onto the beautiful green oak viewing platform, designed and built entirely by women, I thought that saving the world might be good fun here. I watched the sun sparkle on the photovoltaic roof and heard the gentle thud, thud of the wind turbines beyond the reservoir and strawbale buildings and squeezed my daughter's hand.

At community dinner last night, Lucy (who apparently fixes the communal car in her best dresses) asked:

—*What can you do?*

—*Um ... babysitting. Gardening. Oh, and Dan is an artist. I'm afraid Maya has a short concentration span, though.*

—*Have you ever built a house? We're all going to start on a new one tomorrow. Would you like to help?*

I laughed. It felt like coming home.

I never got over my first love completely; I often thought about those hot Cuban nights, but I settled for somewhere similar and somehow deeply familiar, nestled in the heart of Wales. A place where people worked hard and partied easily, and above all, left a small footprint on the earth they borrowed for a short lifetime.

'People often say to us, "You haven't got very much money ... What have you got?" But if you look at what we've got in the site community here, the collective facilities are really wonderful ... it doesn't belong to any of us individually, but it's as if we each had an estate of 40 acres ... we've got access to workshops and tools, a truck, each other's skills and abilities, babysitting, because we share them. We are living, as it were, like the rich.'

Peter Harper, Centre for Alternative Technology

WHAT DID HE SHOW YOU? LOVE!

Elaine Heller

Elaine is a healer who lives in Bristol and has travelled extensively in India, Ireland and Denmark

I am writing this on the sacred Isle of Iona, off the west coast of Scotland. Many years ago another Iona visit took place that changed my life.

Julia, a clairvoyant American healer en route from Findhorn, gained unexpected entry to a shut Iona Abbey, and, sitting quietly got the message, 'Do not go straight back to California, but return to London and tithe your money to the young woman at the British Tourist Authority who gave you your train tickets. Pay for her to become a healer and teacher.'

Julia responded to the mystical promptings and came to watch me doing my Tai Chi practice. Thankfully she saw beyond the willing, yet rather awkward and naïve English exterior, and saw my qualities and what I was in essence.

There followed an amazing few days of my sick mother being given spiritual healing, my experiencing 'visions' and past-life sequences and seeing colours in the aura for the first time. This was the 'free show'. After a few months I was irrevocably committed, via Julia's money, to taking classes in meditation, intuitive massage and fine balancing, plus personal therapy. My first 'openings' disappeared and I was at the start of 25 years of study with my wise and deep teacher, Bob Moore. This delightful, humble Irishman lives in Denmark and for decades I travelled back and forth between the UK and Denmark learning, often painfully, how to be on terms with myself, to work with energy, and develop my sensitivity. Bob has dedicated his whole life to a study of energy and spirituality, and little by little, through his patient teaching of meditation and spiritual attunement practices, I came to know some of the intricate and highly complex aspects of the aura and experienced different levels of consciousness. Always with the simplicity of love, Bob shared his precise knowledge and gave us valuable self-development exercises and an 'overview' of how he saw the functioning of energy and the human energy fields. Gradually I experienced my own freedom and reality and the possibility of at-one-ness.

It's been a great joy to be part of the spiritual family learning these skills with Bob, releasing the unreal and growing in understanding. In my turn I offered help to others through healing and teaching, first in London and then in the south and southwest of England. Gradually and steadily it became the passion, the centrality of my life, what I was here to do ...

It hasn't been easy, and still isn't, yet I can only enter deeper into spiritual reality and let all else drop away. This has meant some tough choices in my life and sometimes the learning becomes frightening and lonely. As I reflect on this, I can acknowledge another turning point in my life, when I sold my house in an idyllic village on the West Sussex Downs to pay for two years' educational training in healing with Bob and two doctors.

I choose then a life of trust and love and my reward has been to be in a position to meet thousands in the heart and witness their growth to wholeness ...

My only income has been what I've earned through healing or running meditation and self-development groups, but I was really paid in smiles and seeing someone leave lighter and more hopeful than when they arrived.

It felt a real privilege to spend my days helping people to move on from their problems, illness, hurts and pain and realise their spiritual longing. Filling the starved places, giving the tools for self-recognition: 'Who am I?' 'What can I trust?' 'What am I here for?' 'How can I help myself?'

So many different people, often with the same profound human need to connect to a non-physical reality based on their own experience. A longing to expand and move beyond the ego and mental and material limitations into higher dimensions. Dropping the fears, the masks, the protective barriers and opening to our True Selves, to the reality of Being ...

My work has evolved as I have, and in recent years I've been very aware that the actual energies in and around us and the earth are 'quickening up' and many of us are being confronted in new ways. In the Seventies, Bob said, 'There will come a time when the earth will need clear thinkers' and my sense is that we are now in that time. Perhaps it's not the eleventh hour but a minute to midnight. Now is the time for us to wake up. I notice that a number of us are experiencing big rearrangements in our outer lives and a need to find what is true security. What was 'fixed' is being moved, frequently through self-confrontation and suffering. I think we are being forced to choose what is good and real ... and now, as I sit in this still, so beautiful and friendly place—I realise that a new octave begins ...

I sense that it's vitally important to regain truth and harmony within ourselves, recognise our Divine nature and to remember again and live according to the pure unwritten laws of the Universe. To have courage to take new directions, to choose for the planet what is sustainable ... for ourselves what is 'permanent'.

I look up at the soft blue-green of the distant hills. I see turquoise and sparkling blue sea, white sands, grasses blowing quietly in the wind and sun. I take in the clear blue light, the vast skies, the sheep grazing, and feel the crystal clarity and deep peace of Iona and wonder where my service will next take me ... perhaps to Arunachula, the heart centre of the world in India ... the cleansing purity of the Ramana Maharshi ashram ... and then ...?

As I turn within, I can feel my 'little self' experiencing anguish over a surrendered relationship and as I allow the longing for another human, I touch into silence, bigness and spacious sweetness of Presence. I'm left with the feeling so well put by Julian of Norwich:

'Would you know your Lord's meaning in this?
Learn it well.
Love was his meaning.
Who showed it to you? Love.
What did he show you? Love.
Why did he show you? For Love.
Hold fast to this and you shall learn and know more about love but
you shall never know nor learn about anything except love for ever.
AND ALL SHALL BE WELL
AND ALL SHALL BE WELL
AND ALL MANNER OF THINGS SHALL BE WELL.'

PLANT ACORNS, GROW YOUR OAKS

Elizabeth Hellmich

Elizabeth is a social activist, childminder, foster carer and neighbour-hood watch coordinator in Bradford

This little contribution tells what can be done if you have an idea and feel sure it will work—go for it and surprise yourself with the outcome.

I am half a century old, but only quarter of a century in my head, even though my body insists on lying some days and tells me it feels like it's about to hit the full 100 big time.

I have lived in the Heaton area of Bradford all my life, but like many big cities, the once-affluent areas change and not for the better. As my two children and 150 foster children (not all at the same time) and many child-minded young ones were growing up and moving on I could see changes in my area that not only affected me but were altering the lifestyle of my children and young people. As my own two were growing up they were saying that when they were old enough they would not want to stay in Bradford. My youngest is an entertainer and lives away for ten months of the year and my eldest came back after university, met her young man and is starting a family, but not too close to where she was brought up, just near enough for me to be handy if needed. I work in the theatre on a semi-professional level, both in stage management and wardrobe. I earn just enough to keep enjoying it and help pay for the voluntary work that I am part of.

Because of the changes in the area, I decided it was time to stop sitting back and get up and do something. I was not alone in this feeling; many others were of the same mind.

Why shouldn't they have the same freedom that I had when growing up and be able to enjoy all the good things, such as a walk in the park or woods, strolling along the streets and shopping without fear of a crime being committed either against them or their friends? Old ladies became fearful, young people were approached by drug dealers trying to entice them into buying into their trade in death and mothers were keeping the youngsters inside for fear of them being 'led down the wrong path'. All this was impacting on everyone's lives, no matter what race, creed or colour. I started a neighbourhood watch on my street and saw what a difference it made—not only did crime virtually disappear, but we became a community in our own right. We have many different religions and races in a small street of fifty houses and we all get along very well. This led me to becoming Chair of the Neighbourhood Watch Association that we set up for the whole of our police division. This worked as well.

From there I took on (because someone asked me a question), a Fireworks Safety campaign, which I have run in Bradford for the last five years. This has made me many new friends nationwide because there are so many groups who also want tighter legislation against fireworks, which are, after all, explosives and on a yearly basis blow off people's hands, legs and faces; in the worst cases, heads are blown off or severely injured.

I have received several awards for my work but would prefer it if the government realised how much of a problem fireworks are and actually did something constructive instead of listening to the ones who shout the loudest because they make the most money. It will be several years before suitable legislation is brought in but it will happen as the voice becomes louder. Bradford has at last listened to the noise I make and I am running a fireworks safety campaign paid for by the council (instead of me hassling anyone with money to buy awards for competitions). So at least my home town realises what a problem it is. The campaign this year involves educating not only the children's first teachers; we are targeting information to them and hoping they will pass it down the family chain.

My main work started after the Bradford riots, when I attended meetings in the area and women were saying that the fear was more than they could live with; they were asking 'what can be done?' My friend Sue and I came home and after a few minutes the idea for the SAFE Project was born. The plan was to find trainers who could teach the ladies how to empower themselves, learn how to make their home, street and environment safe places to be. Because we are neighbourhood watch coordinators and our backgrounds are in education and social services we knew little about how to get things moving. How could lives in the area be changed for the better, and how could we trust, because, after the riots, *who* could you trust? Your neighbour? Friends? Shopkeeper? Everyone was wary of people from other cultures. The answers were 'yes' you could trust the majority, but no one believed it. The negative press after the riots scared everyone and gave the world the idea that certain areas of Bradford were BAD. How wrong were they?

174

There was a desire among the women living in the area to change everything and make it the place they believed it was when they moved here. They wanted to stay and care for their families; problems were not relevant only to the areas affected by the riots.

As the project ran and gained worldwide recognition, we realised that sadly, many people felt the way that we did.

The SAFE Project has been established for over a year and many great and positive initiatives have grown from it.

Women out and about in Heaton and Girlington stop and talk to each other; racial fears are being eroded; everyone involved in the project has made many friends and learned many things reaching across cultures; we are all much better human beings and feel very privileged for the opportunities we have had and will have in the future. The small idea that Sue and I had seems to have exploded into one of those things everyone wants to be associated with. We feel very proud that Bradford is moving forward and that we have been a positive part of this movement.

Since writing this piece we have been given £50,000 to train 14 people who will take the training Bradford-wide. Sue and I are still astonished that there was such a great need for the training when we thought it was only relevant to our part of the area affected by the riots. It seems, sadly, that the fear of crime is greater than the powers-that-be want to recognise.

If you want to do something, don't wait for others, do it yourself; we all have powers within us that we don't know about until we need them.

Whatever your dreams or ideas are—go for it—NOW.

LOVE THE WORLD

Verity Hesketh

Verity is a schoolgirl in Bovey Tracey, Devon. She was 12 when she wrote this story

Hi. *Read this story!!!!* Okay, maybe that's a bit melodramatic. But then, the whole environment is melodramatic. At least, it is now. Hey, calm yourself, I'm just a normal person like you. I'm not a diseased hippy or a drug-taking schoolgirl. Just a regular person, taking it easy. Until now. What the hell happened? Our environment virtually *is* hell. Shock, horror, disaster. Do you realise that the whole world is going up in smoke, just because of you and me? Humans. Coal-burning industries produce most of the sulphur dioxide emissions, and motor vehicles produce almost half of the nitrogen oxide! I know some people are thinking, 'I'm going to put this book down, it's boring, I know all this stuff. On to good ol' J. K. Rowling.' Excuse me? What do you know about it? Keep reading, you ought to. *You ought to.* Our world is more important than a magical soap opera.

Today I was coming back from the swimming pool. I was right at the top of the hill going down to the town. To my right there is a field and to my left a nice lot of trees. A copper beech and some oaks. And you know what I thought? God, I love this sort of thing. The field had rape strung through it and the copper beech looked amazing. The bright sunlight smacked the leaves, bringing out their tiny skeletons. There is a river at the bottom. The light also hit that, scattering tiny rainbows against the side of the mill.

It all changed after that. The cars whirled past me, coughing out petrol fumes. I got as far as the high street; I was opposite the youth café. About three or four teenagers were kicking something about. At first I just thought it was a small ball, then, as I got nearer, I noticed it was a smallish plastic bottle. They kicked it into the road. At last one of them shame-facedly picked it up. But I don't know where it went after that. I saw a lot more cars on the high street as I was walking up. More than I remember from the last few years even.

Just think about it all: large parts of our forests are being burned down to make way for ugly buildings and for farming. The *remaining* plants can't react fast enough to break down all this carbon dioxide. This dense layer of carbon dioxide builds up quickly, trapping the sun's heat and causing global warming. That's just *one* of the key issues in this sad, bad world. And the saddest thing about this world is, people just don't care. Some people are a bit like slinkies, not really good for anything, but you can't help but smile when you see one fall down the stairs. No, seriously speaking, some of us do care, a lot. But we need to make a big impact. I know I keep saying that again and again, but it's just so true.

Bet you didn't know this one. You can tell, just by looking at lichen, approximately how much pollution you have in your neighbourhood. Green algae grow on trees in much polluted areas. Leafy yellow lichen are found on walls in areas that have some pollution. Scrubby bluish lichen are found in cleaner places.

There are no surprises? Not surprising. But you could give people a surprise. A nice one. Whether you are a manager of a bank, or just a common secretary, you could change it. Flip the planned demolition of the environment on its head. Forget the head bit, DESTROY the planned demolition act. Don't get me wrong. I'm not asking a lot. I shouldn't have to. I'm not asking you to crash the president's house or kill Tony Blair. President Bush certainly isn't bothered about our environment. He'd sooner wallow in a pool of cow dung than take the world seriously.

Just to do your bit and spread the word, that if we don't do something now, the whole world is going to be a disaster. A fiasco. A cataclysmic bomb of unhappiness. Do us a favour and start helping spread the culture. The new culture. A new trend. And if you're not careful, you might end up being very unfashionable. We need to make this fashionable. Give the world a chance.

The list below will help to show you how to do your simple part in saving the world. You can do more if you want, but just start on this first.

TOP TEN TIPS FOR SAVING YOUR WORLD

10. Look, I know you have heard this tip a million times before, but relax. You might just read it properly this time. If you already do the following tip, sit back, look smug, and go on to the next tip. So, next time you have a small journey to make, use either your legs or your feet. It's not as if you are going to be spat off a bike saddle like an Australian lager from a trained wine taster's mouth. It's great for your health. It keeps you going.

It is, I have to admit, a very good way to take the world at a leisurely pace. There are still beautiful places to discover! We need to keep it like that. If we don't, no one's going to. *Walking* is also a great way to boost vitality within you, and is a great subject for parties. '*I* walked 15 miles today,' you say nonchalantly to the opened-mouthed spectators. Sounds attractive? Get to it. It's not like it's going to be a hard slog. Remember, it's fun! Just the same with running. Although the fun bit is optional as opposed to walking. Good way to get fit.

9. You can use the environment for purposes other than making natural paper with bits of plant in. For instance: have you always envied Missus Next Door for having a roses and lilies complexion? Here is a rather nice experiment to try out. Save some rainwater. I am deadly serious. Get this rainwater and strain it through a double thickness of muslin to get the impurities out. Apply it for washing your hair and face. It's kind to sensitive skin and gives back a zing to the dullest hair. Often the simplest remedies have the best solutions. Plus, it's completely free and has none of the complications of make-up.

8. Compost. The stuff made out of rotten fruit skins and tea leaves and all the other left-over muck. It's a great way to give your garden (if you have one) good soil. Admittedly, it does take quite a long time to break down all the food molecules (about a year). But it is really worth it in the end. Really, really. Nature is a many-sided shape, so why not try this method to keep the soil, animals and plant life happy?

7. Recycle. Bottles, cans, paper, all that sort of thing. Every time you recycle you are reducing acid rain. Many areas affected by acid rain are many kilometres away from the source of pollution. So make yourself feel good and recycle your recyclables.

6. If you buy products without unnecessary packaging, that saves energy. Go for it! Plus it's a much better way to buy. Fresh fruit and vegetables, etcetera ...

5. All activities that burn fossil fuels cause some acid rain. Not a good idea to have a coal fire. Also, think about insulating your home with insulators so you can turn down the heating and—you guessed it!—save energy.

4. Five minutes to change to green electricity. Turn off the television, computer and lights. A video or TV left on standby still uses 80% of the power it uses when it's on. I was afraid of the dark, but when I found this small, supposedly insignificant fact, I started to turn the lights off. Funnily enough, I'm not scared of the dark any more!

3. Eat *fresh* food and (if you're a bit of a carnivore) eat fresh meat also.

2. Do *NOT* use aerosols of *any* description. They harm the ozone layer.

1. Put a flower in your hair, listen to John Lennon and pray for the best!

To end this 'brief' chapter (note the sarcasm), I want to tell you people to keep your confidence. Even when you get discouraged, it's good to keep going. In fact you *have* to keep going. It's *totally* essential we have your support. Animals, plants, insects, helpful bacteria … The lot. Good Luck!

A TWENTY-FIRST-CENTURY LIVING KIT

Jain Hopkins

Jain was raised in Yorkshire and works as a healer/therapist in Brighton

How inspiring, I reflected, when invited to *Speak Up* and describe what I would do *'if I had a magic wand'*. A chance to talk about my concerns; what great medicine! But my ego was involved and I wondered what I'd have to say. Would my offerings have worth, or turn into mere mumblings?

Over the next few days I realised I had loads to say; in fact, more than I could handle. I wanted specifically to *wave my wand* at the healing needed within humanity. If each individual was healed, there'd be no one to create war or assist in the destruction of the planet or allow the suffering of its creatures. I believe totally that it's important to take responsibility for healing ourselves to ensure that we're no longer willing to support or allow harm, so here goes my magic wand.

In a conversation with a friend, I knew my offering could be contained within the concept of a *Survival Kit for the Twenty-first Century*. The crazy mix of opportunities that has been my life has given me an amazing collection of healing information. The only issue I had with the idea of a survival kit is that I want *more* than survival; I want full-on living in a large, courageous, expansive way that also becomes part of my own character. I know each of us is capable of being bigger, more alive, more creative, more of what and whom we really are, and that this process will automatically bring us to care for others, for animals, for the world, and make us realise that by caring outwardly we are caring inwardly and by caring inwardly we are caring for the universe—which is what matters most of all.

I'm from the north of England and like things to be practical, helpful and down to earth, and therefore want to offer actual assistance and aspects of the learning I have gained while healing myself. I hope this magic wand can produce a spark that will help others ignite a fire. For the magic wand to be most effective, I suggest you read the following slowly and with reflection to see which of the ideas apply to you and how you might answer the questions within a 'continuum framework'. For example, on a percentage scale ranging from 0% to 100%, where are you on this particular continuum or with this particular issue? Then ask yourself if this is where you would like to be.

STEPS

Sometimes change feels overwhelming, especially if you expect everything to change immediately. If you use *steps*, things become achievable and in the end automatic, like learning to drive a car. Initially, change feels tough and confusing, but with practice it becomes easier. Most learning is like this; with practice, it all begins to happen. We are like layers of an onion and need to work with each layer to get to the deeper layer, until finally what is true emerges.

HONESTY/PRETENCE

Honesty that offers space to be real, share what is important and move beyond the superficial is something to aim for. It gives each of us the courage to be ourselves, to stop wearing the corporate or social mask where pretence is the norm, the courage to say we are 'OK' , when inside we feel like dying and need antidepressants and can't ask for help for fear of others' opinions, or we wind up in debt trying to keep up with the image we want to maintain. When we stop pretending, we start living and reduce the weight we carry. Denial of the truth comes out sideways: as anxiety, illness, stress, the killing of other creatures, and even the planet.

The first step is to be honest with yourself. The questions here are designed to help with this process. If your answer is 'I don't know', then guess; imagine a million pounds riding on the answer. In fact, this is the ultimate win. It's about winning your life and being fully alive to joy, pleasure, pain, awareness, courage; it's about everyone winning and not exploiting each other in the drive to get ahead.

CHANGE/STUCKNESS

Too many of us live as if we can't change and are permanently stuck. Is your life how you want it to be? Is the world how you want it to be? If yes, then great. If no, are you addressing your 'stuckness' and trying to get it moving? Do you think others are in control and it is *they* who should change? If that's the case, why them and not you, as this leads you to being a victim, and surely that's not what you want? If you choose to stay small and hidden, there must be some advantage to it. Why would you keep doing something if there was nothing to gain? So what is the gain? *This question is important.* Are you choosing to stay with what is going on because it feels better-easier-safer-less-scary than an alternative?

RESPONSIBILITY

We believe we actually take responsibility, but do we? I find more and more areas in my life where I give responsibility away and expect *others* to fix things or to change themselves. Where are *you* with taking responsibility for *your* life, *your* world, *your* health, *your* relationships, *your* self-esteem? Are you where you want to be?

Being responsible may mean asking for help; the notion that 'I have to do it alone' can block healing. Why do you need to do it alone? Is it too painful or embarrassing to ask for help? If your car breaks down, are you expected to know how to fix it? When you have a problem with your life, it's OK to ask for assistance. It's your life, and if you're not taking responsibility for it, who will? Try different approaches and see what works for you!

INSIDE/OUTSIDE

Society acts as though the answer is *outside,* that others know better than you who you are and what is right and true for you. At times, others do see parts we miss, yet not all the time, because often we know if we ask ourselves what the answer is—we know! Especially when our intuition becomes more fully developed.

SHEEP (ASSERTIVENESS OR IS IT BAA-NESS?)

As humans, we tend to go along with what others say, often without thinking. We act as if we are sheep and find we are following other sheep. What does it mean to be a sheep? Saying 'yes' when you mean 'no' or saying 'no' when you mean 'yes'. How often do *you* say other than what you mean? Do you assert your needs? Are you living your *own* life? (Am I living my own life? Gradually I am learning to, though I still go *baaa* at times.)

PRIORITIES

Who or what is the biggest priority in your life? And the one after that? And next? Keep going until all major items are listed. These may include work, pets, the environment, children; they are your priorities, there is no right or wrong. Reflect on where you are with this. Is it where you want to be? What about others? Is it where you want them to be? What about the world, plants, animals—do they even exist among the usual priorities?

BALANCE: GIVING AND RECEIVING/TAKING AND GIVING POWER

Have you seen those old-fashioned scales that need to be balanced? We humans are pretty similar: on one side there is giving out and on the other taking in. To be healthy, we need to balance giving out and taking in. Do you give and receive in more or less equal amounts?

Another area we can benefit from balancing is *power*. If we constantly give away power (as in co-dependency or passivity), or constantly take power (as in needing to manage and control), this frequently creates imbalance. When there is imbalance, life becomes overly challenging. Do you want others to do it your way? Or would you rather give them your power, then blame them if, subsequently, things don't work out? Wouldn't you rather be balanced, and choose what is right for you in any given moment?

EMOTIONS/RATIONALITY

In our society, we have a tendency to like the rational, logical mind and avoid the emotional fluidity of feelings; logic is manageable, controllable, and emotions fluid and spontaneous. How do you deal with *your* emotions? Do you dump them on others? Or squash them and bottle them, allowing them to build you into a pressure cooker waiting for an explosive release? Squashing negative feelings has the result of also squashing joy, ecstasy (a drug-free version), love and serenity.

SAFETY: RISK OR SURVIVING

How deep do you jump in? How much do you allow yourself to *live* your life, or how much do you try to make it safe and survivable? Or maybe you *don't* want to feel safe and are always pushing and risking. Both extremes restrict life and growth, keep it dull and depressed or so dramatic it distracts from the real you and from what is ultimately most important. One possibility is to allow yourself to grow as the flower you are rather than stay stuck as a small seed safely encased in a hard shell. What would help you move from being a seed to becoming a flower?

DEATH

Most of us are afraid of death. We try to stay small and avoid it, hoping it will go away. Then when we're older, we realise we missed out on truly living. Take a few minutes to imagine the following: imagine you are 40 and how that is or was or may be for you, and then imagine you are 50 and again how that is, was or may be, and then imagine the same for 60, 75 and then 90. At 90, you are dying. Reflect back over your life—did you address what was important? Did you heal what needed to be healed? Did you *live* your life? Evaluate what matters and then live it; don't wait until you are dying to be filled with regret. Live to the fullest instead of to the minimum.

SHOULDS/RULES/I-NEED-TO/I CAN'T

How much do you evaluate what is important to you and how much do you live within rules—the shoulds or shouldn'ts, the can'ts, the 'be perfects'? Initially we may say: I live *my* life, and yet if you take time and evaluate, is this actually true? So often, we have followed these patterns for so many years we don't even see them. What restrictions or rules are you are placing on yourself, on others, on the planet?

SELFISH

Are you worried that if you prioritise yourself, others will think you are selfish? This is a concern many of us have. For example, if you always prioritise your children over yourself, are you showing your children how to

185

prioritise themselves, or are you modelling for them the fact that you always prioritise others? Does self-interest indicate selfishness, or does it mean looking after yourself enough so you can actually care for others and for the world from a healthy position rather than from a resentful or exhausted one?

LOVE/FEAR (OWNERSHIP)

Fear and love are the opposites of a continuum. When we are fearful, we are not loving; when we experience genuine love, fearfulness falls away. Reflect on this. Is what you call love really love, or is it fear? How much of your love is wanting to possess the other, to boss them, to tell them how they should live, even what clothes they need to wear? In my experience, real love is about giving and sharing, not about 'owning', even though sometimes when I use the word *love*, what I really mean is *possession* or *desire* or even *fear*. Are you open to letting love in or are you always pushing it away and then feeling needy?

I want to conclude with a prayer—or maybe it is a poem, I'm not sure—which I offer to all creatures and sentient beings as well as to nature herself:

Love Is

Tend to myself
Do not force myself, allow
Allow the truth
Allow the experience of now
Do not decide what is to be
Discover what is, in the moment
Do not force it to be love
For then it is not love
It is cold and it is false
Allow it to be what it is
And in the allowing, love will grow
Know even in the moment of not feeling love
If what is, is allowed
Love will grow
Love is growing
Love is

186

SOS (SAVE OUR SOULS)

Rebecca Hughes

Dramatist and animal rights campaigner, Rebecca Hughes co-founded Writers for the Abolition of Vivisection

There are a million ways to help our planet recover its glory and there is one way: Shine the Light. This is not New Age gobbledegook, but something that's been said forever. Bring the Light into all the dark places of our hearts and minds and realise, without blame or judgement, where and how we have been acting in such strangely perverse and ignorant ways. Anyone not living in a state of true enlightenment is living in a degree of madness.

We now know for sure what mystics have always said: everything affects everything else. Every thought, word and deed affects all other life forms. It is one thing to hear or say this, but quite another to deeply understand and live it.

Our problem with living in a material world is its lack of response to the Creative/Divine/Eternal Essence because of its fixed nature. Further, materialism, both physical and mental, as lived in most parts of the world today, is the high road to destruction. Do we reach a critical point and turn back or do we take a leap into a higher dimension of being?

Materialism is the addict forever dissatisfied, not caring what is destroyed to apparently satisfy the eternal craving which enslaves us.

I believe human beings want to be rich and provided for, living in abundance, because they have an unconscious soul memory of an unfallen world where there was no battling with physical matter in order to survive.

To retrieve that state, we have to soul-search, not be distracted by imagining contentment arriving through making fortunes, feeding off the adulation of others or wielding power. Those things are also a distorted reaching for connectedness with the Infinite. But the only authority is spiritual.

We are all interdependent, but are utterly responsible for our own actions. The great messenger, visionary and friend of humanity, Reverend John Todd Ferrier, whose writings are known to few, but are the most powerful and transforming I've ever come across, declared the two greatest sins of the West to be flesh-eating and idolatry. If we cause unnecessary suffering and steal the lives of the innocent in order to live off their dead bodies, we are taking death into ourselves, becoming the partner of Death and will remain sick and unhappy and consequently, so will our planet.

The Christian Church is a confused institution which has promulgated a false interpretation of the original teachings of the one called Christ. For the most part, it lacks even compassion for the creatures we should be caring for. Jesushood is the all-compassionate way of life; Christhood something even higher. These are states for all to aspire to. A Nazarene (one from Nazareth) was one who lived a pure and harmless life – a life of Ahimsa.

Isolated in our cars, distracted by the facility of air travel, covering the planet with concrete and tarmac, destroying its rainforests to ranch cattle for meat, plundering and poisoning its oceans, filling our homes with junk, using products and food from across the world with which we have no proper connection instead of connecting in our communities, allowing the miasma of mass market manufacturing to deny individual creativity, exhausting ourselves with electronic pollution and microwaves, changing our DNA with mobile phones, imagining biggest is best when small is beautiful, using brand as a substitute for belonging, wasting resources because we think we can, we allow ourselves to be overcome by the Darwinian story in which 'survival of the fittest' fosters the notion that biggest and strongest are best. As a result, we are reaping the rewards of toxicity – cancer, violence, depression and so much more.

Darwin uncovered the story of our planet, but the challenge is to realise there was something before, an Eden, a Golden Age, an unfallen world, not fixed, full of Lightness and Brightness of being where 'the lion could lie down with the lamb'.

Compassion is the very first step on the path to recovery. It involves constant effort, self-examination – what are our motives? Someone bumps into my car, was I somehow angry that morning to attract that? – discretion, wisdom, the search for true knowledge, a positive challenging of the status quo, respect and open-mindedness. All else is as temporary as sticking plaster.

Paracelcus said, 'There is no death to be feared except that which results from becoming unconscious of God.' That great Goodness is to be found wherever we look for it – in a spontaneous, heartfelt smile, the beauty of Nature, the devotion of an animal, the joie de vivre in the young of most species, in unselfish self-sacrifice, in the sunrise …

Proselytising religion is a huge part of the problem, carrying the idea of separation and judgement, as is fundamentalism with its literal and fixed interpretations.

Women essentially symbolise the embodiment of the Intuition, the 'inner tuition,' that storehouse of soul knowledge which we access by allowing in the Light. It is a long and trying quest, but anything less leads only to darkness and destruction. It is inner knowing which brings change for the better, its truth only tested by results. Fear fuels our bad habits – reliance on the greedy, chemical pharmacopia, which in turn feeds off the horrors of the vivisection laboratories; the constant pursuit of vaccination against the 'enemy', which results in insensitive, shocking and invasive multiple injections into infant bodies, breaking the trust between parent and child; the morbidly false idea of the need for animal protein; mistrust and prejudice where there should be communication.

Love, in its purest, truest form, will abolish our fears. We have to trust in our powers of self-healing; physically, mentally and spiritually reaching for a higher understanding, and the planet will self-heal. Finding that place, even for a brief moment, is a huge release.

Both men and women need to call upon and use that feminine principle of nurture in order that this amazing and beautiful planet with all its generous, abundant life might survive. The pristine essence within us all has no beginning and no end and, I believe, longs to be acknowledged. That longing lives within each of us.

Open our hearts and we walk with angels. Look at the stars, into the heart of a rose, talk to an industrious ant and be humble.

A FEMININE RENAISSANCE

Harmony Between Masculine and Feminine Values

Leonie Humphries

Leonie lives in London, is a social activist, and works with the School of Economic Science, the Progessive Forum and Creating a Sustainable Society

My *magic remedy* for our global problems concerns the harmonious nature of the balance between masculine and feminine. The *caduceus* represents this balance (of pairs of opposites) and the process of transformation. The harmonious relationship between masculine and feminine values could lead to equity and sustainable lifestyles. Today it could be said that masculine values, such as *competition*, currently dominate our social and economic systems, and that feminine values, such as *cooperation*, have been restrained. History shows that up until now, economic doctrine has always been formulated by men, with masculine values at the heart of the ideologies. Global capitalism (or globalisation) is perhaps the final manifestation of the domination of these value systems applied to economics and hence society and the environment.

Today, climate change and other environmental disasters require urgent solutions. Those who are clamouring for a nuclear renaissance as a solution to climate change—picture this: *a speck of polonium 210*—remember the images of the healthy young man ravaged and finally killed by radiation sickness caused by a teeny weeny dose of this terrifying substance? Now picture this—gallons and gallons of the most highly radioactive ('fissioned') wastes from nuclear power plants waiting in what the nuclear industry calls 'swimming pools' to be disposed of—how? (They don't know.) And by whom? Our children? Our grandchildren? (They call it 'discounting the future'!) And where are these swimming pools? They lie beside the nuclear power plants where so-called peripheral communities live—which means those whose voices cannot be heard. Uranium 238, used in nuclear fission to produce energy for our demanding societies, has a half-life of 4.6 billion years. That's the same time it is estimated to take for the sun to turn into a red giant, by which time all life on earth will be dead. And the half-life means that's how long it takes for half the quantity to lose its deadly radioactivity and it takes that time again for half the rest and again and again and again for ever ... for all of it to become harmless. And they keep digging up more and more uranium 238. Where are these mines? They're in the USA, Canada, Australia and other countries, and again peripheral communities live nearby where there are millions of tonnes of highly mobile waste tailings still containing a good percentage of uranium 238 and further contaminated by heavy metals used in the extraction process and susceptible to mobility in air and water, just lying there on the surface, having been dug out of relatively safe rock. Remember Chernobyl? The 'sarcophagus' used to cover the radioactive reactor after the accident is disintegrating and there is a danger of the same dispersal of radioactive material happening again across Russia and Europe—even now. Still think nuclear power is the answer to climate change? What are we doing to our children and grandchildren?

Remember Jesus's words, 'consider the lilies ...'? All he meant was that everything is given. Let's start with faith in that. Let's not do the poisonous stuff. We can provide for ourselves without killing our planet. Renewable sources of energy are ready and waiting to be used and developed further.

Perhaps, if and when more of our men decide to live up to their responsibility as protectors of the whole human family, including future generations and the planet earth, we shall begin to see some real developments towards both social justice and environmental protection. The resourcefulness of men, when the need is urgent, is beautifully illustrated in the film of the *Apollo 13* space mission, where the break-down of essential equipment on the spacecraft *Odyssey* turns the mission to land on the moon into the most potentially disastrous one of all. Yet the determination and ingenuity of all the men involved ensured the safe return of the astronauts. The memorable words of one of the astronauts—'Houston, we have a problem'—might be echoed today on behalf of our own 'spacecraft', planet earth, and there is a desperate need to change course to ensure the establishment of a truly sustainable and equitable future for all. The question is: can our men cope with this challenging responsibility? Perhaps a feminine renaissance is needed to motivate the masculine to take care of the whole of our planet and all its inhabitants: a feminine driving, emotive force, could provide the power necessary to ensure the reforms are delivered.

It is time to develop a new economic and political culture, one which includes feminine values, is based upon human values, and which therefore takes proper care of the WHOLE of humanity and the planet earth. So, if I could wave a magic wand I would like to bring about a radical upheaval to ensure transformation to equitable and sustainable lifestyles. Women could provide the driving force for this radical shift.

I am considering setting up an organisation called 'Emotive Force' to contribute to this feminine renaissance. Any interest out there?!

A LESSON FROM TRADITIONAL SOCIETIES

Jemima Khan

Jemima grew up in London and lived in Pakistan for ten years with the extended family of her then husband, Imran Khan

Despite Pakistan's image as a brutal, uncivilized society—a hotbed of radical Islam and terrorists-in-training—I found that there are many lessons we in the West can learn from traditional Islamic societies.

For me, one of the most important lies in the joint family system in which everyone—young and old, aunts and uncles, grandparents and children —belongs to a highly interdependent community where every member has a role and a place and where there is always a sense that one is inextricably connected to others.

For many years, I lived as part of my now ex-husband's extended family in Lahore. My children visit Pakistan in their holidays and spend time there surrounded by cousins of all ages. Although it was a completely alien concept for me and at times very challenging, I do believe that there are advantages to being part of a society that encourages mutual interdependence and close social and family ties.

In Pakistan, society revolves around family life, allowing mothers and children to be together in a way that would be impractical here. Grandparents, and in fact the whole community, play a crucial role in child rearing. A single mother, a widow, an orphan is naturally absorbed and supported by the wider family or community rather than the state.

As a result, individuals and children in particular, seem less emotionally dependent, as they are in close and continual contact with so many other people of all ages—from babies to great grandparents—and have sufficient emotional and psychological security to become independent.

Within this framework of support, no one relationship has to bear too much emotional intensity or weight of responsibility, and there seems to be less of that needy attachment and insecurity characteristic of Western family relationships.

A traditional society is by its nature inclusive. When I came back to England after almost a decade away, I was struck by how differently we respond to old age, for example. In Pakistan, with every year that passes, a person is accorded more respect. Old people are valued for their wisdom and experience, and their slower pace doesn't seem to prevent them from making a vital contribution to the family and the community. In fact, they are accorded the highest social standing of all. Here in England, old people are routinely dumped on the state to be taken care of and it often seems that with every passing year, a person becomes a little bit more invisible and insignificant.

Children don't fare much better. UNICEF recently released a report which brought together comparative research on the material, educational and emotional state of childhood in 21 developed nations. Many people were shocked to discover that Britain is at the very bottom of the list. Despite living in the fifth richest country, British children consider themselves to be the least content in the developed world. They have the highest rates of underage drinking and teenage pregnancies and saddest of all, judged themselves to be the loneliest children in the developed world, with the unhappiest relationships with their families and peers.

In my view, there is a fundamental need for everyone, young and old, to have a role in and feel a part of some kind of wider community. This may explain the growing phenomena of pseudo-communities such as interactive community web sites and fellowships.

Despite the fact that in the West we are generally considered better off than ever in terms of increased personal wealth and longer life expectancy, if we used GNC (Gross National Contentment) instead of GNP as a measure of 'progress', I'm certain we'd be in for a profound shock. I believe that the breakdown of the Family and society, and the Western model of *individualism* is partly to blame. What we need now is a social revival.

WILDLIFE

Pauline Kidner

Pauline lives in Somerset and is the founder of the large wildlife rescue centre well known as Secret World

Chance brought me in to the world of wildlife rehabilitation and since the early 80s my eyes have been opened to the countryside around me. I have always loved the country but never truly understood the species and their interactions, which are so much part of our lives. From a background of farming, my whole world changed direction and I came into contact with animals that many people never get the chance to see.

Compassion was my first emotion and when faced with an orphaned or injured wild animal the immediate response was to help—relieve pain and try to get that animal better. People, knowing my love of animals, would bring me these casualties and experience was soon to reveal that you cannot save everything, that sometimes you have to let go. I tried to find out as much as I could about the animals I cared for: how to feed them, what kind of care they needed and, if successful, how and where to release them. Over the years and through the support of countless people and the help of dedicated volunteers, I am able to run this very special place called *Secret World Wildlife Rescue* in Somerset where I can touch the lives of many animals, always with the aim of giving them a second chance.

Which animals are important? Which ones should we try to save? Try as you may to ask these questions, there can only be one answer—for each and every being is important to the rich patchwork quilt of our countryside. We embrace the ethic that every animal is important to us— from a baby mouse that will clutch a tiny artist's brush for its milk to the sad sight of an adult deer hit on the road and no longer able to flee from humans in to the depths of the woods.

Is our work really necessary? Yes, in so many ways! Reducing suffering has to be important and often we need to help the people who find, and indeed sometimes cause, the injuries incapacitating an animal that was once a free spirit. We are often asked how we manage to let them go after we have reared them from babyhood, spent so much time with them and are finally going to release them. They soon tell you! Their pen

197

becomes too small and they try to get out, they dig or stretch their wings and you can see them actually being *called* to the wild. If you love them, you will let them go; the one thing that all wildlife wants is its freedom.

The chance to educate people through our work on the need to protect habitat and save wildlife for future generations to enjoy is terribly important. Why are so many things disappearing, where are the song birds and the hedgehogs? Hedgerows are now protected but before that law came into place only a few years ago, in Britain alone in the last 50 years enough hedgerow was lost through mismanagement or being torn out to actually go around the circumference of the world three times. If such a vast amount of habitat can vanish without our noticing, what other huge effects must we be causing during our lifetimes? Our gardens now play an extremely important part in the survival of wildlife and at last people have begun to realise what a rich variety of wildlife they can attract to those gardens and encourage through careful planting and management. But there is still much that we need to do to reverse our damaging human impact on everything around us.

History plays no part in the lives of wildlife—we do not need to hunt. Animals will control their numbers through the availability of food. Why are we so arrogant to believe that we have to be involved in manipulating their populations? You can hunt or shoot a fox, but immediately the space in the social group will be replaced through breeding. Badgers too have been maligned through the centuries and remain persecuted, even though they are a popular logo of our Wildlife Trusts. Even though science now disproves that the culling of them will ever be a benefit for the control of Bovine TB in cattle, many farmers still call for their blood because of an historic mindset. Digging and baiting of badgers still remains a weekend sport in certain areas of our country. But how could anyone who genuinely loves animals look on this as *sport*?

Our countryside is fantastic. There are swifts that leave their nests and fly for two years, never stopping until they are old enough to breed— flying thousands and thousands of miles; eating, sleeping, mating, preening entirely on the wing. Who wouldn't marvel at such tiny birds! Butterflies can at times travel all the way across the sea to other lands. There are so many animals that we glance at without realising the incredible journeys they make and the lifestyles they lead. Even though there are many species that need saving in other countries, we must never lose sight of our own fragile earth here in Britain. There is so much out there needing our care! I cannot offer too much encouragement for you to find out all you can about the country we live in, and do whatever's possible to help to protect it for others. As Chris Packham rightly said, 'You don't have to go to the ends of the world to see beauty; you just have to learn how to recognise it.'

SACRED SPACE

Lucy Lepchani

Lucy is a community arts practitioner and poet living in Devon

Recently, some children in my quiet English country town vandalised a public building. In a way, it is not surprising: consider the content of many young people's computer games, the themes of many television programmes, and the radio and television news that tells us all, and within children's earshot, of atrocities in the world. These atrocities associate 'us' gloriously or victoriously doing it to 'them', but when 'they' do any harm to 'us', they are clearly the bad guys. We also hear about our helpless dependency on earth's resources, that it is we who are destroying the planet, and must change our lives, while impersonal governments endorse tonnes of explosives to destroy landscapes and topple buildings abroad, their authoritative media voices telling us it was the 'right' thing to do. Confusion reigns. We swallow down whatever we can determine as 'good' and buy another distraction. Fiddling while Rome burned was lightweight by comparison.

The child vandals, who turned out to be only 10 years old, surreptitiously entered the building whilst it was unlocked, yet temporarily unattended, and set off all the fire extinguishers, leaving a layer of thick white chemical dust all over the CCTV cameras, and then on absolutely everything else. Then they turned on all the gas taps of the kitchen cooker, closed the doors, and left. Further destruction was avoided because, luckily, a passerby smelled the gas.

It was hardly an act of drunken and reckless spontaneity; the children were sober, and arrived masked and disguised. As a result of the damage, many bookings, community activities and services were cancelled, rescheduled or relocated; efforts that had been made were left with disappointed results. I am sure that in this instance, individuals will recover from their losses and inconvenience, insurance will take care of the costs; and I am sure the children, who have been caught now, were somehow punished; but the fact remains that the destructive acts carried out by these few rippled throughout our community and touched the lives of many. Isn't this a symptom, in a microcosm, of what is going on in the whole world? Including all of us, you and me, us and them? Acts carried out by a few hands that create a great ripple effect; and aren't we all, metaphorically, setting off the fire extinguishers and leaving on the gas taps of the planet?

In western society, our survival is inextricably linked to destruction, as every new resource used and discarded is a resource used up. However, if we recognise the problem as 'us' and 'ours', we have already taken a first step to turning things around. The children, when they destroyed the town hall, viewed the building as belonging to 'them'—those other people— and not as being part of their own community resource, and the community as 'us'. It is this perception of separation that alienates one from the world and from others, from a greater sense of belonging than we already know, and from being worthy to belong. To 'belong' in any community or society is to be valued by it, to be sacred to it. Why do we, so often, not 'belong'?

I perceive the cause to be that our culture does not recognise the importance of acknowledging what is sacred. Sacred: with regard to all of the places we occupy, the other people and cultures which we encounter, and all the resources we use. 'Sacred' is, traditionally, an esoteric word; the concept is removed from everyday, ordinary life. This is a loss; one that we perceive unconsciously, but that no less dulls our senses to a greater depth of experience and connection to our world. No wonder we 'need' more and more things. A cultural heritage of monarchs and patriarchs has decreed our existence to be entirely mundane, 'less than'. We are conditioned to disassociate from everyday miracles everywhere we look, every time our bellies are full of something nourishing and bountiful, every time we feast our hands or eyes on what we already have. Things like clean running water; children who did not die routinely of diphtheria or tetanus or suffer rickets; bodies and minds that can reach their amazing potential; the presence of music, gardens, harvest, dance. Is this why people sometimes seek to mask their dim reality with drink, drugs, danger, and even more 'things'? Authoritative traditions and self-delusion insist that we experience miracles only via the alleged experts, those who claim to know about such things. We are taught that sacredness lives only in churches or temples, and that we might only taste or handle it if we read the book, wear our Sunday best and wash our hands first; that it requires po-faces and hushed tones, and somebody better than us to lead us to it.

Be warned: herein lies a trick. Of course all Holy places—churches, mosques, synagogues, or whatever—are sacred; but this quality does not stay contained behind the door when we leave; and neither is it the preserve of those who claim a connection to faith or religion. To believe these things would be to fall for the lie at the root of all 'them' and 'us' conflicts.

To close any chasm that divides us—race, creed (or none), gender, age—we have to learn to accept that those things which are held in esteem by others are worthy of esteem—even if we do not accept this within our own lives and practices. It is the responsibility of each of us to our own personal freedom, to value the personal freedom of others; and in making sure that harm is not done to others, we take care of ourselves. We must redefine, re-discover, re-learn and reclaim the fact that we are all sacred. Us and them. We are all made from the same atoms that have trailed around the starry universe since the beginning of time. We; Us; everything.

If I can do one thing in my life to change the planet, then it is this: to do my small part to actively create, maintain, or re-create, sacred space: keeping the back garden in order (easier said than done); cleaning up some litter in a park or play area; letting my children grow up experiencing nature as miraculous; spending time with friends when they are needy as well as entertaining, and being grateful to have had that chance; praising people for their efforts; campaigning for better public transport, cleaner rivers, safer streets. Appreciation is the harvest of reclaiming one's own world as sacred: being thrilled at the first signs of spring, and acknowledging its miracle; being thankful for water running from the tap; whispering 'thank you' through time and space for the secrets left in stone circles; doing a private, crazy dance for joy at my new winter boots; saying cheers for the effort someone else has made to produce a bottle of wine; or lighting a candle on my mantelpiece altar in memory of someone passed on.

We reclaim the world, the ordinary mundane world and bring it to its full life when we make it sacred in our own, simple ways. The effects of reclaiming this kind of creativity in one's own hands ripples outwards, touches on the lives of others. How about flushing some rose petals down with the sewerage sometime as a symbolic offering of thanks and appreciation to those who maintain the sewers? Or if you are wealthy, sending a donation to their union?

Imagine how society could be, all of it, if our creative imaginations ran beautifully wild in reclaiming sacred space: children might learn songs in school about the workers who produce their chocolate. Old people's homes might produce storybooks celebrating the lives of their residents. Policemen might dance in the High Street at full moon. Shop managers might even replace the chocolate bars at the checkout with ceiling mobiles to entertain the babies, rather than grab a chance of even more profits; oil companies might clean up the mess. If those of us who are able could better practise these things, what might happen in time? Please try it. Children could be unavoidably influenced by a culture that honoured the connectedness of all things, regardless of what they possess or consume. This alone is a good enough reason to get on with it. In ways that are within our ordinary reach, it is possible to perceive and experience the world teeming with miracles; and as we belong to that world, so it belongs to us. Waiting for a messiah to come, or for the day of judgment, or for the experts and world leaders to get together and sort it out, is to deny our true worth. The future is poised in every moment, and that is held in all our humble hands.

This is not a new idea. Neither is it an unworkable or impractical suggestion. For example, many of the Lepcha people of Sikkim have continued to honour their 'old' religion of making shrines everywhere they live and go, despite outward appearances of conversion to other religions. For these people, creating sacred space is a daily spiritual practice, connecting everyone in the entire community and for generation after generation. Lepcha society has one of the lowest crime rates in the world, and the people have the anthropologically documented disposition of being 'happy, unsophisticated people'. Their rich folklore, the lack of warfare and arms trade in their culture, and powerful cultural mythology, are rooted in the value of living in harmony with the earth and everything on it.

There is also the worldwide environmentalist revolution—seeking to move away from consumer values and find sustainable connection with the earth; to relate to the planet as a living entity, or alternatively, to value the soil itself as an absolute treasure. With its advocates proclaiming effective solutions, like renewable energy, composting and recycling our waste, it is also re-defining the term 'sacred'. Transforming waste into a resource is a mundane miracle. Every compost heap is an altar; creative, practical, pro-environmental choices are new-made daily rites in which everyone can participate, and which define us all as priests and priestesses.

The 'magic wand' to change the world is as real and effective as we allow it to be. It's as easy as playing 'let's pretend', and weaving it into our adult responsibilities. The 'inner child' is as sacred as our actual, worldly children; it is an aspect of ourselves that is crucial to planetary survival; and losing the ability for imaginative play is a deep wound in all humanity.

We must play, imagine, transform; consume resources, but if we could acknowledge their true, far-reaching value, we could consume less devastatingly. To begin with: support UNICEF, Fairtrade, Greenpeace, Action Aid, the Lion's Club or the Women's Institute; or imagine our ancestors walking beside us, keeping us company when we are alone and in doubt. Spend more quality time with the children. Plant vegetables.

Once, long ago, our communities sat together by the fire and told stories, awestruck by the storytellers' skills; or they would dance and play music together as part of their celebrations, ceremonies, rites of passage, and mystical experiences of God. Life is structured very differently now; but our own hearth, the town hall, the pub, or the local meeting place in high street or mall is the heritage of that communal hearth. Here is where to begin saving the planet; and no matter what challenges life brings, remember we do have that wand, the power to reclaim what is sacred; and that Heaven itself is already present on the earth—if only we have the courage and the imagination to look.

NATURE FULL OF BUDDHA

Ingrid Lever

Ingrid, who works in Bristol for the local government, describes herself as a 'Buddhist-style do-gooder' with a small farm in Somerset

When I was a child, I read a book about a log cabin full of animals. Inconvenient animals. Attractive animals. All in the depths of a dappled wood. I wanted that house and that steady, anchored place slowly merging with earth. And now, with my folly figured in Pan who plays his pipe on the old metal knocker on my door, I have my paradise, my deep *riving* and rooting into one special patch. The buzzard swerves low, flapping for height; my cat curls into sun at my feet. In the barn, the second brood of swallows chatters at each feed. The sheep, young Poll Dorset ewes with tight teddy-bear coats and dapper fringes, are quiet for once—all too plosively eager for food and hugs.

And the house? It has offered its store of surprises: waking up to a bright green cricket on my pillow; waking up to a sheep on the stairs; watching the determined route of a rove beetle as it crossed the carpet; chrysalis cases halfway up walls; sweeping the woodlice out—to have them unroll and march right back over the threshold. Butterfly wings in the loft hint at bats. That American cabin had raccoons under the floorboards, a woodpecker hammering at the gable end, and termites slowly chewing it all to dust. All very unwelcome when house prices are high and having one's castle may promote a drawbridge mentality. (I war with myself over what I want versus what would 'maximise my assets'. Hard, sometimes, not to feel a sucker heisted by myself.)

So far, the biggest challenge to my conscious *laissez-faire* with nature was the appearance of the flying ants. My first summer in the house, on a humid heavy evening, myriad small black ants began running up the walls of the old bread oven. Before long, large winged ants joined them, climbing in an ungainly way. And then—flight! And landings: broken wings, scuttling bodies, just feet away from where they had started, exploring the cracks between the floor slabs, landing on me. Revulsion! (I love bees, but don't much care for insects—an irrational division, I know.) I attacked with fly spray, I stamped and squashed. It was over anyway by the next day.

I did the same the next few years, no longer shocked, but prepared—and still a little revolted. And then for a few years I just let it happen, but closed a few doors. (They never seemed to succeed in founding new colonies.) I watched and wondered at the sacrificial plenitude of it. At last, I dug and shovelled the earth below the oven and killed them. Now I am reminded of them on humid nights, or when I see the colonies in the terrace sending forth their awkward adventurers. (I'm glad, on the whole, that praying mantises are not part of our fauna—eyeballing one once on a screen door was quite enough.)

This house going down to earth is the same reddish crystalline dolomitic conglomerate that the city of Wells is built of, cemented with red clay and gobbets of lime, probably without foundations, on hillwash and the alluvium of our little river—where once I saw a dipper, bursting with shrill effervescent song, and once a flash of kingfisher. Grey wagtails nest in the old school walls above the stepped weir. Water voles are long gone—though my neighbour shoots mink when he sees them.

The valley is a sort of flyway: herons and whistling winged ducks beat up and down. Rarely a raven (sometimes mobbed by the wood's crows, who also foul the buzzards) will drop its magical *krok krok* into our nether world.

In this valley and village, I sense the slow churn of time, the slow burn of continuity. I have buried my dead here: cats and sheep, chickens slain by the fox. And the dissenters by my top field buried their dead in a rough green enclosure with low rubble walls. Their names cannot spring out at us. Here is nothing but hogweed and cranesbill, strimmer and sheep. In my garden below spade depth lurk walls—double-dig and you find them. A small silver coin of Vespasian, with his great bull neck and firm chin, emerged from the potato patch a few years ago (of the four emperors in that year of emperors chronicled by Tacitus, the victor). Digging the garden invariably turns up crocks, bits of metal (the cottage was the wheelwright's and then the tinsmith's), stems and bowls of clay pipes; rarely bones. (I manure too well for bones to last and so, I imagine, did my predecessors, dunging the ground from the 'two-holer' next door as well as from their beasts.)

Planting a new orchard, I hit the corner of a wall below the plough line in one of the pits: nothing on the ordnance or tithe maps to say a building was there. The lane behind the field is Old Street. How *old* can a street be that the people of this *old* village called it *old*?

I try to live lightly in this ancient place between the springs of Wells and the Roman manufacturies of the Fosse. I harvest hazels from the hedge each spring, with the smaller hazel poles used for runner beans and peas, and the rest for kindling and firewood. (The cycle of coppicing also provides a range of habitats, as well as marking what I can manage by myself.) The boundary sycamores are pollarded every few years, yielding wood that dries quickly and burns hot. Meanwhile, my work in the city (the most truly unsustainable thing I do) adds a supply of skip wood to the fire. All is not carbon-neutral though, as I buy in coal. If I could afford to, I would put photovoltaic panels on my large south-facing roof. (But I can't.) Things even doubtfully biodegradable (just how much cotton is actually in those socks?) are chopped up and added to the compost heap—which in a garden full of slag from the forge is essential to plant, and to my health.

Compost heaps and piles of hardcore awaiting jobs make good homes for the slow worms, whose sheer bronze and turquoise colouring is a sudden delight. I do, for all that, use Round Up on (some of) my abundant nettles—working full time and living on my own, invasion and overthrow always threaten. And because I deliberately leave the garden alone over the winter, the abundant cover and detritus means an army of slugs for the summer: a 'mastication of molluscs' scour my seedlings, so that sometimes slug pellets must augment sharp sand to enable anything to grow. Set against this, I have decaying log piles for invertebrates, bee tubes for the mason bees, and a long season of flowers to sustain my kitchen, my spirits, and nectaring insects.

I feed the birds with seed (dusted with cayenne, which fazes the squirrels not a jot) throughout the year—and my summer reward is pale copies of the parents coming to the feeder. A few years ago, I planted a mixed native hedge—not strictly true to the area (and laced with intruders, like pyracantha), but chosen because it would provide a range of food, cover, berries and nectar for bugs and birds. Fast voles share the garden with my cat, fleeing between banks of flowers. Most native plants that seed in are welcome—feverfew, fat hen (a mildly nutty addition to salads), tutsan, scarlet pimpernel, foxglove and mullein. The orchard is for the badgers, for noisy fieldfares, for smart sheep who remember their favourite tree and, now and then when time and weather are on my side, for me.

This is no idyll, no paradise garden in four parts watered by rills. There is casual death in it, frequent disease, and many disappointments. (The ruby chard that was to glow in my autumn garden germinated poorly, and that which emerged fell victim to slugs and pigeons.) Sometimes a flurry of grey feathers on the grass means a kill. The sparrow hawk plunders the small birds, the feeder suddenly emptying in a frantic flutter to cover and silence. A cat comes home crippled and dying from some catastrophic fight.

Yet the turn of the seasons always brings something new: bullfinches in spring on the fringe of the garden (let them eat their fill of buds); goldfinches plucking the teasels; a roe deer hart ambling through the frost of my winter field; dragonflies hunting for mates overhead. This is, so far as I can make it, a safe haven for 'all god's chillun'. It is solace for working—so unsustainably—in the city, and maybe penance too. Some kind of payback for the negative impacts of food miles and petrol, and the generation (with the help of business) of a great deal of waste. As Gerard Manley Hopkins wrote, 'Sheer plod makes plough down sillion shine.'

Just like the kids picking a few bluebells, the small actions of lots of people, many times repeated, can add up to benign or harmful outcomes for our world. I see how I live as just a start, capable still of much refinement—but such little beginnings, mirrored by ever more individuals, are the best hope we have of a healthy and beautiful future for ourselves and earth, our home.

I plod in hope.

WHAT WILL THE WOMEN SAY?

Mary Lidgate

Mary, who lives in Teignmouth, Devon, works to empower women to 'speak up'

What is your image of you?
Are you a figure clearly outlined
separated from any backdrop or scenery.
A figure 'stood' alone.

Yet this is not the human condition
for we are air dwelling creatures
totally immersed in a dynamic ocean of gases
through which we are constantly engaged in an intimate and sensual
relationship with air and every living thing on the planet
from first breath to last gasp
not alone
not separate
we smell, taste, touch and see through a vibrant interface of air
we passionately embrace our lover
taking their breath into our lungs as they take ours
and
as we bellow abuse into the face of our enemy so too
we take *their* breath into our lungs as they take ours
we are all one
with all people and all life.

So what is climate change to air dwelling creatures?
It is a dramatic imbalance in our ocean.
The complex system of life in our ocean of air
dependent on an intricate balance and exchange of gases between living
things, the oceans of water and the earth itself
is being de-stabilised.

Women have traditionally held communities together
we understand relationships

we must reclaim the one we have with air
our breath of life.
Understanding climate change is to re-engage with our human condition.
It could bring a time of innovation and creativity.
Or
become another excuse for bitter competition, recriminations and inter-community hatred as resources start to run low.
What will the women say?

'IF THE EARTH WERE ONLY A FEW FEET IN DIAMETER'

Caroline Lucas

Caroline, a Green MEP for southeast England, is originally from Malvern and spends half her time in Brussels

> *'If the Earth were only a few feet in diameter, floating a few feet above a field somewhere, people would come from everywhere to marvel at it. People would walk around it, marvelling at its big pools of water, its little pools, and the water flowing between the pools ... The ball would be the greatest wonder known, and people would come to pray to it, to be healed, to gain its knowledge, to know its great beauty, and to defend it with their lives because they would somehow know that their lives, their own roundness, could be nothing without it. If the Earth were only a few feet in diameter.'*
>
> (Joe Miller, 1998)

I love these words, from a poem by Joe Miller, because they beautifully express how the key to saving the world is to change our relationship with it. We live in an age of technical fixes. As evidence mounts ever higher of the breakdown of our ecosystem: loss of biodiversity, increasing desertification, and—most urgent of all—accelerating climate change, governments increasingly attempt to reach for technical solutions.

And yet it's clear that, while new technologies must certainly play a part, on their own they can never be enough. Climate change, for example, isn't essentially a technical challenge—it's a social challenge, a moral challenge, a challenge to the way we see ourselves in the world. To achieve cuts in greenhouse gas emissions in the order of 80–90% in the next couple of decades, we don't just need different technologies. We need different cultures, different measures of progress, different expectations—and, crucially, a different sense of our relationship with the earth.

That means that we need to reassert the biological limits of the planet, and to remind ourselves that, no matter how sophisticated we think we have become, we are nonetheless entirely dependent for our survival on the basic physics of the universe. Unless we recover a sense of ourselves as part of nature, rather than separate from and superior to it, we will find it extraordinarily difficult to rise to the challenges we face.

And chief among those challenges is to design a different economic system, which is both sustainable and equitable. It's clear that we can't seriously address climate change using the same economic paradigm that got us into the problem in the first place. The bottom line is that an economic system, based on the ever-increasing throughput of natural resources, is patently unsustainable. Whether based on the assumptions of Karl Marx or those of Adam Smith, modern economics is about endless, infinite economic growth. And yet the reality is that this kind of growth is impossible in a finite world.

The next few decades will be decisive in determining whether we can build the public and political will to act fast enough to set the world onto a more sustainable and socially just path, or whether we will simply go down in history as the species that spent all its time monitoring its own extinction, rather than taking steps to avert it.

For me, the political process is crucial. I believe we need urgent political action to put in place a binding, legislative framework based on major investment in renewable energy, energy conservation, demand reduction in the North, and a major redistribution of resources to the South.

But to achieve that, in turn, we need a different mindset, a different relationship to the earth and to each other—we need to imagine what it would be like, if the Earth were only a few feet in diameter ...

214

ALL IS ME

Realising One's Kinship

Karalina Matskevich

Karalina, born in Belarus and now living in Surrey, is a Biblist and theologian and the wife of an anti-nuclear campaigner

I love the marginal. Things in transition, things between here and there fascinate me enormously. Probably because I have always lived in the borderland. I come from a country that lies at the border between East and West. Culturally, the language I speak (Belarusian) is getting close to extinct, and so my life dream (translating the Bible into it) puts me well away from any prospect of status or security. Politically, having once been a dissident under the communists in the former USSR, I still feel like one now, living under western democracy. On the whole, everything I have ever associated with was outside the main stream, the power, the status quo.

I think marginality is a great privilege, as it allows you to see and to approach the world differently (children who know better often relate being 'different' with being 'special'). Joining the perspective of the few brings you nearer to understanding the perspective of one, which is, I believe, the only true perspective. The reason why I often feel at variance with the principle and practice of democracy: the beauty and the truth of the manifold here could be (and is) reduced and subjected to a power, an order, a structure. That order may work very well, or it may well not. (Think of all the democratically elected dictators, one of whom is presiding right now in my country, or the mess the world democracies have created globally.) Of course the mechanism could be 'upgraded' endlessly, but even in the best-functioning political systems the voice of the majority, concerned with needs, does not necessarily express the highest values of its individuals, concerned with goals.

For it is in the individual consciousness that the connection with the world is realised. For no man is an island. All is one, but on the other hand, all is me. And because of this I believe that everyone is responsible for everything. I mean—is already responsible, and always has been, whether or not he/she realised it. And the only way forward is to make that total responsibility conscious.

In 1986 Belarus was contaminated with the fallout from an explosion at Chernobyl nuclear power station. I remember how most people then measured the danger from radiation by the distance separating their homes from the reactor. People who lived 300 kilometres away felt better than the unlucky ones who lived only 100 kilometres away, and the latter in their turn pitied the ones who lived at the 30 kilometre distance. I heard one woman from a village just outside the 30 kilometre zone say, completely seriously, 'We must be all right here, as they evacuated to us people from all the hamlets nearby.' A few years on from that we found that no one was (or *is*) all right. Because the winds blow, the rivers flow, the plants grow, the animals graze, and we humans breathe it in, drink it, eat it, and are part of it all. And while men at the top are still covering it up and say we are fine and mix up radioactive meat with normal in order to feed the hungry—we are still witnessing the truth that all is one in the sad reality of empty maternity wards and sick children (90% of the kids starting school in Belarus are diagnosed with some kind of illness), and in the rising rates of young and middle-age cancers, strokes and heart attacks.

Nuclear power for me demonstrates very clearly the issue of total connectedness and total responsibility: even if we humans separate ourselves from the rest of the universe in our decision-making, *thinking* faculty, the universe in its response to us will make us *feel* that the separation is only illusory. It will make us feel physical pain, as that seems to be the only thing that really touches us. In Belarus we have felt and experienced it, and keep doing so now. But do we all need to wait until the risen sea washes away our house in order to experience oneness with the world?

I believe that everything will change and the world will be transformed, once everyone stops sleepwalking and takes up their responsibility as the 'king of the world'. For everyone *is* the king (only he thinks he is a shepherd boy). Where it's possible to do it politically, go for it, make your voice heard—but the main change, I believe, should happen in the attitude that governs our everyday choices.

Think of nuclear power plants that the majority is benefiting from now at the expense of those who will live on the land tomorrow. Think of the tips which everyone sends their rubbish to and no one wants to live near. Think of powerful cars we buy, new runways we build, new weapons we create. Think of that and make a different choice. The choice, governed not by the need, but by the goal. For it seems that the noblest job for a human being is that of a cleaner. Cleaning and healing the world after us.

TWO ROUTES TO CHANGING THE WORLD

Baroness Sue Miller

Sue, a Liberal Democrat baroness in the House of Lords, is a spokesperson for the environment, food and rural affairs

ROUTE ONE

Thinking about saving the world is depressing—depressing because the enormity of the task and the impossibility of making an impact on global problems like climate change, wars, starvation or torture seem to be far too great. What difference can one woman make?

A few exceptional women have made a difference by their work or their example—recent examples could be Mary Robinson who, as President of Eire, created an atmosphere of reconciliation. She understood the power of symbols—every evening she would place a candle in the window of her official residence. Aung San Suu Kyi, under house arrest for years in Burma, remains a powerful advocate for, and symbol of, the importance of democracy. In the United Kingdom Helena Kennedy has waged a one-woman crusade for women's rights. Wangari Maathai of Kenya, who in 2004 won the Nobel prize for peace, realised that saving the environment is a key to social stability and peace. But these women are the exceptions.

Most of us must change the world by working together. My own entry into politics was as a result of the women's Greenham Common protests. I felt that, important as Greenham was in opposing the introduction of land-based nuclear weapons into the UK, protest was not enough. I had to try and influence a world into which I had now brought children and which was becoming more dangerous because of man.

And that would be my starting point for saving the world. We live in a world that has been run according to the principles, beliefs and drives of man.

Now get me right—this is not an anti-male diatribe. There are lots of men I admire, many I have learned from and a few I have loved. However, often the ones in that list would include those who have a strongly developed set of principles that would be seen as 'feminine'. Ghandi, for example. Historically, men have fought to gain territory, expand their wealth, get *their* hands on the resources. If they have not been fighting literally, then they have been fighting metaphorically in the stock exchanges, the market places and the institutions of the world. The fight and 'winner takes all' principle means there must be losers. Losers are generally those who are more vulnerable or weaker—either actually children and women, or those whose ability to fight is weakened—the poor, the less educated, the isolated.

The second half of the twentieth century may not have seen a world war but it was dominated by the development of a competition culture. Cooperation is seen as a weak option. Cooperation and consensual working is effortful and time consuming. It involves continuous dialogue and good networking skills. It is quicker and easier to allow a culture of *the strongest wins*—and strongest usually means richest as well. This is true of the political party system, the corporate world, national wars. However, the natural female attributes of negotiation and sharing need to be in at least an equal balance to the male attributes.

Suppose for a moment women ran the world. Women were heads of state, presidents of companies; as a matter of course, not as exceptions who have to prove how 'tough' they are and so take on a male mantle as a working mode. I do not believe women's priorities would be the same as those of their male counterparts. The USA spends $400 billion—yes, $400 billion per annum on arms and military action. And further billions on space exploration. I don't believe the women of America would choose those spending priorities. Here in the UK less than a quarter of our MPs are women. Action to remedy this has been given a dirty reputation—positive action, it was called. The media—run by guess who?—said that second-rate women might get chosen instead of first-rate men. Well, they might, but no one is claiming under the present system that all the men in politics are first rate.

If we want a different sort of a world vision, different spending priorities, different ways of solving disputes—then let's try a world based on female priorities. We women will have to get stuck in. Express our views, define our priorities, stand for election, go for that job, support those who share our principles and oppose those who don't.

It is called democracy, but democracy is still failing women. It is devalued, undervalued and sneered at. But it is also the way women will change the world. Women must use it, revalue it and make it work for them. Then they can save the world.

ROUTE TWO

Food. Food really can change the world for better or worse. On the one hand, ready meals full of additives and the cheapest meat that has been raised under the worst conditions, and lots of salt to make it taste better, growers pushed to destitution as they receive so little for their produce while middlemen make a packet, and the meal eaten alone as you dash from place to place. A nation hooked on quick fixes, functional food and eat-alone food. How sad.

The alternative? Schools teach cooking as a core skill. Farmers and growers sell their food at the farm gate. Supermarkets opt to stock local food where they can, the price you pay is no longer the price of the food travelling hundreds or thousands of miles, the food is fresher. Seasonal food is great—sensible people don't want strawberries in England in December. Small producers in the developing world find hundreds of outlets for their fair-trade goods and no longer need aid. Suddenly everyone realises that preparing and eating food *together* is one of the most social and enjoyable activities there is. Women are not expected to wind the clock back to the 1950s and do all the shopping and preparation and anyway, men are as good at cooking—and they love it.

Why not?

CHANGE YOUR DIET, CHANGE THE WORLD

Heather Mills

Heather Mills is a model, and campaigner against landmines

If we're lucky, we can all experience a 'eureka' moment that changes our lives forever. Mine was at the Live Eight concert when a young African woman standing next to me shook her head at the sentiments being expressed and said she wished people would talk about livestock. She explained that in her home country there were fields full of lush crops destined to be exported to Europe to feed our dairy cows and other farmed animals while African children starved to death.

As a vegetarian, it was a shocking revelation for me that I was still contributing to the despair and deprivation of some of the world's poorest people. And so I checked it out with Viva! and the Vegetarian & Vegan Foundation—two campaigning organisations of which I'm patron—and had it confirmed.

More than that, they revealed the appalling cruelty of the dairy industry and the fact that milk is not a health food at all but contributes to a whole string of 'degenerative' diseases – the diseases of affluence such as heart disease, some cancers, strokes, diabetes, obesity and so on that are at epidemic proportions and kill huge numbers of people in the West. I couldn't argue with it, as the evidence on health was set out in stark scientific terms in a report called *White Lies* that contained over 200 references.

The truth is, I should have realised from my own experiences that there is a big question mark over dairy. When I lost most of my lower leg after being hit by a police motorcycle, a persistent infection in the residual limb refused to clear despite endless antibiotics. Nothing worked and eventually the bone became infected, resulting in the amputation of a further two inches from my leg.

A friend recommended I go to the Hippocrates Institute in Florida, which had helped to cure her breast cancer. In a leap of faith, I checked out of the London hospital and went to the US where the Institute immediately required me to come off all antibiotics and other medication and applied wheat grass and garlic poultices to the wound. They also insisted that I ditch all dairy products and meat and adopt a wholefood vegan diet containing zero junk food. In just one week the infection had cleared up and the healing process had begun. It was quite literally amazing. I had my first prosthetic leg fitted while at the Institute and was bought my first pair of roller skates!

For various reasons I didn't stick to a vegan diet when I was back in the UK but I am vegan again now thanks to that chance encounter. The more I discover about cow's milk and dairy products, the more I am convinced that my decision to avoid them is the right one and it's the right decision for anyone who cares about their own or their children's health.

But avoiding meat and dairy is much more profound than that. Yes, it is the healthiest choice that anyone can make and, yes, I know I am reducing my exploitation of the world's most impoverished people, but there is something else which is equally profound – I am dramatically helping to reduce my impact on the world's environment. Whatever decisions we take in life and no matter how convinced we are by our reasons for making them, it's always gratifying to have confirmation that we're right. I know that since its birth in 1994, Viva! has been urging people to go vegan in order to save the Earth, while the big environmental organisations have remained silent on the subject. At the end of 2006 came a report which stripped away all pretence that our diet doesn't affect our future.

Livestock's Long Shadow wasn't written by some small, committed pressure group but the United Nation's Food & Agriculture Organisation and it was shattering in its exposé of animal farming. It maintains that livestock are at the heart of all the world's great environmental catastrophes – and you can pick almost any one you choose!

The accelerating loss of rain forests and the remorseless spread of deserts, overuse of fresh water and water pollution, loss of soil fertility and acid rain, antibiotic resistant superbugs and loss of species – the list goes on and on.

The one that shows most clearly just how reluctant our government is to act to save the world is global warming. Livestock are responsible for a staggering 18 per cent of all greenhouse gases – far more than this when CO_2 is included from slashing down and burning trees and undergrowth to grow grass and fodder for animals. The Press and the government remained almost silent on this landmark report, turning instead on the budget airlines, which produce only three per cent of greenhouse gases.

At least now we no longer have to agonise over what precisely is the best way to save the world — the evidence is set out starkly. More important than anything else is to change your diet – go vegan!

THE ENVIRONMENT, ABOVE ALL!

Mo Mowlam

Mo, who died in 2005, was former Secretary of State for Northern Ireland, and latterly a writer and broadcaster. She was originally from London

'The most important aspect of our lives, which we ignore at our own cost, is the *environment*. Everyone must make an effort to do what they can to help protect the environment. Government must be lobbied, Europe must work together, we must act *now* if we are serious.'

MOUNTAIN ENCOUNTER, 1979

Mary Morton

Mary, who is active in theatrical events, is a poet and writer-member of Moor Poets in Devon

The mountains behind Dubrovnik are the biggest rock garden in the world. From the pretty village where the river Ombla slides, jade green and fully grown, from beneath a massive cliff of limestone, the road winds up and up through a landscape punctuated with pencil slender cypresses, cistus (rose and white) swathes of pale iris, candy-pink convolvulus with silver leaves and blue-grey tall veronicas.

When I got out of the bus at the top of the escarpment, the signpost pointed, starkly, to the road to Sarajevo, across the jagged karst plateau—twinkling with mica when the sun shone, but today, under a lowering sky, the rocks were dull and leaden. Notebook in hand, I began to walk along a hilltop track, my purpose to note and sketch some of those astonishing wild flowers, but the sullen sky heralded rain, stinging with a threat of hail, and I beat a hasty retreat back to the café standing alone by the bus stop.

There were no other customers in the bleak establishment, which had metal chairs and tables and was bare of decoration save for a few international advertisements—Coca Cola, Nestlé chocolate, and the faded photographs of two young men below a Croatian flag.

The woman who served me coffee was as stark and uncompromising as the room. Old, she must have been, though her back was as upright as a lance. Pale eyes, in a face that might have been hewn out with an adze, and a straight-drawn mouth that had long forgotten how to smile. It was an uninviting appearance, but the rain was lashing down by now, there were two hours to pass before the return bus for Dubrovnik and, although I had only a few words of Serbo-Croat, I determined to try and strike up a conversation with her, and we found we had a passable command of Italian in common.

'German?' she had enquired, and when I explained I was British, 'Ah! British.' Her comment was as expressionless as her face. The dialogue languished and I cast about for something to say. My eyes fell on the photographs on the wall. 'Your sons?' I ventured, 'Fine boys!'

'Fine boys!' she repeated. Was there a spark behind those flinty eyes? 'Fine boys! True enough. But they should, today, be fine men! They should be working the land with their father. They should have given me fine boys and girls to be grandchildren to me!'

'They died ...?'

'They went to fight with the partisans. They never came back to me. Stepan ... Tomas ... I don't know where their bodies lie. I got word they were dead, that is all. The Germans came to the house—not this house, the one they burned. They shot my husband there, on the doorstep, because he would not tell them where the partisans were to be found.'

Unable to find words, I muttered, 'You must be so proud of them ...' It sounded feeble.

'Proud! That is what it says on the tablet there, "Presented to Jana Novaca, proud mother of Heroes"! Oh yes, they killed some Germans and then the Germans killed them, so they are Heroes. And somewhere in Germany, there are women who look at the pictures of their dead sons and read, "Proud mother of Heroes".'

'I am so sorry ...' I felt I must make some comment here. She stared at me as though she had never seen me before and then recovered her manners, pouring me a second cup of coffee.

'And you,' she asked, 'have you a man?' I nodded. 'And did he fight? Does he live?'

(My darling Peter, I thought—braving the Russian convoys—torpedoed in the Mediterranean—driving your landing craft ashore on the Normandy beach on D-Day. How dare I feel almost apologetic to admit that you survived it all?)

'Yes, thank God,' I confessed.

'Oh, God!' The old woman's voice was rueful. 'What does God have to do with war? Jesus Christ (she crossed herself), He spoke only of Love and Peace—He never told us to kill—Allah taught his people the same. It is men who make the wars, not Gods. Men! Stupid men, Stupid, stupid men! Revenge! Honour! Die gloriously for your country! So the young men go and, yes, they die. What is so glorious about that?'

'Do you never wish for revenge on those who killed your sons?'

'To what purpose? My sons would have killed them.'

'So you have no hatred for them?'

'Hatred is a sickness, like cancer. It is the hatred that kills; the hatred and the greed and the pride of stupid men. Why should I hate the men that killed my men? I tell you, Gospodina, if I could meet the mothers of the young men who killed my boys I would take them in my arms and we

226

would weep together.' Her voice went on, lapsing into her native language and she turned away from me—to look once again at the photographs? To regain her composure?

As she turned back, the sun came out. The mountains sparkled for a moment and the ramshackle bus drew up outside. I rose to take my leave, uncertain of what I could do or say.

'Addio, Signora, and thank you,' I said inadequately, and held out my hand. To my surprise she put her own hands on my shoulders and, drawing me towards her, kissed me, her cheek hard against mine.

'Goodbye,' she said, in English, and then repeated the valediction in her own language. On impulse, I threw my arms round her and she responded with arms as hard and strong as steel bands. I felt the tears welling in my eyes, but her face was still as expressionless as ever; only those eyes of hers, unfathomable as the pale waters of the Ombla River drawn from its hidden source deep in the heart of the mountains, what secrets did they hold?

I climbed aboard the bus. The woman, standing in the doorway of the café, raised one hand, in farewell? In benediction?

We rattled down the long hill between the glowing flowers towards Dubrovnik, the sunset and the silvery arc of the sea; towards modern comfort, peace of mind and loving company. Behind me, the woman— what was her name, Jana?—in her bleak house at the mountain crossroad, lived with the memories of her dead husband and her vanished sons and a heart that had known twenty-five years of loss and loneliness, that had been hardened by endurance but had never yielded to resentment and desire for revenge. 'I tell you,' she had said, 'If I could meet the mothers of the young men who killed my boys, I would take them in my arms and we would weep together.' And the God whom she believed in, who had nothing to do with war, would bless them even as she had blessed me.

Humbled, I felt a warm wellspring of admiration, no, of love for this new friendship. I, so rich in worldly blessings, and this strong woman, alone with her loss. I had given her nothing but an embrace and a string of platitudes; she had given me, out of the depths of her stark experience, her conviction that Faith, Friendship and Forgiveness were paramount, and that these are not to be attained as by right, but, sometimes, only through deep suffering. Wondering, I realised that not once in our two-hour encounter had she ever smiled.

All this took place long ago. I say, 'All this,' as though it were some-thing of note, something more than a trivial encounter on a holiday years past. But it must have been, else why have I remembered it all this time?

Jana's country was plunged into war again, old wounds were opened, old hatreds revived, and other wars, other hatreds, more bitterness, greed and covetousness have since defaced this lovely planet which was delivered into our care and keeping. Since then there have been more wars, more hatred, terrorism, sudden death and anguished mourning, some recent and painful even as I write. But still the message of that stern and lonely woman rings as true as it did that day in the glittering mountains. Only Love, only Forgiveness, only our shared Humanity can outface the sickness that besets us, and has always beset us. Only so can we move towards the sunset through the glowing, silver-leaved flowers.

MAN AS THE MEASURE OF ALL THINGS

Elizabeth Nathaniels

Elizabeth, who lives in Hastings, is a social activist, journalist and interior designer

War on terrorism and war on the environment endanger the future for all of us. What role can we play as women to save the world?

We can define and value our own innate common sense and fundamental nurturing ideals to rid ourselves of an inferiority complex, and we can find our own voice in a world where man, *qua* man, has hitherto been the measure of all things.

War on terrorism is an excuse to perpetuate violence anywhere and at any time. Powerful leaders merely have to dub someone a terrorist to be able to lift the usual checks and restraints on human rights, without first inquiring as to the reasons for the horrible frustrations which bring about terrorist acts in the first place.

War on the environment is less overt. But the steady erosion of environmental and indigenous human rights is manifest in great leaders' ignoring of their own chemical and industrial weapons of mass environmental destruction of climate and life, and in their failure to abide by international agreements.

So what can we women do to save the world?

Gandhi provided a clue when he said in the 1940s that 'in war against war women ... will and should lead', and then went on to explain that women should shed their 'inferiority complex' and 'find their place in human evolution'.

But how do we shed our inferiority complex when the world is still ruled and defined by men – and man, *qua* man, is indeed the measure of all things? And, having found our place in human evolution, what can we do to save the world?

For eons, the emphasis has been to establish male virtues and values as the norm against which the female is not merely different, but deviant. No wonder we have been suffering from an inferiority complex. What can we do now to establish the best of the female values and virtues, name them, take pride in them and finally, activate them?

Useful clues can be found in the work of feminist psychologists and theologians of the 1980s, in the writings of the Bahai faith and in some fundamental precepts of ancient beliefs, especially Taoism.

American psychologists and theologians at Harvard in the 1980s had some interesting stories to tell about the way in which women's moral development and highest aspirations were discovered to be different from those of men. Different but *equal*. Different but equally admirable. For instance, a man will die or kill for his ideals and beliefs. A woman tends to preserve life at all costs.

For example, the masculine abstract ideal prepared Abraham to sacrifice his own son to demonstrate the supremacy of his faith; while on the other hand, the woman who came before Solomon was willing to relinquish the truth of her own motherhood to save the life of her child. Shakespeare personified the feminine ideal of commonsense, humane justice versus the abstract letter of the law by making his great advocate a woman, Portia, disguised as a man, 'in order to bring into the masculine citadel of justice the feminine plea for mercy' as the Harvard developmental psychologist, Carol Gilligan points out.

To rid ourselves of our inferiority complex, we as creators and nurturers of life should celebrate our strengths as women. Our role models are there: the mathematician nun, Dr Rosalie Bertell, who spoke out fearlessly against lying statistics about allegedly safe levels of radiation; the brave ecologist/politician Wangari Maathai, who plants trees by the million in Kenya; Dr Rachel Carson, who noticed that the birds had ceased to sing: the economist Emma Rothschild, who revealed the fallacies behind the idea that the military industrial machine was good for the economy, and Dr Helen Caldicott, who dubbed that same machine 'the sacred cow that no one touched'. And finally we have those everyday heroines among us who sacrifice careers to nurture children and care for the aged at home.

Girls should not be ashamed of playing with dolls. Women priests should not shun a priestess' robe in favour of the male dog collar. There should be Nobel prizes for noble parturitions.

So can women then, as creators and nurturers of life, come forward as preservers of life on earth? And should woman, *qua* woman, become the measure of all things?

Rather than fall into the same trap of the past, we can welcome the loving spirit behind those great men who called forth the feminine principle, from Mahatma Gandhi to Archbishop Desmond Tutu, and work for balance, above all. In the spirit of the ancient Tao which recognized the equal importance of yin and yang and in the words of the Bahai saint, Baha'u'llah, let us remember:

230

'The world of humanity has two wings – one is woman and the other man. Not until both wings are equally developed can the bird fly. Should one wing remain weak, flight is impossible.'

A SHIFT IN THE ECONOMY

Helena Norberg-Hodge

Helena, an author/anthropologist familiar with Ladakh, and founder of ISEC lives in Devon

I had never been interested in economics, thinking of it as a dry and boring subject. My thinking changed dramatically when I ended up on the Tibetan plateau in Ladakh in 1975, before 'economic development', and I was forced to see how the economy—that is, subsidies for transport and centralised energy, industrial agriculture and medicine—completely transformed a whole society. In a region that had never known unemployment, time pressures, toxic pollution or family breakdown, I witnessed how outside economic pressures gave rise to all these problems in less than a decade. I witnessed how the cornerstone of the economy— farming—was destroyed in the name of progress. It became very clear to me that the same global economic system that was affecting Ladakh was having an impact around the world in every culture I was familiar with— from Sweden and the United States to Mongolia and Kenya—and that everywhere the trend was to separate people from the sources of their food and to create dependence on imports from further and further away.

At the same time, consumer culture images in the media made the young feel that their culture, their language, their food, their clothing, their skin colour were all inferior. The end results were lack of self-respect, despair, and growing anger at the system that so marginalised them. And all the while, economic breakdown was actually 'growth'. It became very clear to me that we urgently needed a fundamental shift in the economic policy.

For the past 25 years I have been speaking to audiences around the world about these issues. In the 1990s I felt demoralised by the lack of understanding of the issues, particularly in the western world. Governments and big businesses had come up with a new label—calling it 'sustainable development' and 'economic globalisation'—and the idea was that this was new, when it was actually fundamentally the same old tired formula for generating 'growth'. But many people—including the proponents—fell for the rhetoric.

Now, as the world stands on the brink of perpetual violence, terrorism, war, and ever-greater environmental breakdown, people are waking up by the millions. The growth and awareness from Ladakh to London and New York is very clear to see. It is exponential. Communication between the divides, North and South, environmental groups and labour unions, is breaking down as people recognise the need to reshape and redirect economic activity.

Around the world literally millions of grass-roots initiatives show that people from all walks of life are longing for a deeper connection to the natural world and to one another.

We all need to step back and look at the bigger picture to recognise that the way governments use our taxes to stimulate growth is actually responsible for exacerbating, if not creating, a social and environmental breakdown. We need economic literacy campaigns, campaigns that dispel the myths around growth and so-called free trade. Don't shy away from thinking about the economy. Don't leave it to the 'experts'—their vision is so narrow, they might as well be one-eyed. We urgently need the Bigger Picture. Something that is easier to see when you haven't been narrowly trained in a particular field. We need to recognise how the invisible hand of the global market operates to silently divide us from one another and from the earth. It may sound unbelievable, but understanding these connections is actually incredibly empowering and I feel very hopeful that we can succeed in turning things around before too long.

The dominant view in the media and even academia is that the multiple social and environmental crises are due to over-population, some sort of evolutionary 'progress' which can't be changed, or because of innate human greed. When you look more deeply, however, it becomes apparent that the most fundamental root cause is misguided economic policy and this is far easier to change than human nature.

A DEEPENING OF LOVE (FROM DISMEMBERING TO REMEMBERING)

Marian Partington

Marian, who lives in Wales, has written a book about forgiveness after her sister was killed by Fred and Rosemary West

In 1973 my younger sister Lucy claimed to be doing 'the opposite' of those around her (mostly me!). We were both in our final year of studying for a degree in English literature (I had predictably 'dropped out' for a year or two). Her passion was for medieval art, literature and religion. She was received into the Roman Catholic Church in November. Five weeks later we were both at home for the Christmas holidays near Cheltenham. She both admired and disapproved of my lifestyle. 'Living with' my boy-friend, hitchhiking alone, wearing Mr. Freedom trousers. We did, however, share a love of T. S. Eliot's poetry and loved to discuss the mystery of the 'intersection of time with eternity'.

On 27 December 1973, she went to visit a friend in Cheltenham. She left her friend's house to catch the 10.15 p.m. bus home and was never seen again. She was labelled as a 'missing person' for twenty years, and in March 1994, her bones were unearthed in the basement of 25 Cromwell Street, Gloucester. Then she became labelled as a 'West victim'.

For the whole of the Rosemary West trial (October–November 1995) I had a sore throat. I knew that it would not go away until I had spoken and been heard. In December 1995, I began to write. On 18 May 1996, the *Guardian Weekend* published a long essay I wrote, entitled 'Salvaging the Sacred'.

Writing became my way of searching for meaning. I began a painful inner journey from the dismembering of Lucy's body to the re-membering of the sacredness of all forms of life. Writing became a way of allowing myself time and solitude to experience my grief, by finding words and images as a structure for my own healing.

Sometimes I felt that I was risking the disintegration of myself without the assurance that a new whole would emerge. But I did not seem to have the choice to turn back. I was rescuing and reclaiming Lucy's truth and finding a depth of compassion I had never known. I felt I was being given an enormous gift I must share with others. The response to that essay was deeply encouraging. I received many letters. Each one reflected the best of humanity. Each one raised us all through its act of loving kindness.

Rosemary West was fifteen years old when she was abducted from a bus stop and raped. She was nineteen years old when Lucy (21 years old) was gagged into anonymity, raped, tortured and killed, or left to die. She is one of the few of the 74,000 prisoners in Britain who will probably 'never see the light of day again' (i.e. be released). I have thought a lot about justice in relation to murder. I don't think there is any human sentence that can appease or repair the devastating loss of a loved one to murder.

I figured out (in my head) during a Buddhist retreat in 1995 that working towards forgiveness offers the most creative, positive way forward. But how to do it? I made a vow to try. I could understand that it would involve giving up all hope of a better past and would be the kind of full stop that would offer a new relationship with the present moment, with myself and with my environment.

My initial motive for beginning this journey towards compassion was for the sake of my children. I have realised, in terrible depth, the reality of the cycle of violence and abuse: we pass on our unresolved pain to the next generation. I have been trying to explore my feelings and integrate the dreadful reality of Lucy's death in a way that does not pass on my struggle with anger, bitterness and grief as well as the aftermath of a difficult trial and media coverage. I needed to know how I could use my life to stop this cycle of violence/abuse and revenge, without denying the devastating effect it has had upon us all.

But my immediate experience, after this vow to forgive, was murderous rage. The emotion rushed up from my navel, dashing its heat and power against the inside of my skull; swilling, scouring, and eroding like a river in flood. It had no logic, no reason. Its energy was terrifying in its involuntary seizure. I pulled my hair, banged my head on the bed, screamed, rushed outside and stamped and clawed at the earth. I had no words, just a roar. My desire to forgive was premature, pretentious and impossible. But in that moment, when the rage seized me with a physical power that obliterated thoughts, I was connected to all humans who have killed. I could never lightly dismiss murderers again. The hope of forgiveness became more urgent.

On another retreat in 2000, after my interview with the Ch'an (Chinese Zen) master, grief flooded back again, and my desire to breathe returned. His words challenged every cell in my being: '*Just know that your suffering is relieving the suffering of others.*' Does he mean that by staying true to my own unresolved pain, not trying to bypass it (by

236

denial), allow it to destroy me (suicide), dump it on others (murder), I will eventually find the place of peace that allows me to express my life in a way that is genuinely free of all negative impulses?

I thought of Rosemary West and tried to say to her, in my head, I am feeling sick with pain, but I hope that it might help you in some way. And then the most profound realisation of the depth and extent of the suffering she has created for herself filled me with a heartfelt response of really hoping that this method works for her as well as for me. I could feel her terrible isolation in a society that hates her, and how irrevocably her family is wrecked and fragmented (dismembered). While I was experiencing this compassion (empathy with suffering), my isolated pain was transformed into a feeling of spacious ease that connected me with all forms of life. It felt like 'the intersection of time with eternity'. Yes, in that moment forgiveness was spontaneous.

I have chosen to work towards reclaiming the sacredness of my life in honour of the sacredness of Lucy's life and ultimately the potential sacredness of Rosemary West's life. It seems meaningless for her to be simply locked away and written off without any hope of change. Is that the 'punishment' that our society desires? I would like her to be released within herself, to be able to unravel her delusions and find some sort of truth. I know that with professional help she is moving in that direction, away from cruelty towards compassion for herself. I wish her well.

Sometimes I feel overwhelmed by the fact that I may never have explored these depths if dear Lucy had not died in such a terrible way. I feel joy and a deep gratitude to all those who have supported me on this journey. Thank you, Lucy. Your life and death have deepened my knowledge of love.

Gradually, by staying true to my inner daily practice of prayer and Buddhist meditation, opportunities arose for offering the compassion that I have experienced in a more practical way. Unexpectedly, I began to work with those who have committed serious crimes as part of the Restorative Justice Project in Bristol prison and more recently as a contributor to the Forgiveness Project (www.theforgivenessproject.com).

This approach to crime, as harm done that needs healing for all those affected by it, is a natural expression of my own experience of re-membering. Those labelled and kept apart as perpetrators, victims, and their communities can move towards the deepest form of justice, a process of reconciliation and forgiveness through which one is freed from all hope of a better past. The 'dis' (apart, asunder) moves towards the 're' (afresh, anew)

May we move from dis-membering towards re-membering the place of enlargement, acceptance and belonging. As Lucy wrote in one of her poems:

> *Things are as big as you make them—*
> *I can fill a whole body,*
> *A whole day of life*
> *With worry*
> *About a few words*
> *On one scrap of paper;*
> *Yet, the same evening,*
> *looking up,*
> *can frame my fingers*
> *to fit the sky*
> *in my cupped hands.*

FIGHTING FAITH

Sister Phyllis CSC

Sister Phyllis, a nun, originally from the Solomon Islands, now lives in Richmond

Do not repay anyone evil. Be careful to do what is right in the eyes of everyone. If it is possible, as far as it depends on you, live at peace with everyone. Do not take revenge, my friends, but leave room for God's wrath, for it is written: 'It is mine to avenge; I will repay,' says the Lord. On the contrary: 'If your enemy is hungry, feed him; if he is thirsty, give him something to drink. In doing this, you will heap burning coals on his head.' Do not be overcome by evil, but overcome evil with good.

(Romans 12:17–21, NIV)

In the centre of the city of Honiara are the four Anglican religious orders: the Franciscans, the Melanesian Brotherhood, the Sisters of the Church, and the Melanesian Sisterhood. These religious orders are different in their own rights, but they keep the same vows as other communities do. The work each of these communities is engaged in deeply is mission and evangelism. Sometimes they do missions together when it is required, but otherwise each community has its own programme.

In the South Pacific, to the north east of Australia, Melanesia stretches in an arc of islands from Papua New Guinea, through the Solomon Islands, to Vanuatu. Within the Solomon Islands there are six bigger islands which are inhabited and many other smaller islands, some of which are volcanic, and others are resorts. There are a lot of differences in the Solomon Islands, with different cultures and customs and different languages. This sometimes makes communication difficult for people. Despite culture, custom, language, amd even race differences, Solomon Islanders always united as one people. For many centuries people from the isles lived happily together, until June 2000, when the happy isles were challenged by a civil war which hardly got a mention in the western media.

The tension was between Guadalcanal and Malaita. Both islands are in the Solomon Islands. During the height of the tension the only people who could mediate between the two warring factions were the brothers and sisters of the four religious orders. This may sound weird to some, but in reality this was what was happening. We went out to the two warring parties hoping to convince them not to fight. We went to them without any weapons in our hands, except the knowledge that we were doing it for the good of the people, our nation, and even for those who are in the warring factions. This meant that whatever happened it was for the betterment of our country, because we love our country. It was a sad thing.

As a member of the Community of the Sisters of the Church I was amongst those able to mediate between the two warring factions. I would drive a two-and-a-half ton truck across enemy lines, transporting people who were homeless and delivering food from the town to cut-off rural communities. It was not easy since I had to go through check points with a truck full of goods. It was so frustrating when at times I was told to turn back or to take with me just a couple of bags of rice to the hundred souls out there waiting and starving.

On several occasions I had to face a gun held to my head. For me it was part of my calling to serve people. I had to show people that we belong to God and this is how we should treat each other, instead of fighting each other. Through missions which the sisters and brothers had conducted on each side of the divide during the war, we had built up relationships with both militia groups. Because we had helped them, they trusted us and we could go places others couldn't. They had great trust in us—there were times they wouldn't listen to women, yet they respected us.

As a result of the tension many people had lost their lives and many others were left homeless. You could not imagine this would happen in the Solomon Islands. It will be an experience that will live in the minds of people for a lifetime. Everything was chaos during that time. There was no law and order. Generally speaking the whole country was affected and everything was in stand-still. All the offices were closed, only a few shops were opened. People did not know what to do. Everyone was in terrible fear and because of that, many had gone home to their own island. Even the government could not do anything at this stage to help the people and the country. The government members were also threatened. Everybody was helpless and hopeless during that time. The only hope people had was to seek help from the Churches. People's eyes were open to seeing that, never mind whatever happened, good or bad, there is only one person who is in control of everything, and that is God. People seemed to be very near to God during those times of hardship.

After everything had quietened a bit, the government asked for some assistance from outside the Solomon Islands to bring back law and order to the country. In 2002 the Regional Assistant Mission to the Solomon Islands (RAMSI) went to the islands. This was led by the Australian military force. They disarmed people with guns and captured those who caused violence and had them put in custody. They did a tremendous job. Since then the Solomon Islands have returned to normality.

Law and order returned and people moved freely again, but the mission of the sisters and the brothers continues. Day and night people came for help for either physical, mental or spiritual needs. We, the sisters, at times ran out of room to put up families. There was not enough space to accommodate them, especially mothers and children. Sometimes we put two families together in one room. This is against health regulations and even our culture. However, these were difficult times and we thought that it was best that they had somewhere to rest.

Moreover, as problems increased in our city, one aspect of work that the sisters are engaging in heavily is helping women and children who have been abused by husbands and fathers. The sisters had been involved in this work for quite a long time, but recently a place has been built purposely for this ministry. Before, it was separated from our home, and we used our own resources to support those women who came to us for help. At times we didn't have enough to share with them or to provide for their needs, but the most important thing for them to know was that we cared. It was quite understandable when those in need arrived at the door expecting someone who really cared about them.

However, the sisters did not all live on the same island; they live and work in several different islands. In this way our ministry work is extended to people in other parts of the country. The work that the sisters do varies from island to island depending on the need there is. Normally, the ministry most sisters engage in in rural areas is often to go on mission.

On the mission they would spend weeks and months with the people in the rural area, giving encouragement, teaching children at Sunday schools and taking services and studies for adults. These activities would be done during evenings. In the day time people would work on the farm, fetch food for the family and do ordinary everyday work. In this case the sisters would also go with families to help the mothers in whatever work they may have planned for the day, whether it was to carry wood home for the fire to cook food for the family, or to help carry the food home, or to fetch water for cooking. It all depends on what has been planned for the day.

There is a great contrast between the rural life and the city way of living in the Solomon Islands. In the rural areas, life is much slower and organised and the needs of the people are different. In the city, life is much more demanding and problems increase every day. In the midst of this, we are to be 'the best of citizens', as Augustine put it. But what should we be doing?

Although our general task is to offer what little help we can to all people in need, most of the time our heart goes to women and children as they are the vulnerable and the victims in our society.

Practically speaking, we can do such things as donating time, but just as important, we can listen. We can also be an influence on those around us and befriend those who find themselves shunned by many.

NINE AND A HALF RIDICULOUS SUGGESTIONS

Lucy Pinney

Lucy, previously a columnist for The Times, *is an author living near Honiton*

I'm not very good on big issues. For me, it is tiny domestic details that make the most difference. So my changes to the world would be small. My only vaguely political suggestions would be:

1. An agreement that whenever town-dwellers pass a law only affecting the countryside, country people should be allowed to reciprocate. For instance, when Westminster made it impossible for farmers to get rid of a dead sheep without paying around £25, under my system, people in remote village halls could have spent long, merry evenings deciding whether to reclassify coffee as toxic waste and demand that customers wear full protective clothing to drink it in urban cafés. (And, of course, fill in a 23-page form in triplicate.)

2. In a similar vein, a cunning way of reducing air traffic (and global warming) might be to demand that every air passenger who owned land (even if it was only a town garden) had to either plant a tree or a square metre of vegetables each time they made a round-trip. This would also have the spin-off effect that so many vegetables would soon be grown in this country that none would have to be flown in.

But then I have other suggestions that aren't particularly environmental, but seem just as pressing to me, like the need for:

3. An agreement by all publishers and editors that whatever is done to an author's work should also be done to that author's *name*. So, for instance, if an article or novel was savagely cut, then the author's name should have whole sections cut from it too. And, of course, if an editor was to be creative, and insert their own words, then bits of *their* name should pop up in the author's. This would ensure that if a person called, say, Flabbery, was to cut bits out of this piece and insert their own annoying jokes, complete with exclamation

243

marks!!!, the work would appear under the name Luc Pinflab, and none of my friends would ring me up to ask what I was doing writing such bilge.

4. A very small, discreet system of marks inside the back cover of each book—perhaps a triangle, circle and square—to indicate whether a story had a straightforwardly happy ending, a bitter-sweet one, or was unrelentingly grim. I don't know about you, but I hate reading a book, and getting deeply and lovingly involved with all the characters, and then having it all turn out wrong in the end.

5. A PG version of every 15 or 18 film. For the past twenty-eight years, due to faulty birth-planning, I have been accompanied everywhere by at least one small child, and it is very annoying not being able to see popular films (unless they are PG or 12A). It's annoying for the child too: how are they to understand popular culture or make sense of whole episodes of *The Simpsons* if they haven't seen seminal works like *The Godfather* or *Hallowe'en*? I cannot even watch these films on DVD without having a large blanket ready to throw over my small companion(s) at crucial moments. And even if I do get to watch 18s on my own I don't enjoy the sex and violence. Like plenty of other people, I'd much rather it wasn't there at all. So why aren't there bowdlerised PG versions? Imagine the joy of finding out what the PG versions of *9 and a Half Weeks* or *Kill Bill 3* were like.

I have also often longed for the following to be invented:

6. A hireable, very soft padded room, locking on the inside, so that it would be possible for an exhausted adult to nod off while safely minding a hyperactive toddler.

7. An ultra-efficient household lie-detector, so you could find out, once and for all, who ate all the gherkins—and whether your husband was being unfaithful.

8. Some way of storing housework energy in a battery, so that you could scrub floors in a frenzy when doing displacement activities to avoid filling in your tax form. And then tap into it all a year later when you were feeling genuinely exhausted and frazzled.

½. Special ear-muffs so that parents could clearly hear film soundtracks, radio plays, their partner's jokes, the latest album from Amy Winehouse, etc., while simultaneously filtering out toddler tantrums, sibling rows, small computer fanatics describing (in exhaustive detail) how a game works, and teenage girls complaining how badly they have been parented. This only counts as half a suggestion because some of it could be accomplished by using an iPod.

9. A small, very fast robot that wandered around, scooping up litter and chewing gum and keeping a sharp eye on passersby. If it saw anyone throwing litter, it would fire a sticky, compacted pellet of gum and paper at them, as a reproof. The wonderful thing about this invention is that it would not only clean up the streets but amuse bored children, too. And who knows? Hours spent teasing the robot and dodging the gum might even solve another problem—obesity.

MONEY AND THE EMPEROR'S NEW CLOTHES

Susana Piohtee

Susana, a social activist living in Hereford, is a Tenant Participation Compact Development officer

'You what?' exclaimed a friend I hadn't seen for some years when I told her I was in the middle of writing an article about money and the economy. We had trained together to become psychotherapists, and were having a 'catch-up' session in my garden on a rare warm summer's evening.

She, it turned out, had achieved her goal of becoming a psychotherapist, with an accountant and a waiting list. My own precarious debt-based financial circumstances sprang into focus and I felt a twitch of envy move in my heart.

But, as we chatted, it seemed that my friend was not able to whole-heartedly enjoy her success, despite having 'made it' professionally. Indeed, she screwed up her mouth in a wry gesture and lamented that she found it disconcerting to discover how many apparently successful people, in the relative safety of a psychotherapy session, admit to feeling insecure and unfulfilled. The pressure to achieve, the need to constantly be competing against others was leading to breakdowns, depression, sickness and collapsing relationships, never mind disruption to their 'professional development'. Almost as an afterthought she reluctantly acknowledged that she too had begun to feel pressured, anxious about whether she was 'good enough' compared with other therapists.

'Doing therapy ain't what it used to be,' she quipped.

I agreed, and we talked about how the inherent challenges of practising psychotherapy had been compounded by all sorts of additional challenges related to its shift from a vocation to a high-profile, money-making profession; and how this affected the relationship between client and therapist as well as between therapists themselves. It had always been my contention that work of any 'therapeutic' nature must remain a vocation.

'All of which,' I explained, 'is why I decided I would never be able to make psychotherapy my main source of income, and is part of why I've become involved in all this stuff related to money and economics. I want

247

people to wake up to the insanity of our economic system. Economics is like the engine room of our society. It's where we control the way we go about providing for health, education, the environment—you name it, all the things that we need for daily living.'

My friend was looking puzzled. 'But isn't it a dry old topic by your standards? I remember you as the person who used to get into such a strop about having to spend time keeping accounts and retaining all your shopping receipts for the tax man when you started up your own practice.'

She had hit the nail on the head, highlighting the very reason I had become interested in the matters I loosely describe as 'economics'. Always an independent thinker, a desire to 'be different' and single parenthood had left me with a financial status usually referred to as 'on the poverty line'—I was pretty much a failure by the standards of our society. I had been faced with the 'dryness and rigidity', the sterility, of our current economic system often enough to evoke within me a perverse interest in a subject about as distant from my usual interests as can be imagined.

I set out to explain. 'The way I see it, our economic thinking is completely out of balance because it's founded wholly upon male values and has a mantra that goes something like, "*The only way to succeed is to compete with everybody and for everything.*" This thinking creates a fear-motivated cycle of "*Attack to win and defend to protect what you've won*" —and it sucks the life blood and creativity out of countless millions of individuals. Its rules and regulations favour those who "make and amass money", but actively discourage those of us who desire to use our energy, strength, skills, creativity, logic and common sense for the benefit of our planet, or our "communities"—you know, real live people, instead of for the benefit of business corporations! It's a system that's actually life-threatening!' I squeaked indignantly as I ran out of breath.

Her quizzical silence encouraged me to continue my scary mono-logue—scary because I wasn't able to tune out the icy internal voice asking, '*Who do you, a mere woman, think you are to make these judgments?*'

'We need an economic system that is life-*enhancing*—"juicy", fluid, imaginative. It's got to lubricate "exchange", if you see what I mean!' Her eyebrows raised slightly as she nodded, not unaware of the image I'd just conjured up. 'In other words, it needs some powerful female input. It's time for men and women to work together. Men need to respect and value "feminine intuition" much more. You know how much I appreciate "things masculine", but I've come to the conclusion that men are not best suited to being in charge of economics; after all, economics is basically housekeeping—whether house means a cardboard box or our global home! Most men, *especially* those who have reached top positions of influence, are still dominated by the need to achieve, to win. In their minds that means beating off the competition. Men seem to see most things in terms of competition. I'm not saying there's anything wrong with competition per se; I know some people who can't be bothered to get off their asses to do anything at all if there's no chance of proving they're "better" than somebody else. But we've got to find a way for that urge to compete to be harnessed constructively so that a *communal* benefit is its aim. When competition is about the need to prove you're better than somebody else, or you're right and they're wrong, it can only result in a field littered with "losers" feeling bad about themselves, and the results just become progressively more destructive—maybe think "terrorism" here! Doesn't business talk ever remind you of a battleground—*cut and thrust, crippling competition, hostile takeover*?'

Nothing was going to stop me now, but a deep breath was needed before I launched into the next bit:

'Women, whether we care to recognise it or not, whether we *like* it or not, are dominated by the need to nurture, to protect. We're used to putting the needs of others first and are more inclined to see things in terms of cooperation. You can't spend nine months with another being inside your body sharing all its resources and every second of your living without learning about the ultimate benefits of cooperation—i.e. life!

'I am just so fed up with hearing our "leaders" tell us *there isn't enough money* for inspirational education, proper health care, quality housing for all, healthy food—you name it, any basic human need. And we, the public, swallow it, even though we constantly see examples of plenty of money being available to make yet more money! I feel so frustrated by the insanity of it all!'

I drew a breath and continued before my friend could stop me.

'Do these "leaders" truly believe it when they say "there is not enough money to go round"? Think about it —is money a natural resource that is scarce? No, it's not! It might have been once upon a time, but these days most of it is quite literally something that banks create out of thin air in the form of debt—97% of currency circulating in the UK is in the form of debt! We both know what problems being in debt can bring people! But the banks call it "credit" and have the cheek to charge high rates of interest to individuals and organisations that borrow the phantom stuff *and* make huge profits for themselves in the process—actually it's called usury!

'Did you know that most people haven't a clue about the way banks work? Not only do they create money out of nothing, they can choose *who* they lend it to; so they're not only controlling *how much* money is available but also *what it's used for*. Just think of the power that gives to those who own the banks!'

I had finally gained my friend's full attention. 'Surely that can't be right? That would mean it's banks that really control things and not the government,' she interjected sceptically.

'You got it! Banks and their associated corporations. And that's why there's never enough money to provide decent public services: because the government itself has to borrow from the "central" bank *at interest* every time extra money is needed for public services. And, of course, that's why we have to pay so much in taxes—and that's another whole big issue!

'And if you ask an economist why the government doesn't just create money itself for funding public services, most of them look supercilious and bang on about it not being as simple as that; about inflation, and "experts" who understand the complex monetary system being the only ones to understand it.

'For a long time I believed it—surely the "experts" *must* know best, even though what they were saying sounded pretty illogical to me. Then one day I came across writing *by an economist*—an amazing man by the sound of things—who totally supported my own view that our whole economic system—and that includes things like the crazy belief that an economy is only successful when it's continually "growing", and the way our tax system penalizes those who are "productive" and benefits those who sit upon huge personal fortunes in the form of "land"—is one big scam. From then on I just got more and more involved and discovered more and more people who think like I do. It was amazing.'

I gave her a couple of quotes that had been introduced to me whilst planning a series of workshops entitled '*Money Talks—but should we believe what it says?*' 'What about this beauty, straight from the mouth of famous banker Mayer Amschel Rothschild himself, way back in 1790: "*Give me control of a nation's money, and I care not who writes its laws.*" Or the words of Josiah Stamp, 1920s Governor of the Bank of England: "*If you want to be the slaves of banks and pay for the cost of your own slavery, then let banks create money.*"'

I could see my friend was beginning to get rattled, but chose to ignore it and plunged on: 'It's the belief that money is the key to prosperity that really bugs me. We live in a society where nearly all our actions, and even our thinking, are dominated by dependence upon money. The word "economy" seems to have become synonymous with "making money". We have elevated money to a mythical status; and it's a myth that needs debunking. Our credulity in its power would be touching if it wasn't so dangerous.'

'But that's true, isn't it? Without money we can't do anything; well, you know what I mean, we can't actually survive without money!'

'I know what you mean, but it's only true because we *believe* it to be true! To say we can't survive without money is a fabrication, just like "The Emperor's New Clothes". The power that money exercises over us is way out of proportion to its actual value. We've created a self-fulfilling prophecy. It's as though we're under a self-induced spell that prevents us from using our knowledge, our skills, our labour and the world's very abundant resources unless we've been "switched on" by money. But once enough of us *wake up* from this spell and come to our senses, we stand a chance of reclaiming "money" for what it truly is—a means of exchange, and if we choose, a tool for doing good business—business that produces and/or distributes "good". There are lots of groups and individuals, some of them quite influential, exploring and campaigning for all sorts of alternative economics. But as always with these things, it needs mass support before politicians will begin to take any notice.'

'Yeah, and isn't that the problem?' My friend was gathering up her things. 'Don't you think most people are happy with things the way they are? After all, you can't say our economy hasn't raised living standards enormously. I'm really enjoying my new-found wealth!'

I had to challenge her. 'Are you? Your standard of living might be better than it was, but what about your quality of life? You've just been saying how unhappy your "wealthy" clients are, and you yourself; despite earning plenty of money. And why? Because *having* to "compete" with others *all the time* is frightening. Just use your imagination to follow through to the logical conclusion of everybody striving for "the competitive edge" all the time.'

I stopped speaking, noting from my friend's expression that she'd had enough of my lecturing. I shrugged. 'Look, I'm not intending to have a go at you personally (though I suppose in a way I was); I just think we *all* need to begin taking personal responsibility: stop relying on the so-called experts to tell us how to manage things that deeply affect the lives of each one of us, and listen to our intuition and use our common sense. Look at all the misery in the world—so much of it is due to people's belief in the power of money to bring them prosperity. Ask yourself whether competing for material wealth is actually resulting in the sort of things people everywhere say they want: peace, freedom from fear, being loved and loving?'

My friend raised her eyebrows quizzically and checked her watch. 'I've got to go! You know what? One thing hasn't changed about you; you're still a crazy idealist. I can understand where you're coming from and I think I can see where you're going; but I'm not sure *I* want to go there. It's taken me a hell of a long time to gain my bit of material wealth and I'm not knocking it. It's giving me more freedom than I've ever had before,' she alleged, a touch defiantly. 'And I intend to enjoy it!'

'Of course; I didn't mean you shouldn't,' I agreed hurriedly, wondering if I'd just managed to lose a friend.

After we'd said our goodbyes, I went inside feeling despondent and berating myself for being too challenging. How could I possibly help 'save the world' when I couldn't even encourage one more woman friend to question for herself the myths upon which our economy is built, to see how we are brainwashed into happily leaving unquestioned and unchallenged the influence of those 'experts' whose 'expert advice' has led to greater and greater affluence for a small group of international 'elites' at the expense of hugely unnecessary suffering for many millions of humans, and a war-devastated planet?

Since that meeting—some years down the line now and after which that friend went her way and I went mine—it has been confirmed to me over and over again that one change, a truly important change amongst myriad changes that need to happen before our world can be safe, is for the current imbalance between masculine and feminine to be righted. And that will only happen once enough women reconnect with their own inner wisdom, the Divine Feminine, and begin to seek the information that will enable them to question and challenge the status quo and to work side by side with those wise men who also understand the need to include a feminine approach in all decision-making processes.

Once we have reconnected with our very own and very powerful inner wisdom, we become more discerning about which external sources of 'expertise' we give credence to, whether it be the preacher, the insurance broker, the economist, the politician, or even the celebrity columnist.

Once we begin to trust the voice of our heart, we commence reviving the power to cast off the money myth to which we have been in thrall for so long.

252

PENNEY'S RANT

Penney Poyzer

Penny is a writer and broadcaster on green issues, and lives in a pioneering 'eco-home' in Nottingham

I've been in a bit a ferment recently and think quite possibly I am moving into my eco-freako, feminist-radicalist phase. I'm probably borderline menopausal and a bit psychotic—but in a good way.

What the planet needs is for a lot of us women to go a bit barmy and stop conforming to what the ads on telly tell us about how every aspect of our lives should look, smell and be revitalised with *pro ketamin B* with added botox, or whatever.

I know this message is stroppy and believe me, a couple of years ago I honestly would not have presumed. But I was younger and more patient then. The time to give a shit about what people might think has gone: I'm a woman on a mission and my oestrogen is turbo-charged.

For the last couple of years I've felt that women have been pretty passive over this whole Climate Change thing. Women make *all* the major consumer decisions for their families. They have an immense effect on the amount of waste, chemicals and energy used in the home—because they manage the show.

A survey in Spring 2007, carried out by the Women's Environmental Network and the National Federation of Women's Institutes, showed that the vast majority of women surveyed said they were *'very concerned'* about Climate Change. They also wanted it to be made 'easier' to live more greenly, to have good quality information, etc., etc. All positive stuff, but way overdue and, well, a tad passive. Now we have this information, what do we do with it?

Well, I would suggest we need to be thinking beyond our next batch of mains-powered room fragrances. We need to get aware and *evangelise*—which is exactly what supermarkets, car manufacturers and banks are spending millions on—telling us and their shareholders how wonderfully green they are.

Picture this. You wake up to a breakfast offered to you on a neatly laid tray. The perfumed steam of freshly brewed organic coffee mingles with Ethically Baked, Real French, All-Butter Croissants. Mmm ... totally delicious, utterly seductive—and immoral. We can't afford this kind of lifestyle anymore. The cards are maxed and the interest rate keeps on climbing.

Women, put down your cleaning products, switch off your iron and forsake Fern and Phil for five minutes. Sit back, have a cup of tea and question where all this stuff is leading your kids.

We need to become an army of conscious consumers—and to become conscious pretty damn quick. We can't buy our way out of this one. It's simple; we have to learn to live with less stuff.

Women are bloody brilliant, scarily strong when we want to be and potentially awesome as an army of change-makers. Let's get busy and have a boogie while we are at it!

WHY DAISY HAD A POINT

Liz Reason

Liz, who lives in Oxfordshire, is a policy analyst specialising in energy/ climate change

I went to a school that prided itself on educating the 'crème de la crème'. No doubt relying on the notion of cream always rising to the top, they gave no career guidance, other than the expectation that you should go to university, whether you had a clear idea of what you wanted to do or not. So like many girls, I knew only that I wanted to do something 'interesting and useful'.

As a result, like many people, I left university with a degree I had found boring and no idea about how I might spend the rest of my life. So I did two years' voluntary service overseas. Then I trained to be a teacher. And then I met Daisy the cow.

Daisy was a cow of two halves—a man in the front legs and a woman in the back. She was walking the streets of Cambridge to make a plea for vegetarianism. This was not the 'I'm a cuddly animal, please don't eat me' kind of a plea. Daisy's rationale was that she ate a lot of grain and was an energy-intensive way of supplying humans with food—7lbs of grain in fact, to make 1lb of edible Daisy.

Now, I have to say that this was news to me. And as someone who'd never really stopped to think about whether I should eat meat or not, it's a message that packed a punch. I'd lived in Africa, so knew that we in the developed countries took more than our fair share of resources and, what's more, took it for granted that we should. So I stopped to find out who'd brought Daisy to the streets, and found myself talking to Cambridge Friends of the Earth (FoE).

To me this all proved a heady brew and I was hooked. Hook One—use fewer resources for our own sake and for the sake of the planet—was a message that addressed my instincts; Hook Two—here is something that is fundamental to the culture we have constructed and which we don't think to question—probably dangerous; Hook Three—people want to believe that technology would provide answers so that we would never have to address how we need to rationalise/ration our use of resources— human behaviour at its best and worst.

So for the next few years, I set about re-defining myself from a modern linguist to an energy policy analyst, with jobs in fuel poverty, energy efficiency and consumer representation. These all helped me to understand different aspects of the policy process, including the ways in which we create problems, which then have to be solved! For example, mass cheap house-building led to hard-to-heat homes, led to fuel poverty … Why didn't we think to build homes with a good energy performance? Because we took energy for granted.

Gradually, I became more dissatisfied with campaigning. There was something about being always on the outside which, I felt, made those in the mainstream able to dismiss non-conformist views as 'not understanding how the world works'. Joining the 'real world' would give me more credibility.

And that's what I decided to do. I wanted to understand what the incentives and disincentives provided to business were—what led them to behave in certain ways? Given certain incentives, were their decisions uniformly inevitable? And if we didn't like that behaviour, what other incentives could be provided to get outcomes in line with what was desirable?

The key message FoE was out to promote was that we use all our resources without reflecting on the impact on other humans and on the planet. This made sense to me. So I decided to attend one of FoE's meetings to find out more. And that's when I discovered energy policy.

Now if there's one thing those living in the twentieth century took for granted, it was energy. Ownership of cars was designed to allow all of us to travel further, faster, and more frequently. Our homes would be warm all the time, requiring us only to turn up the thermostat, not carry in the coal. We could live in a world of constant daylight and on-stream entertainment. Consuming fossil fuels like there was no tomorrow, consuming calories like food producers were going out of business. By the beginning of the twenty-first century, air travel had become 'a human right'; we put on jumpers and jacket to go into the office from outside, because 'no company will rent a building without air-conditioning'. There are many places where it is no longer possible to see the stars.

At the time I joined FoE, it was embroiled in the Windscale Inquiry, putting a professional and rationally argued case against the development of the site in Cumbria for more re-processing of nuclear waste. Fundamental to its arguments was cost. When the first nuclear power plant was opened at Windscale, the headlines had read 'Nuclear power— too cheap to meter!' FoE argued that this would not be the case, that nuclear power was a complex technology, fraught with environmental risks, and subject to wild cost claims from the state-owned Central Electricity Generating Board. How much cheaper it would be simply to use less energy—the term 'negawatts' was coined to describe the low-cost reduction in megawatts of electricity demand.

I realised that, whether I liked it or not, money talks and I had to understand the money before I could really get in and influence policy. (What a delicious irony that the development of the electricity market highlighted the true high costs and risks of nuclear power, which had to be retained in the state sector, proving in hard investment terms what campaigners had been arguing for years.) I knew that what really drove decisions was the economic and financial framework within which business operated, often referred to as 'the free market'. I soon came to understand that there is no such thing as a 'free' market. Every market is regulated—for safety, to prevent the abuse of market power, the simple rules of trade between different market players. Arguing that their 'freedom was being curtailed' was an excuse for companies to fulfil short-term aims at the expense of the long term.

When the restructuring and privatisation of the electricity supply industry gave opportunities for the development of renewable electricity projects, with colleagues I set up a company to undertake wind developments in Cumbria. We wanted to show that wind projects could be developed which were financially attractive and appealing to nearby residents. We succeeded and the number and capacity of the wind farms we started continue to expand.

We decided to build a house that used 75% less energy than the average—and did so—and its energy performance is exactly as predicted.

The electricity market also created a need for those who understood the rules and the impact on future costs and profits. So seeing another opportunity, we set up a management consultancy that specialised in the energy markets, advising those making major investments in new power stations and companies.

As a leading consultancy in this field, we were soon working for major market players in the UK and Europe and being employed by government to assist with policy analysis and development related to integrating green energy and energy efficiency in the new market environment. This really helped me to understand where the money was, and how to make rule changes to move the incentives—and the money—onto players in the market to create a greener world.

And then I came to realise—like many others—that climate change is coming upon us at a much faster and more furious rate than we had expected. I decided to leave the consultancy to set up *Reasons to be Cheerful*, to help implement the many policies designed to reduce our reliance on fossil fuel energy more speedily and effectively. And that's where I am now.

I want to help communicate the link between our thoughtless energy use and climate change. If carbon dioxide were purple and had been visibly clouding our skies with smog, we would have acted to curb our emissions a long time ago. I want to get effective action to minimise the energy use and carbon dioxide emitted by our buildings. And I want to help get the incentives right to encourage investment in activities and products which will lighten our footprint on the planet.

Along the way, I've realised how important it is that we take personal responsibility for our actions and their outcomes. That's what I do. It's caused me no grief; in fact, I've had an enjoyable and healthy life. I'd like to hear politicians dare to say: 'If you want rights, you must fulfil your responsibilities, and that goes for climate change action too. If you want a planet, you must have less of it for yourself.'

There's a virtuous circle in all this—fewer calories consumed, whether food or fossil fuel, leads to a healthier, less stressful life in better networked communities. And we preserve the planet for future generations. There are some reasons to be cheerful!

My heart sinks when I hear young women say: 'I don't know what I want to do for a job, but I'd like to do something interesting and useful.' Yes, of course do something interesting, and please do something useful; but also follow the money!

THE NURSERY CLASS

Phillipa Reynolds

Phillipa, born in New Zealand and a teacher for many years, now lives in Devon and is active in a local peace group

The troubles of the world seem to be very great … there are 'wars and rumours of wars', starvation in poverty-ridden countries, and disasters, both man-made and 'natural' in many places. How can I, one western woman, help the situation? It seems impossible to alleviate any distress.

Sometimes I think that the world situation can be compared to a nursery class, of say, 3-to-4-year-olds. There are a lot of things to play with … there is a sunny place to play, and a sheltered space inside if the weather is bad … There are plenty of things to play with … more than sufficient for each child. All is peace and quiet. There is an air of purpose, a sense of concentration, of enjoyment.

Suddenly, the peace is shattered. An 'incident' has occurred. The place is loud with shouts, screams of frustration, anger. Arms are flailing, feet are kicking, toys and chairs are knocked to the floor. It is chaos, mayhem. But the nursery teacher is quickly in action. She sorts out the 'troublemakers', soothes the injured, comforts the crying ones and exudes such a sense of loving control and orderliness that soon calm is restored, the children are quiet and once more playing happily together.

What happened? How did she restore peace?

She is a very wise, experienced teacher. First of all, she came to the aid of those with injuries (real or imagined). She put plasters over scratches and cuts with appropriate soothing words. She dried tears with words of comfort and a loving cuddle. She reprimanded the wrongdoers. She spoke to the class, saying, 'There are plenty of toys for all of you here. You do not need to hoard toys to stop anyone else using them. You should never snatch, or take by force, any toy from any other child. You should *never* gang up with anyone else to frighten or take a toy from someone else just because you want it at that moment! There are *plenty* of toys for you all. Remember our "Code". We do not have bullies here. We share what we have. We do not use force. We help the younger and weaker ones. We speak gently and quietly. But we can still have fun and enjoy ourselves.'

Perhaps the world, our nursery class, needs to take a few lessons in behaviour from our fictional class. What lessons can be learned? Perhaps our 'teacher', maybe in the guise of the United Nations Secretary-General, needs to say to all countries:

1. There is plenty. The earth has many resources. There is enough for you all … if you share them … and use them wisely.

2. Don't hoard your resources. Use them. Be inventive. Find new ways of using them more efficiently, and use them for the benefit of all. Use them in peaceful ways. Don't use them to produce weapons that can kill and maim people.

3. Work together with neighbouring countries to build up your economies for the good of all.

4. Help the weaker ones in the international community. Give them what they need—food, clothing, medicines, tools, skills, and so on. But with all your giving, make sure you do not send your unwanted "rubbish", things from your own country, inferior goods. Help them to "pull themselves up by their own bootstraps".

5. Don't "gang up" with other nations to bully the weaker ones to fall in with some plan that benefits only you.

6. Do not use force against another nation to get what *you* want.

7. Be grateful for your environment. Just as the nursery class had a bright space, shelter and pleasant surroundings, so nations have a wonderful environment in which to live and grow. Don't pollute it or you will destroy it.'

Do you think the nations in our present day will heed such advice? If they have as much sense as the nursery children, they will.

THE REVOLUTIONARY ECCENTRIC

Dame Anita Roddick

Anita was the founder of The Body Shop

'Never doubt that a small group of thoughtful, committed citizens can change the world; indeed, it's the only thing that ever has.'

(Margaret Mead)

Every real and good change of significance, every revolutionary idea, every heartfelt gesture that changes one life or a thousand, was once seen as eccentric. Leaders are few and followers many, for a reason: Change requires bucking the status quo, and bucking the status quo requires a willingness to be perceived as crazy, dangerous, or ridiculous. Like entrepreneurs, revolutionaries, activists, and changemakers of every stripe lead because they cannot follow that with which they do not agree, or which limits their imaginations. They change the world because their passion and conviction will not allow them *not* to.

Not all revolutionaries set out to change the *world* per se; they set out to change *their* worlds. And in so doing, they often change the way one person, or a few people, or whole communities, or entire nations, or the world thinks and operates in some significant way. 'The world' doesn't have to be literal; real change can be small scale and still be revolutionary. All it takes is an ability to see other possibilities, and the willingness to help others see them, too. As someone once said, 'We are only limited by our imaginations.'

I, for one, didn't set out to change the way business operates. I just wanted a means to support myself and my two daughters. When I first applied for a loan to start a small hair-and-skin-care shop in Brighton in 1976, the man behind the desk looked as if I'd asked him to shave his head. A woman? Running a business? How preposterous, he obviously thought. Weeks later, I went back to the same bank with my husband in tow. We had the loan in minutes. That banker could not see beyond his own nose. My company went on to show how business can be done differently worldwide, showing that women can indeed run successful businesses, and that businesses can indeed have compassion—and just plain passion—at heart instead of pure profit motive. Many people had said it was not possible. Today, The Body Shop is among the most recognised and admired brands in the world, with shops in over 52 countries, and fair-trade agreements in a dozen more benefiting local communities in some of the poorest places on earth. Time and again I was told it couldn't be done, that it would not work, that I was insane. I was not limited in my thinking to believe that business was just financial science; I sensed that it was also about trading and bringing your heart to the workplace.

In my travels for The Body Shop over the past 29 years, I have met thousands of activists and businesspeople, entertainers, theologians, women's groups and anti-globalisation activists, native tribes and vagabonds. I have met the Dalai Lama and Nelson Mandela. I have spent days deep in the Amazon rainforest and on the streets of London among the homeless. And I can spot a revolutionary from 100 paces. First clue: Everyone thinks they're crazy or dangerous.

I think of some of my personal heroes and see how they fit this description: Jesus Christ, Joan of Arc, Gandhi … the list goes on. They were tenacious and driven in the extreme. They refused to say, 'This is how it's done; this is how it is' or especially, 'I can't.'

Not everyone who changes the world is a household name, much less a martyr, but they too, can and do change the world. I think of the twenty employees of The Body Shop who went to Romania with me to help repair and re-equip the orphanages there, and the two who ended up staying and starting Children on the Edge, a non-profit group that is systematically deinstitutionalizing the children of Romania. I think of the shops that joined our campaign with Amnesty International and mobilized thousands of shoppers to sign petitions and send letters, ultimately freeing 17 prisoners of conscience around the world.

I think of Ken Saro-Wiwa and the rest of the Ogoni people in Nicaragua who stood up to Shell Oil, which was occupying and polluting native Ogoni tribal lands. Their bravery cost many of them, including Ken, their lives. But it focused international outrage on exploitation by multinational corporations, especially those which are backed by corrupt military regimes.

I think of the five or six people who helped The Body Shop Foundation establish the Amazon Co-op in Brazil, where eleven tribes who had been on the verge of being driven out of their native territory by disease, illegal logging, and the incompetence and corruption of the local government now have decent health care, clean water, and three of their own businesses, including a 'green pharmacy', an eco-lodge, and an Internet café.

I think of the Angola Three, Black Panthers who stood up against corruption and abuse inside Angola Penitentiary in Louisiana, and who were framed for crimes they didn't commit and thrown in solitary confinement for 31 years. They are still there, but their hope and determination does not fade with time. When they finally are free—and I have to believe they will be—I hope the corruption and injustice at the heart of their stories will be exposed in a way that changes a deeply broken criminal justice system.

There are thousands more, of course, whose impact you feel every day, even if you have never heard their names. You'll know them by that slightly crazy gleam in their eye. *And then you will see how this world really does need more of these wonderful heretics.*

ACTION AS PEBBLES

Jean Schulz

Jean, born in Germany, was wife of the late Charles Schulz, creator of the Peanuts cartoon strip. She helped develop Meals on Wheels and lives in California

I think it is important to go about with the knowledge that our words and our actions do have an effect in and on the world. We don't have to be sappy-sweet about the things we say, but we should be aware that we don't know where other people are in their maturity and development, so as we make our way through our days we should be careful as we would be if we were speaking in front of a group of 10-year-olds.

My father told me a story to illustrate this. It stayed with me and I tell it when the occasion arises.

This was in the Sixties. My father ate his lunch at the typical-for-the-day drugstore lunch counter. One day a woman came to sit on the adjacent stool. 'You don't know it,' she said, 'but you saved my life.' My father was surprised to hear this. This was a person he didn't even recognise. The woman explained, 'I was planning to kill myself and my plan was set. I stopped in here and sat next to you at the counter. I don't really remember *what* it was you said to me, but I remember that you gave me a small shred of hope, and after I left I realised that suicide was no answer to my pain. That was eight months ago. I feel better now and I just wanted to thank you.'

And our actions TOO. Each action is like a pebble in a lake, sending out ever-widening rings which may be supporting positive and strengthening reactions, or imparting negative reactions.

This is what is meant by community: living as though everyone is important to everyone else.

People now talk about curbing their impulse to anger when small things happen in traffic situations. They do this because there are more volatile people out there in cars, with small consciences and with guns, who think little about the consequences of their actions. But actually, we should be giving people the benefit of the doubt, smiling apologetically instead of raising the fist, letting them in instead of cutting them out. We don't know what they may have just gone through, what their sorrows are, what their major deficiencies are. We do know our own strengths, our own intent and we can act on it in a posititive way to spread positive energy.

This is not a call for perfection or to take the fun out of life. I think one of the best things we can do for others is to develop our own sense of humour and learn to laugh; at ourselves, and at the troubles of life.

So any time you think you are small or insignificant in the world, think again. Your actions, your words reach far beyond what you could imagine. It is scary.

Beyond all this, be sincere, not serious, and learn to laugh.

SEEING AND FEELING ONE

Karen Eberhardt Shelton

Karen is a poet, writer and photographer who was born in California and lives in Devon

What a challenge it all is! Over the years, I've read books that were a call to think and act, have joined organisations trying to stop war/help the earth/protect animals, and encountered a range of deep thinkers that have made a difference in how I live by planting themselves in my consciousness, and thank goodness for that.

David Orr, a visionary educator of our era, said, 'Education ought to begin with the *power of language, appropriately and carefully used.*' The way we speak is how we think; how we think is what we say. I agree with him when he says 'It's not just about houses or water or any particular system. It *has* to be about how we think. The ultimate object of ecological design is the human mind. The object is to overcome those parts of the human mind in the culture that give rise to illusion, greed, and ill will', to which I would add apathy and indifference. William Blake is an example of someone who thinkingly came to understand his connection to the divine in nature. He knew it was there if you looked with the right eyes. He also saw art as an act of worship. I suspect what he meant was that 'to realise our oneness with the web of life—there is no force on earth greater than this consciousness'.

This makes me realise that as a writer I engage in countless acts of worship. Bringing together this book is one. To use my writer's voice to *Speak Up* feels utterly divine. (I can't imagine being a writer of adverts or pop lyrics or sales hype; what a waste of energy!) A Seneca Native American named John Mohawk wrote a piece titled *From Miracle to Magic* in which he talked about 'acquiring the consciousness that embodies the essence of the spirit of life in, not just the world, but the entire universe'. Acquire that consciousness and you can't rationalise pollution or chopping down rainforests or doing the myriad horrible things that humans do. *Shared consciousness.*

Dan Dagget, an ecological maverick I recently discovered, describes how we 'live in a world of relationships', a reality that touches me like nothing else. He continues, 'Humans have a relationship with and responsibilities to nature as predator as well as prey, as starters of fire, as slowers of water, as spreaders and cultivators of seed. We can't break up with nature, with the other components of nature, with the other humans living within nature. There's no place else to go.'

Then there is Paul Hawken (whose six books have been published in some 52 countries and 30 languages), opening minds to the concept of *natural capital* (everything that comes from the earth) being confused with *industrial/manufactured capital,* to the point where 'We are using more of what we have less of—living systems and natural resources—in order to use less of what we have more of: human beings. The only viable future for business lies in adapting to ecological principles grounded in social and economic justice.'

Read Thom Hartmann's *The Last Hours of Ancient Sunlight* (oil equals sunlight), or Brian Swimme's *The Universe Story*, Edmund O. Wilson's *The Future of Life*, Lewis Thomas's *The Fragile Species*, and Thomas Berry's *The Great Work*. Bill Bryson's *A Short History of Nearly Everything* is a sublimely accessible account of how 'everything' fits together. There's no excuse for not knowing, not caring, not living lightly on the earth! 'Wisdom begins with the sincere desire for instruction', it says in the Book of Solomon.

So here I am, trying in a small way to make the world a better place. How one goes about this has been in the back of my mind all my life, but only lately, after climbing to the top of the hill and looking around, feeling my back go creaky and no longer having the knees to run a 10K, I see masses of tragedy occurring everywhere, and realise a different approach is needed, a more suitable agenda. I've done the peace marches and sit-ins, waved my flag and signed petitions, gone to meetings, attended hearings, written to the governor, the president, put placards in the window, and the earth-wrecker's ball rampages on and on. We've got masses of organisations each doing good work, but none of them effecting a global impact. Why not find a way to change attitudes right from the start? There are more than six billion humans eating, breeding, fighting, building, producing, travelling, wasting, and not one of them is capable of providing water for that six billion; only earth knows how. But we don't reflect on that as we destroy our way through life, and nobody seems to have figured out how to teach children to 'realise their oneness with the web of life', so now what?

I'm lifting my magic wand (her name is *Eve*) out of the family trunk. I'm going to take her wherever I go and when I see a person doing something bad for the earth (doesn't matter if they're one-legged, president of the world or have ten Ferraris), or something cruel or mean or stupid, I quietly go up to them and tap their shoulder, upon which Eve instantly deposits an invisible sheen of mutant DNA. If I catch them up to no good a second time, *ting,* tap two. More day-glo DNA that won't brush off. If a third tap's in order, there's no warning, no falling shadow, no throat clearing, not a whisper; it's just *poof,* instant, magical, gentle disappearance—that person never to be seen again, not even by worms. They vanish without leaving even a smudge, dark glasses or a tie, and certainly nothing of a 'designer' nature.

If there were fewer people in the world, it wouldn't be so hard to keep track of them all. Right now we're swarming around everywhere like huge colonies of wood ants looking for more places to build giant nests. I would place a cap on population. How silly for the French to encourage women to have more babies. Maybe France can afford them, but the world as a whole can't. As Gandhi used to say, 'There's enough for everyone's need, but not for everyone's greed.' There's a surplus of greedy people filling their hampers with everything they can grab, and that's absolutely, unsustainably Not Right. There's not enough to go around for billions of humans (ever hear of a *finite* earth?), and it's ridiculous to try to gouge every last goodie out of this unreasonably depleted larder, so it definitely makes sense to cut back on numbers. How 'bout 2 billion, max? And no cheating.

Otherwise, it's the *rivet* thing. Simon Barnes, a nature writer I like reading, described how the planet sustains itself through biodiversity. There are uncountable entities, big and little and mostly microscopic, scrambling around everywhere creating a strong tapestry of resilience and ability to adapt, co-exist, meet new challenges. But when you remove a few here, a few there, it's like popping rivets out of an airplane. A few missing rivets don't make the plane drop from the sky, but remove too many and reach that critical point, the poor old plane plummets like a concrete turkey. Everything on the earth is a rivet of one sort or another, so how many and which ones do we eliminate before we crash? Who wants even a minor crash?

Maybe we should start with what's broken and our lack of connection to the earth that leads to ever more brokenness. Basically, we're disconnected. Otherwise, you wouldn't be reading this book—because there'd be no need for it. So what to do?

Let's get realistic and practical. Everyone from the age of 12 up would have to read Brian Swimme's *The Universe Story*, I mean *everyone*: doctors, scientists, technicians, teachers, computer nerds, old ladies in bingo halls, and maybe especially politicians, because they're the ones who make the unrealistic rules … They'd also have to read Jennifer Ackerman's *Chance in the House of Fate,* and for good measure, all the other books I mentioned earlier. *And* they'd have to discuss and be tested on them to make sure they understood the message. *CONNECTEDNESS, LIVING IN RELATIONSHIP TO THE EARTH and becoming co-managers of the entire eco-system* would form the basis of education. It would be engrained in all children everywhere that they are *completely* dependent on the earth, to the point where they can't take their next breath without it, and must care for it as if their very lives depended on it. Which they do, silly. They would come to automatically feel it's unthinkable to do anything anti-earth. Eventually it would get to the point where, as grownups, they'd do away with phone poles and masts, the roar of traffic, having to live and work in dull, drab buildings with nothing green around them. They'd lower the population, be happy with less, live in harmony. They'd embrace *Natural Capitalism* (earth's storehouse) and thereby 'eliminate the whole concept of waste through better designs that adopt biological patterns, processes and natural materials.' (Amory Lovins). They'd learn that 'We can't liquidate the earth's capital and call it income. Services, products and relationships must address this issue … The first rule of ecology is that *everything is connected.*' (Paul Hawken). START WITH KIDS. Most grown-ups are too stuck in their ways.

We'd set up a framework for 'where to start' and how to do it. How do we learn to become intelligent? All kinds of people would have to get together in conferences, workshops and seminars and figure this out. How do we make ourselves realise that *actions speak louder than words* and that action which shows itself to be in collaboration and harmony with the earth needs to express itself as capable of this deep, deep compassionate intelligence, which is innately made up of the ability to both see and feel from the depths of one's being—right down inside the twists and turns of one's personal section of coral reef. (Coral reef: as in a solid but flexible structure made up of masses of collaborative organisms each doing their thing while simultaneously allowing the others to thrive. A kind of *walk your talk* system geared to infinite sustainability.)

The earth isn't going to get better until more little human babies right from the time they start talking are brainwashed, not into being clever members of the profit-based Liquidation Establishment, but into wanting to *see* and *feel* and be deeply intelligent individuals. And when we have enough of them—little yellow drops being dropped into a sea of blue that make the blue sea finally turn green—the whole planet will rejoice. But only if millions and millions of yellow drops are added to the blue sea—it won't turn green otherwise and will remain stuck in despair.

If we understood the importance of true *intelligence,* we'd put the acquiring of it at the top of the list and start figuring out how to cultivate it in people. It's startling to realise how *few* humans are deeply, consistently intelligent, and lack a deeper insight with which to examine and question everything that comes their way. The nice people in my village can't even manage to pick up the litter around their homes. That's a sure sign something's missing.

So to narrow it all down, even though my magic wand *Eve* has been out consistently doing her job and is quite weary; to ensure that she'd get a pension in her old age, here's what would need to happen so that magic wands were no longer needed.

1. *Speak up*. Care enough to have a point of view, then utter it. Let your mind come out of your mouth—when the need is there. Just damn well speak up!

2. Remove all guns. That means ALL. Every last one. Bury them in the ice and silica of a dead planet 2 million light years away. No more killing instruments.

3. Design a small model country where they do everything right, and draw up some kind of collaborative blueprint for figuring out answers to problems as they crop up. It helps to see that it's possible.

4. Employ the bottom line starting at the earliest levels of 'education': *compassionate seeing and feeling.* Without it, we're lost. With it, we'll be the flower of the universe.

5. Reduce the population. We'd go mad if there were as many badgers or buffalo running around as there are people. It's not fair for one out-of-balance species to consume so much. Restore balance by keeping reproduction to scale.

6. Learn to do what's useful. How to sew, cook, grow a garden, change a tyre, forgive, build a straw bale house, harvest hemp, practise conflict resolution and mediation, keep a realistic balance sheet, identify birds, know what's genuinely important ...

7. Put a clamp on computer games, with a reinstatement of real games: putting on plays, kite flying, swimming in rivers, telling stories, contests, using imagination ...

8. Stop the abuse of others. No more 'using' of animals, no more blinkered cruelty—factory farming, and all the rest. We should be ashamed of such practices. To want to go on hunting is to reveal your lack of 'connectedness'. If you *feel* for the fox and *see* your mutual

relationship with the earth, you couldn't possibly want to treat it like an 'other'. (If you do, I will send *Eve* after you.) *Connectedness* would also mean no war or religious intolerance, no gay bashing or bullying, no ethnic hatred, no polarisations. When you *see* and *feel* your connectedness, you cannot kill and maim.

9. Return to our highest calling: restore the land, protect the seas, clean the air, protect biodiversity, activate the earth's stewards. Do for the survival of everything all that which is required for ourselves. (You wouldn't let your car exhaust blow back in your face, would you? Why should it contaminate anything else?)

10. None of this genetically modified nonsense. (Most of our ideas turn out to be wrong. This is one of them. Unless you are God, you don't mess with nature's blueprint.)

11. No waste whatsoever. Recycle everything! Produce nothing that can't be returned in some way to its natural design, or reused as some natural variant of the original. Natural Capital is limited, and therefore must be kept turning over and over and over … 'We *all* live Downstream; there is no *away*.'

12. Soil, water, air, microbes, bacteria—in collaboration, requiring our collaboration. It's so simple! Without them, we perish. *We can't take our next breath without the natural world!* You think I'm exaggerating? Go try it.

We could easily 'save' the world simply by understanding it. That would mean understanding ourselves, that we are no different, we are it. What we do to the world, we do to ourselves. Basic stuff. Get back to basics. Therein lies the plot. Play, read, learn, think, grow an imagination! SEE. THINK. FEEL.

I want Eve to come home to a good night's rest. But as long as deviant, cruel, selfish, greedy, ignorant, thoughtless, careless, indifferent, petty, heartless, small-minded people are milling around doing their part to undermine the integrity of the natural world, she'll have to go about zapping bodies and making them disappear. It's that or *wake up* and get our act together. It's better for unappreciative humans to disappear than to have the entire earth dissolve into a complete mess of permanently sabotaged designs, opportunities and wonders. This 'Global Warming' caused by humans should be somebody's idea of a global joke, but don't laugh. It's a real phenomenon we've foisted on ourselves, as though we thought it clever to pick apart that which sustains us. Now I have no choice but to Speak Up for all I'm worth, over and over and over to help save this magnificently awesome, *irreplaceable* planet. Now get on and do *your* part.

The Not Knowing

Humans tell their stories as though nothing
tied them to the ground;
their characters relate to other humans
but not the effects of fallen leaves or tides
or barbed wire running beside a stream

Humans tell their stories as though
the only dialogue was between themselves,
as though they lived in a soapy vacuum
inside a brick carapace that hummed electrically
without knowing what powered the switch

As though banners hung above the streets
declaring **Here, only humans are in charge
and all the rest is beneath us**

So you retire to Florida and play shuffleboard
and knit and tune out plankton and ozone
and seismic shifts;
the whole vast irony of life
immersed in a sea of neon light

You know a *little* about how society works;
in other ways you are the natural world's worst
morons, the Milky Way's most miserable misfits
the duds who swear on designer clothes
and cars and planes and things that never breathe

Why, you even choke the breath
out of the packaging of your own kind
as though killing what you love
would fix the thing you aren't

A PACKAGE OF TRANSFORMATIONS

Clare Short

Clare has been Labour MP for Birmingham Ladywood since 1983

What we need to do is end the wars in Iraq and Afghanistan by withdrawing; insist on a peace deal between Israel and Palestine by giving each a state based on the 1967 boundaries set according to international law; put in some peacekeepers to stabilise the two states; and insist all *weapons of mass destruction* are removed from the region—this would deal with the problem of Iran's nuclear programme.

This package would transform the Middle East. The United States would no longer have to prop up a series of oppressive governments, and democracy could spread through the region. Having thus delivered a political route to justice, we could all unite to prevent the spread of terrorism.

With this big, bitter division removed from the world, we should focus on basic development for all people so that extreme poverty is no longer a fact of life. This is now achievable and not very costly.

In such a world, we could all work together to massively reduce carbon dioxide emissions to prevent global warming from wiping out human civilisation and many other living things. We must all then learn to live in a less greedy consumerist world. If we do, there will be more equality within and between countries and we will have more time to enjoy music, art and poetry, to appreciate nature and be kinder to each other.

EVERY DAY IS EARTH DAY

Penelope Shuttle

Penelope is a poet, radio dramatist and a regular performer at poetry festivals

For the past thirty seven years, I've had the good fortune to live in a beautiful part of the world, in the far west of Cornwall. When I first moved here in 1970 I think most of us were oblivious to man-made threats to the environment. We were living, though, in a paradise of fools.

Cornwall, in all its beauty, was idyllic, and seemed as if it would always remain so. Yet that was not entirely true, as the history of Cornwall is also industrial, and post-industrial, and the mining industries had left their dark stain upon that purity.

Long before 1970 the first voice had spoken in warning. In her famous 1962 book, *Silent Spring*, Rachel Carson demonstrated how pollution was destroying the environment. She knew this from her scientific background, and from having been brought up in Pittsburgh, which in the mid-twentieth century was a very polluted city (though now, thanks to Carson's work, a greening city).

She said,

> 'Over increasingly large areas of the United States, spring now comes unheralded by the return of the birds, and the early mornings are strangely silent where once they were filled with the beauty of bird song.'

And as the seventies turned to the eighties, and the eighties to the nineties, and up to the present day, her voice has been joined by many other voices. But who is listening to these voices? Are they/we preaching to the converted? How can environmentalists, poets, artists, all the concerned, get across to the general public who remain oblivious to the duty we all have to preserve and sustain the environment for those future generations who, unless much much more is done, will look back at our generation with bitterness and rage? How can we get our message across to the politicians and industrialists who run the world, not caring if they run it ragged?

To paraphrase Carl Jung, we must remember that as human beings we are the second creators of the world. We are the completers of the world. Now we have to heal the world as part of our completing of it. So we do it by speaking out, we do it by our actions.

My daughter is a professional environmentalist. Sometimes she gets downhearted, and she says, 'Mum, I wish I'd never trained as an environmentalist, because I know just how bad things are, and just how short a time we've got to take action ...' And then she gets on with her job, hoping there is enough time.

Maybe there is enough time. But maybe only just enough time. And only if the world takes pity on itself; only if every individual wakes up enough to remember that we all live *in the great house of the Reverend Mrs Earth and Doctor Waters* and we must care for it.

Every day is Earth Day. Do you want bird song, or can you live without it?

WITH MY HAMMER …

Shannon Smy

Shannon, born in Sheffield, now lives in Somerset and is founder of the music group Seize the Day

Sometimes, when I'm having a rough day, someone smiles at me and that's enough … I've spent weeks of my life walking up and down lines of security guards and police, talking to men whose job it is to stop me from protecting trees. Mostly they agree that we need to stop building more roads; mostly they know that we just fill every road we build; mostly they are worried about the consequences of climate change … Mostly they think it's too late.

We'd talk …

'Have you got kids?' I'd say.

'Yes,' they'd reply (mostly).

'What kind of a future are you offering them if you've given up on the world?' I'd say. They'd look at me for a while, and then shrug.

Sometimes I'd push it and say, 'You might as well go home and kill your kids right now then … if there's no hope!' It wasn't my most positive line so I didn't say it much, but I thought it a lot …

There were over 800 security men at Newbury guarding the diggers and the chainsaw crews, and I had successes with some of those men. We wrote a song together once—that's what I do, write songs. It was a cold March morning and I kept thinking, 'What are we doing here?'

'What *are* we doing here?' I sang it over and over as I did my rounds. After a while one of the policemen yelled, 'Can't you think of any more?'

'You think of something more!' I yelled back … and so it started.

The team leader opposite me, 'Dave the red-hat', wrote the first lines to wild applause from his mates …

> *Chainsaws gleaming as the trees are screaming for mercy,*
> *Trees are falling as protestors are calling for mercy.*
> *What are we doing here? What are we doing here?*

We wrote five verses between us in the end—I just kept going up and down the lines singing the bits the last guys had written and filling in the gaps …

279

The next day, I took a film crew round with me—but the men who'd written the song had already been split up and moved, as a consequence of getting too friendly with me. We filmed the song anyway, and it was shown on BBC2.

I know those men will remember me; after two months I got to be friends with some of them. They saw how much I cared and I saw that some of them did too. We gave each other back some hope.

In the last weeks when it was nearly all over, one of them carved me a stick from a felled tree. He explained that the symbols on it 'were runes of protection and courage'. It was an incredible gift and I still have the poems two of them gave me in that last week.

That was the year we formed Seize the Day, and I've been performing in this radical, political folk-band for 10 years now. We've toured India and America, played Seattle during the WTO protests, won a Radio 3 World Music Audience Award, and performed on the Main Stage at Glastonbury Festival ... I've been interviewed by Radio 4 and been the 'pick of the world' for my *Everywoman* interview on the World Service. I've appeared naked in virtually all our broadsheets and tabloids—and yet, you have probably never heard of me.

Is that good or bad? Both probably. I've never publicized the band with my activism but I've used the band endlessly to promote direct action and all the campaigns we've been involved with. Sometimes it's really important for people to know who you are, who's making the protest and why, to be able to identify with a person or group and sometimes, it's better that the protest speaks, not the people doing it. Even when the actions themselves are heroic, it's the image which people remember.

I can tell you for certain that taking my clothes off in public is *NOT* my idea of fun. I, like most women in this country, have been led to believe that my body is ever so slightly less than perfect, and should under no circumstances be shown in public.

Unfortunately, it was too good an idea, and so five of us, three women and two men, spent three hours stark naked, five storeys up, on the roof of an advertising agency in the middle of Soho ...

As you can imagine, we got plenty of media coverage for our 'Naked Truth' protest, with its banner saying 'End the Genetix cover-up'. It was one of the actions which helped open up the debate in our country, leading in the end to the defeat of GM foods at the check-out. It only took the well-planned actions of eighty or so people, but to do it, those people had to overcome their fears of failure, exposure and arrest.

I know from the messages I get from many new activists that songs which celebrate that courage are often what inspire people to take action themselves.

There are many mysteries and coincidences in life and some change our lives forever.

On 30 January 1996, I woke up to the radio coming on. I have to confess to not being one of life's early-morning Radio 4 listeners, so I'm surprised I didn't turn it off. The main story that day was about three women who had broken into a British Aerospace base and, having disarmed a Hawk jet with household hammers, had called security and handed themselves in.

Six months later the exact same thing happened again. I can honestly say I had not listened to Radio 4 in between. The main story that morning was the astonishing acquittal, by jury, of the now four women who had tried to prevent 'a greater crime' being committed by our government. It was simply the most inspiring modern-day story of courage and commitment that I had ever heard and not only was it true but it had made me cry.

I wrote the song 'With My Hammer...' in 1997. I gathered every piece of information about the case that I could find—newspaper articles, witness evidence, and letters they wrote to each other in prison. I wrote the song using their words and feelings wherever I could. It took a week, sitting on the side of a mountain overlooking the Himalayas in India.

I've sung that song a lot now and it's had a direct effect on my life. I stand on stage singing it with as much passion as I can and when I get to the chorus, anything I'm scared of or avoiding just pops right into my mind:

With my hammer I break the chain, I will not remain in silence ...
I will stand and I will defend my right to fight against violence ...
No prison can contain the freedom that we gain when we move
*   through fear.*

I went to prison and to Palestine because of that chorus, and I was scared of both. My prison visit was short and not particularly sweet, but I'm no longer scared of 'gangs of lesbians' shaving my head and injecting me with heroin! I met some great women in prison, mostly women who'd had hard lives, women who were trying to even up the balance a little ... and got caught.

Palestine was harder somehow. A friend told me she was going to join the International Solidarity Movement (ISM) out there for a fortnight, to try and stop the levelling of Palestinian homes in refugee camps, to take part in marches in Bethlehem and Jerusalem, to visit Gaza and Hebron … and to stand in front of tanks. I couldn't believe she was going—she had three children! She might be shot in crossfire! Or blown up by a suicide bomber! I could not imagine anything more frightening. And then she rang me and said she couldn't go.

All I could think was that someone had to go—but that sure as hell didn't include me! It took me four days. I knew my partner would love to go—fear just wouldn't figure for him. But me, I was running hard. It was one of those real teeth-gritting, hold-your-nose-and-swallow-your-medicine-decisions. I was scared—so I went. (Don't you just love your own head sometimes!)

I'd love to be able to say that all my fear completely dissolved when I set foot in Palestine, but not a bit of it. When it was really hard I cried, and that made a difference …

The night after we arrived I found myself at the front of a march from Jerusalem to Bethlehem. The idea was that the 'Internationals' protect the Palestinians by surrounding them on all sides. What that meant for me was that when it came to the road block—the rows of soldiers and tanks, the rows of soldiers with really big guns, I was being pushed right up against them. As you can imagine that was *not* the day I overcame my fear.

We were threatened and tear-gassed and I faced young men with big guns pretty much every day. I remember looking into the eyes of one soldier as he fired his gun into the air. I think that is what changed it around for me; he was more scared than I was in that moment.

In my time there I met some incredible Israelis and Palestinians and one day at a refugee camp met a child who'd been shot by accident. He hadn't spoken for seven years. I held a young woman's hand as she cried—it's her headscarf I keep my video camera wrapped in.

I'm grateful for the changes that trying to change the world has made, and continues to make, in my life. I know that my biggest challenges are fear and hopelessness and that I am at my most powerful when I act despite both of those feelings, and preferably not alone 'struggling through', but with love and support. It's not always obvious what the best thing to do in any particular situation may be, but my experience has shown me that it's usually better to do something than nothing.

And so I come to my last story. I was once running a market stall when I saw a man shouting at his two-year-old little girl—she was crying and he hit her. I went over to him. 'Excuse me,' I said, 'do you know the time?'

'Yes,' he said, 'it's 2.30.'

'Thanks,' I said, 'my watch stopped over an hour ago'—we smiled at each other. 'I couldn't help noticing how beautiful your little girl is.' His smile broke into a beaming grin.

They came past my stall later and I gave the little girl a candle. She knew I cared and her dad and I chatted for a while. All parents love their children.

She smiled at me as they walked away. I know I changed the world that day.

WATCHING THE WORLD GO BY

Mary Taylor

Mary is an English social worker living in Suva, Fiji

The response is always the same when I say I live in Fiji: *how wonderful that must be and how lucky I am*. I try not to be too dismissive, but many of the problems that we see in the world today can be viewed as if looking through a microscope in Fiji. Everything is on a smaller scale and so it is easier to make the observations, to see the changes and to watch life in action.

Fiji is developing. Some would say that is a good thing, but to watch a country slowly take on the trappings of the developed world and 'make progress' is often not a pretty sight. Money starts to take control in a society where not that long ago it didn't really matter so much and with the interest in money, there seems to be an associated lack of responsibility about what happens around us. Suva is the capital city in Fiji and it is growing very fast; where once there were palm trees, there are now concrete buildings absorbing the country's oxygen.

More and more cars appear on the road with each passing month. They aren't small cars either, they are very big 4-wheel drives using large volumes of fuel; not just in moving along the road but through the air-conditioning that keeps their passengers cool, even when they are parked and waiting outside shops. Our fuel has a high sulphur content, so of course this doesn't help the level of air pollution. Buses and taxis are the main offenders, belching out black fumes as they go by. This is not the image the tourist has of a tropical island. There are attempts to control the problem but you still see the black smoke—I have started to think the buses are immune. Sadly, most of these buses do not have windows, and so the passengers get their daily dose of sulphur, and perhaps now they are addicted.

Then there is the litter. This is a major problem and every day you will see people throw rubbish from vehicles. Lately there seems to be the strange phenomenon of rubbish piles on the side of the roads. Garden waste is put outside for the council to collect in Suva. Sadly, it is not recycled. Until quite recently these piles of garden waste used to remain purely heaps of grass cuttings and other green waste from the garden.

Now there seems to be some sort of epidemic in which paper and plastic appear from nowhere on these piles, growing out from between the green, ugly and white. Again people do not seem to care, or perhaps they do not notice.

The supermarkets have vegetables on their shelves imported from overseas. It is likely they were poor quality in the first place, cheaper of course, but when they start to rot, they remain on the shelves looking dejected and sad and exuding negative energy.

So we have air pollution, poor quality food and litter, but people don't seem bothered, or perhaps they do not notice. There are other problems too, but these are of a more political nature and for now I just want to talk about the things we as individuals can change or attempt to alter.

Why do we all seem to care so little these days, always rushing here and there, never having a minute to spare for anyone? It isn't just a lack of concern for the planet, it is also a lack of concern for each other, and of course the two are very connected. We talk less but we communicate often and at length by email—though sometimes that communication is limited to forwarding a joke, a story or a series of pictures which are trying to tell you about yourself or the world, or something. At work we send emails to colleagues in the next office instead of knocking on the door, sharing a cup of coffee or even just exchanging a few words on the phone. Is it because with email we are in control, we can choose when to stop the interaction?

Then there is 'My Space'. I only recently discovered this when I was in the UK on leave. I was amazed and, I have to admit, somewhat cynical. Here we are in a world where we really do talk less and exist more and more in our own 'space', yet we tell strangers details about ourselves that often only close relatives know. Is there some connection here with reality TV?

I have also noticed that throughout the world my friends often comment '*I am so busy*'. My mother didn't say that and neither did my father; they seemed to have a lot of time on their hands, or maybe that was because I was a child and I had a lot of time on *my* hands. So is it a lack of time that is affecting the human race and encouraging or nurturing selfishness, or is it that we just have evolved to be 'more selfish'? Some would support the latter, perhaps saying there are too many human beings in the world and so we have become less trusting because we have to hang on harder to what we have. But I find this hard to accept. I think we do have a population problem but I am not convinced that this is the reason we all care less for ourselves, for each other and for the planet.

I do find myself saying many times that if there were more women ruling the world then it would be a better place, but there are, of course, examples of women who have been in power and who have been very uncaring and very aggressive. However, I think as females we care more for those around us, especially in the traditional family setting. When I look around me at work, it is the women who are always there to listen if a colleague needs an ear.

However, I also believe that time is an issue. If we are always rushing around, then we do not have the time to see, to think, and to step back and reflect on what is happening. I try as much as possible to 'live in the present'. This is quite a recent change in my life and it happened because I realised what was happening, how much 'rush' there was and how little I was actually enjoying everything around me, or not even enjoying it; it was more a case of just observing and noticing. I also noticed that when I rushed less, I enjoyed 'the little things' and actually achieved more in my day and reached the end of it in a happier state. If we slow down and take the time to look around and observe, then we would 'see'. When we rush, we don't 'see', and it is because of this that we do not notice what is really happening.

I don't think addressing the world's problems is just a case of *individual* responsibility. Of course governments have responsibility and increasingly there is corporate responsibility. In Fiji, some of the big companies could be made to accept that their presence makes a significant contribution to a problem. Most of the litter we see is from junk-food outlets, and of course the inevitable plastic bottle that once contained some fizzy drink not only does little to alleviate one's thirst, but also plays a significant role in damaging one's health. (Lifestyle diseases are also on the increase at an alarming rate in Fiji.)

So I would argue that if we could just slow down a fraction, we would enjoy our lives more and we would then have time to take on board some of the problems around us, either on a small scale or globally. Why the constant rush and why are we all so busy? I do know that in my job, the Internet and email really have not done me too many favours. In my profession, colleagues from afar ask for your opinion on a paper or a proposal, and it means that information addicts can impose their addiction on you and send you a document you must read, which you do, but if you don't, the guilt flows freely. Even if you have surpassed that guilt problem by now and are more able to hit the delete button, your time still goes. So I do put some of the blame on this computer age of ours for stealing some of that precious commodity.

287

Then there is satellite TV and DVDs and games and so much other stuff, and at work we are expected to come in early and go home late, and oh yes, don't forget to work through your lunch hour as well. Thus not only are we in too much of a rush to care, to notice, we are also too tired. We seem to be living in an age where being busy is the norm, and if you are not busy, then there is something wrong.

A very good friend in the UK recommended a book a week or so ago and as I was there at the time, I bought it. This morning I decided I would look at the first few pages and this was after I had written the first two pages for this piece. The book is *Pure Bliss* by Gill Edwards, and in the opening pages she defines 'Hard Time' and 'Soft Time'. 'Soft Time' is exactly what I am talking about here; a time of 'being', where you can feel more present and alive, and where you can live a meaningful and purposeful life, a life that really makes a difference. Gill Edwards believes that most of our stress is created by us and so can be controlled by us. A while back I would have disagreed with her completely, but not now. It is really up to us to control the 'rush' and try and be as much as we can in 'Soft Time'. It is in that Soft Time that we will be able to have an impact on ourselves, on those close to us and also on those beyond our immediate circle. We will enjoy life more, but we will also have the time to 'see' and it is only when we 'see' that we are likely to take action.

WOMEN RALLYING FOR CHILDREN AND EARTH

Nancy Todd

Nancy, an author who lives in Massachusetts, is co-founder of the New Alchemy Institute

The women of the world, the daughters of the earth of the early twenty-first century, are faced with two dominant agendas—not to mention a plethora of only slightly less urgent issues—and none bodes well for either the near or the long-term future. A number of women today feel so strongly about their nations becoming involved in military confrontations that they are appealing to women around the world to rise up and 'be outrageous for peace'. Theirs is a call to reorient governments to focus on nurturing, compassion and non-violent resolution of conflicts. 'Because of our responsibility to the next generation, because of our love for our families and communities and the countries we are part of, we understand the love of all mothers for their children, and the driving desire of that child for life.' They are exploring and educating on issues ranging from civilian casualties, to military budgets in relation to unmet human needs, the need for stronger international institutions, and the environmental consequences of war.

By examining the environmental consequences of war, these women are drawing attention to what is likely to prove the ultimate issue of our time. The potential for suffering, as earth's essential life-support systems weaken and fail, staggers the imagination. As ecologist Gregory Bateson foresaw many years ago: 'If you see the environment as yours to exploit, and your survival unit as your people and your country against other people and other countries, and if you have an advanced technology, your likelihood of survival is that of a snowball in hell.' What renders both the scenario of war in the Middle East, or anywhere, and that of ecological collapse as uncalled-for as they are intolerable is that we now have the conceptual framework, the technologies, and the practices which could form the foundation and infrastructure for a sustainable and more secure world.

The only lasting effective defence is prevention. It becomes necessary therefore to look at the root causes of terrorism and to begin eliminating

289

the social conditions that feed and motivate the pathology of hatred. As one terrorism expert at the RAND Corporation admits, 'Stability is an anathema to a revolutionary movement like Hezbollah.' In light of this, world-class energy expert Amory Lovins urges that we take decisive measures to establish sustainable societies by striving for energy independence, developing a non-provocative form of defence, helping make other nations more secure and redirecting economic investment to address social needs.

A future citizen of the world we are trying to create lives about five minutes' walk from my house, down the road, past a seasonal pond and along a woodland trail. He is a small boy by the name of Quinn. 'Quinn Todd of Sippewissett' he will explain to people asking his name. Quinn Todd is quite tall for his age, and sturdy. He has tufty dark blond hair, sapphire blue eyes and an expressive face. He often gestures with his hands when he is explaining something he feels strongly about. His fantasy life is rich. In the course of a day, or even an hour, he can be Peter Pan, Captain Hook, Tarzan, Superman, Batman or Buzz Lightyear. He has or can create appropriate masks and costumes for all his heroes and envies those who can fly. When he was younger he put out most of the backs of the larger members of his family as we attempted to swoosh him about in personal-flight simulation.

Whatever the connection to his affiliation with superheroes, Quinn's defining characteristic is an innate courtesy unusual in a small boy, analogous to what the French call *politesse du coeur*. He is, for example, exceedingly forbearing with his television-illiterate grandparents and patiently brings us up to date on the happenings of his favourite programmes and videos. Faced with something he doesn't care for at the dinner table, he does not respond by fussing or emitting loud 'yuks!' Instead, gazing steadily at you, he says, 'No sanks.' (To be quite fair to him, his pronunciation is now no thanks but his younger 'No sanks' has become part of the family lore.) His pattern held even at the doctor's office when he realised he was about to have a shot. 'No sanks!' he announced, alarm evident in his voice, and again louder with a mounting note of desperation, 'NO SANKS!' before he burst into tears and submitted to the inevitable.

He can, of course, like any child, be a royal pain at times. Quinn Todd of Sippewissett is neither saint nor angel. He has to be reminded from time to time about pleases and thank yous. Yet he has a kind of empathy that is rare. In a group of adults he always makes sure the other people around him get to greet each other by name. One day when I stopped for a few minutes, he asked me anxiously if I had said 'Hi' to Dave yet. Dave

290

was then in another room but it was important to Quinn that I go in and acknowledge him. Another time when his grandfather had dropped him off at day care, he marched him up to his teacher, tugged at her shirt and announced, 'This is my friend John.' One autumn he built a little house of twigs in our front yard and filled it with acorns for 'my friends, the squirrels.' He has spider friends as well.

Yet even from his relatively secure vantage point, Quinn senses that all is not well with the world. After the terrorist attacks of September 2001, picking up on his mother's shocked grief, he patted her hand and said reassuringly, 'I know what. No news. OK? Then we'll be happy again.' No—or less—news and we would all be happier. If fate is kind to him, Quinn may not be directly affected by war in Iraq. But I cannot get away from the thought that somewhere in Baghdad—or Teheran or Tel Aviv or Beirut—there is a small dark-haired boy as quirky and full of love and promise as Quinn. Is there a bomb smart enough to spare him? Can we ever dismiss the life of a child as unavoidable collateral damage in service of a greater cause? Or is the possibility equally frightening that, in a society dominated by privation and fear, such courtesy of the heart withers before it finds a chance to take root and grow?

On September 12, 2001, in the aftermath of the cataclysm of the previous day, the Masters of Holistic Science students at Schumacher College in England met their programme co-ordinator Brian Goodwin and their tutor Jordi Pigem. Stunned, they attempted to grapple with what had happened the day before, grasping at straws for some kind of intellectual and spiritual comprehension. The students were from a number of countries, including the United States. Gradually their discussion led them to believe that actions such as the terrorists' attack, or indeed most of what we do, ultimately can be traced to the way we understand the world. If a culture or an individual is motivated by a worldview that has at its core a deep-seated sense of anger, fear and distrust, this will engender a drive for control over perceived enemies or other obstacles, human or otherwise. In western culture's science and, through science, most of society has come to view the natural world with an abstract objectivity. Through this type of detachment, the living world recedes to an entity removed and apart from ourselves. Water, for example, is not seen as a necessary and sacred element but a resource or, worse still, a commodity. This results in a near-complete alienation from nature and only the most token acknowledgement of human dependence on the biosphere as the source of life. Such fear-motivated need for control cultivates the hatred necessary to strike out at other people and

291

cultures. It is as true of terrorists as it is of those who would inflict excruciating suffering upon many to eliminate a few like Saddam Hussein and his lackeys.

Ultimately, as Buddhism teaches, true security lies not in defeating one's enemies but in not having enemies. What would happen if we attacked Iraq or the tinderbox that is the Middle East with unpredicted kindness, as the women calling for a pre-emptive strike for peace are urging? What would we have to lose if we redirected some of the trillions we spend on weapons to helping desperate people obtain clean water, sanitation, adequate food, health care, education and meaningful work? Would they still hate us?

It was Carl Gustav Jung's conviction that our understanding of spirituality was not a journey toward perfection but one toward wholeness. In their struggling with the implications of the attacks on New York and the Pentagon, the participants in the discussions at Schumacher College also explored a worldview that is the polar opposite of the one arising from anger and fear. In the long run, our only hope lies in embracing a worldview that emerges from love and trust. A person or culture so inspired, like Quinn and his friends the squirrels and the spiders, embraces diversity. Rather than distancing itself from other cultures or from the living world, this way of understanding the world draws us toward engagement and participation. And from such immersion grows a sense of connection and belonging; of belonging to place and to community, to the human family and to living earth. It is a process and a practice of healing and of homecoming and something women understand and can yet bring into the world.

WAKE UP, YOU ADULTS

Anna Maria Vallario

Anna Maria is a teacher from Wales, and currently lives in Bristol

Where do I start? I would like to ask the question: WHO ARE THE CHILDREN WE TEACH?

For me, as a mother and a retired primary deputy headteacher, they are the jewels of our world, they have so many facets that shine out in the purest form of innocence and trust.

In my role as a teacher and facilitator, they taught me so much. The greatest gift I had from them was to see them shine out in their magnificence, even the children who came to me with deeply dysfunctional behaviour. How did that happen?

As a teacher I had choices; not so easy these days in the current educational climate of information and an over-burdened, knowledge-based curriculum. Yes, I had to teach the children academically based requirements, but I also chose to facilitate their learning by providing opportunities to let their spirits sing—to open them to learning which was alive and meaningful to them. I taught through a child-centred approach, reaching the *whole* child, at a level they individually understood, and they were motivated, so they wanted to learn. This is when they shone and I knew I was a part of a miracle of life. I felt like I fed them through my heart and they lapped it up. There was no failure: each child learned and succeeded at their own beautiful pace and level of understanding.

We shared a world of awe and adventure as we explored life together, and it was wonderful to see the children's faces light up as we delved into the world of story—the sharing of feelings, passion and enjoyment. Every area of the curriculum could be used as a route to positive development of the individual child—for example, artwork. This was valued by every child, without exception. In fact, everything the children offered in their efforts was of value and this made them shine all the more. These words feel flat on a page of writing; no words can express what can be seen in the eyes of a child when they feel worthy.

My style of teaching was firm and on occasions very strict, but the children knew I knew them, I knew how they learned and above all I believed in them. In this current climate, attainment targets and constant testing do nothing for the whole child, except to label and judge, and in many cases very cruelly and harshly, with so many children written off!!

Children need encouragement and plenty of praise and opportunities to succeed in their own way, to be encouraged to find out how they feel, who they are and to be able to express who they are. What power we wield as teachers and adults. What a massive responsibility we all have.

What do we give our children in education these days? Good teachers yes, maybe, but what a dysfunctional education system we torture our children with. Who is asking the question, 'ARE OUR CHILDREN BEING EDUCATED IN THE FULLNESS OF WHO THEY ARE?' That would be a very wise society. No, the questions asked are, 'Who's reached which attainment target and how many?' Numbers, numbers, hoops and more hoops! Can't people see that we are failing our children? Is anyone listening to what the children are saying? Are we so arrogant as adults that their views and feelings don't count? All we have to do is ask pertinent questions and observe them in the school environment. In a recent visit to a primary school, I was appalled by the number of children who had become totally de-motivated by what and how they were expected to learn. What was also clearly evident and, for me, very alarming, was the lack of confidence in the children; they saw themselves as failures and I felt the death of their enormous spirits.

In my experience, only a small number of children are seen to succeed and feel successful in this numbing, number-crunching philosophy. When are we going to wake up to the fact that knowledge on its own is sterile, that it sinks into the mind and often disappears? This is how I feel education is today. What are we saying to these beautiful souls who entrust us with their personalities and emotions? I left the profession six years ago due to ill health and the stresses and frustration of not being able to give the children the learning environment I previously saw working successfully. I miss the children and the opportunities to get the best out of each one of them.

Now is my chance to change things, if not through government legislation (how did education get so interfered with, by people who seem to know nothing about educational psychology? It makes me feel so angry), then through this book. If I could change the world I would make it possible for all children to succeed in something, anything that the individual could feel proud and worthy about. I would love to nurture children in all their facets and for us adults to believe in them. My changes would incorporate teaching from experience and the heart, allowing each child to come to learning from their own place of understanding and being.

I believe that we are all much more than our intellectual minds, that we respond to life through our feelings, so I would make this fundamental core of how we exist on this planet central to education. I would like to make it possible for children to learn to know themselves with acceptance and love and in doing so encourage our future generations to take a more responsible and caring role in their lives and their environment.

We have all been ruled by our heads for far too long; now is the time for our beautiful hearts to conquer this world.

BUILDING BRICKS FOR A BETTER WORLD

Elsie Walton

Elsie, now deceased, was head of a primary school, and a Methodist preacher in Somerset

If I could save the world, I would do it by persistently urging my contemporaries of whatever creed, colour, calling or culture to read day by day by day God's definitive word to His Creation in holy scripture.

God is the same God whether we call ourselves Muslims, Jews, Sikhs or Christians; even agnostics and atheists. He is the 'otherness', the numenism, the Spirit behind the everyday reality of our earthly lives. It has always, always been so. Through prehistory human beings have always been aware of this—of this something beyond themselves. They raised the menhirs and standing stones and phallic symbols to reach out to the 'Invisible', the definitive, positive Creator. They buried their dead in the foetal position of an unborn child as though they instinctively felt the continuity of the Life Force in Resurrection. Men like Abraham communicated with this invisible power as friend speaks to friend, even though not one of their five senses identified Him. God was revealing Himself progressively through His chosen people in every age.

This is the instinct that distinguishes us from the rest of Creation. It is the ingredient inherited by every human being, whether it is acknowledged or not. We are all the same in the eyes of God—all of us—the wise who worship Him through their own faith as well as the ignorant who ignore Him.

God has only two rules for living the good life: to love Him and to love everybody else. These are the two rules that answer every question, every doubt and apply constructively to every human situation. Moses, inspired by God, wrote down the tenets of the original Covenant in the books of Exodus, Leviticus and Deuteronomy, and Jesus, God incarnate in our humanity, explained and interpreted them through teaching, parable and example. He said things like: 'If someone strikes you on one cheek, turn to him the other' and 'If you are asked to go one mile, go an extra mile just for love.' He said, 'The Sabbath was made for the benefit of man, not man for the Sabbath.' He said, 'Sell what you have and give to the poor.' He said, 'If you want to be first you must know what it means to be last and least,' and, 'The master must be ready to be the suffering servant.'

When they brought the woman taken in adultery for him to agree publicly to her being stoned to death, he said, 'He who is without sin cast the first stone,' which puts us all in our place.

What a saved world we would live in if these were the rules we kept. If I wanted to save the world, I would have to insist that everyone knows and lives by the rules God has given us through the men and women like ourselves, held in the grip of God.

But the very word I use—*insist*—is breaking God's law and rejecting God's own attitude towards His human creation. The word 'insist' implies egoism, judgmentalism, 'I know best-ism'. It says, in effect, 'Give up your freewill, your democracy, your man-made denominations, your contrived rituals and do as I say.'

But God never insists. We make up our own minds. We form our own opinions. We come to our own informed conclusions. I must know in my innermost being that God is not just loving, He is Love itself and the only way to save our world is to acknowledge this Truth and live like God among our own contemporaries, as Jesus did.

This requires the empowering of the Holy Spirit that God gives us when we ask and seek and find, because we believe.

A LONG-TERM PROJECT

Fiona Walters

Fiona lives in Devon, where she has restored a Victorian apple orchard. She is a lawyer.

Until recently, I didn't feel I was able to contribute to making the world a better place. But, of course, it is a mass effort in which we all must play a part. I care about the English countryside. Conceivably, this is a selfish indulgence on my part from which I gain huge fulfilment. Possibly it underpins a greater personal ethic to be in harmony with the seasons and make a small contribution towards the preservation of a delicate environment on our vulnerable planet. Whatever your verdict, hopefully my actions will speak louder than these words.

In 2004, Ben Bradshaw, MP (the then Parliamentary Under Secretary for the Department for the Environment, Food & Rural Affairs) presented me with a DEFRA conservation award for the most outstanding restoration of agricultural buildings on Dartmoor over ten years. It was very surprising to be given an award for something that seemed to me to be an obvious and necessary task to undertake. Two years prior to this event, with the help of my partner Anthony, I had purchased a sad old house, barns and neglected lands known as 'Druid'. This small estate became the subject of extensive renovation. Particularly in relation to the range of eighteenth- and nineteenth-century barns, we sought to repair the existing buildings in sympathy with the purpose for which they were originally intended. Previous occupiers of the property had over hundreds of years carefully considered Druid's intrinsic natural advantages and had built accordingly, without ostentation. This building work was a short-term project.

The Druids (rather like the aboriginal people in the southern hemisphere) understood the land and their place within a natural order. To that end, 'Druid' is sited well on the southern fringes of Dartmoor. It is located high enough, at 600 feet, to avoid the low-lying seasonal frosts of the neighbouring stannary town, but nestled into a hillside to avoid the harsh winds of Dartmoor. I have been able to grow more tender plant species than would normally be expected to survive here. Previous Victorian planting of a palm tree in the garden indicated that I could be more adventurous in this regard. However, I am reluctant to describe the site as a 'microclimate'; nor can I report that there has been a gradual climatic change, because I haven't lived here long enough. The farmer tells me that summers are hotter and drier. He has been a resident in the area for over thirty years, and I listen carefully to what he says as he understands and cares for the locality more than most.

At the beginning of the twentieth century, there was a relatively clean and stable global environment. The global economy now produces as much in seventeen days as the economy of our grandparents, around the turn of the century, produced in a year.[1] The cost of our present economic prosperity is a deadly legacy for future generations.

With this in mind, self-sufficiency in relation to water, heating/cooking and food supply is the longer term objective at Druid, without using our resources intensively. This aspiration is no more than our ancestors enjoyed here.

In relation to a water supply, the property benefits from a number of natural spring-water sources. One of these springs constantly feeds a 6,000-litre water tank which we buried in a hillside. Its overflow is piped into a natural stream which in turn flows into a small lake. Unfortunately, this flow is not strong enough to generate electricity. However, the water collected in the tank is used to irrigate the gardens when necessary. Sewerage is processed through a 'klargester' in which micro organisms act as a filter. I am told the resultant water from this process is drinkable.

With help, a kitchen garden was created in the first months of living at the property. This comprises beds of rotational vegetable crops, asparagus, and a fruit cage. Although the land does not benefit from any organic certification, everything grown (generally from seed) is planted with no assistance from fertilisers or pesticides. The first crops were tasty, but unreliable and malformed. After much perseverance with composting, tilling and weeding, the produce now is very satisfying. Delicious vegetables sustain us, our extended family and friends.

Another significant achievement here has been the restoration of an ancient apple orchard. The planting scheme was based on an early Victorian plan which had been found and passed on to Devon Orchard Link for historical referencing. After hours of tree detective work, grafts were taken from the old Druid apple trees, some of which were unrecognisable. The orchard had been systematically used as a tip over the years, and it took many weeks to clear the land to make it possible for sheep and other stock to feed safely on it. Allowing sheep in the orchard was the most effective way of fertilization. Hedges had to be re-laid and specific areas were left untouched and remained overgrown to encourage wildlife. Again, with expert assistance, a number of very old fruit trees were revived. Gentle pruning has encouraged the trees back into production. In addition, over 100 new fruit trees have been planted. The trees are never sprayed with chemicals, nor are they fed artificially. We are now in the third year of apple juice production. It is without doubt the best apple juice I haved ever tasted.

Any meat (fowl, fish, or four-legged) we consume is locally sourced and not intensively reared. As far as heating and electricity are concerned, we are currently researching the best way to use our available resources with the latest proposals for alternative fuels.

It has been immensely satisfying to observe the restoration projects and know that future generations will benefit from them. Significant financial investment has been made, but it is worth every penny to provide for the posterity of Druid. The local community has also been uplifted by joyous performances of Shakespeare in the grounds; a Nativity play which progressed from outdoors under a spectacular starry galaxy to inside the barns, truly experiencing the humble, but magnificent spirituality of Christmas; and young musicians playing music in the house at different times of the year. Most important to me, the hard work and way of life at Druid has been witnessed by our young daughter, who despite being raised in the country, does not take for granted the value of living harmoniously within the environment. Her generation are acutely aware of the necessity of finding an alternative way of living. We must all be wise and brave enough to halt the age of self-interest before it is too late.

Note

1. I.S. Postel & C. Flavin, Reshaping the Global Economy, in L.R. Brown, ed., *State of the World 1991: A Worldwatch Institute Report on Progress Toward a Sustainable Society*, Allen & Unwin (1991).

FAITH IS AT THE CORE

Jill Weston

Jill, who lives in Hertfordshire, is a Quaker peace activist and special-needs teacher

Passion lights the fire, it gives energy, vision, a sense of mission. All essential. But the passion has to be grounded in reality to give staying-power when times get hard, and they do, often.

The lessons I've learned on my journey so far are these:

Faith is at the core of it. I didn't know what faith was until I met Quakers. I was trying to learn how to love at the time. I'd made pretty much of a mess of it up till then. I was lucky enough to have some intelligent and long-suffering friends, a lot wiser than me, who were helping me along the way, keeping me just about together, a sticking-plaster job. It had to be done, as I had two children and they were suffering a lot as a result of my incompetence at being a decent human being, let alone a loving mum. I don't suppose it was really my fault; I was spoilt by a confused and unhappy mother who finally finished her own life, neglected by a father who had wanted a boy second time around and instead got a clingy little mouse whom he thought of as immature and unpredictable, which was true but didn't help me much.

It was the early Eighties; Greenham Common time, and I went on an anti-Trident march from Faslane to Glasgow. They had gouged out half a mountain to house the nuclear submarine in the loch at Faslane. On the walk I met some Quakers who so inspired me that the day after I got home, I went to the local Meeting House. The warden came and found me in the library, offered coffee and cake and listened while I blurted out my guilt at being unfaithful, and how I wanted to start again with my wrecked marriage. She told me the story of Jesus and the adulterous woman and how he protected her from her accusers: 'Let him who is without sin cast the first stone.' This simple, tender story of forgiveness, and the kindness of the warden, changed my life. Stumbling often on the way, capable of the same hardness of heart and self-righteousness as those religious men, I've been given the gift of faithfulness like a candle to keep alight. From the faith comes love and hope.

But there can be dark nights. Last night was one such. I lost my faith and cried into the darkness, full of self-pity and fear. Then, on this Easter Sunday morning, I got up, went running, had a bath, had breakfast and cycled to the Quaker meeting as I do almost every Sunday of the year. In the meeting, where in the deep quiet I continued the battle to keep the vision and faith, there was a mystery about Nelson Mandela's struggle and his courage in breaking the law. But I've discovered this is not the way for me. Rather than the heroics of self-sacrifice, I've had to learn the more mundane lessons of responsibility, starting with the husband and two children whom I didn't know how to love. Being a Quaker is still teaching me how to be responsible, moving outwards from the faith that's inside, doing the duties, the caring, going to meetings, cooking meals, growing vegetables, keeping healthy in mind and body.

Other ministry this morning was about how important it is for all cultures and races, from aboriginal to European, to be free to follow their own beliefs, however different from ours, this being particularly relevant in the context of Iraq. But it was the mention of the carpenter, in words that reflected a deep appreciation of the simple, profound guidance he gave, that brought me back to my basic lesson: keeping faith. I realised afresh this is all I need to know, this and forgiveness.

When the meeting ended, I shook hands with the man next to me whose political outlook is very different from mine, but who is kind and cherishes the United Nations as I am learning to do. I realise that recently I am learning to value even more the faith that takes me into all nooks and crannies of relationships with people and that demands that I be not judgmental, not even towards George Bush, Tony Blair and Geoff Hoon. This is the way to reconciliation and peace.

This doesn't stop me telling the world about the injustices and corruptions of capitalism and of this war. I try, having learned a lot from my partner, to live an alternative lifestyle, travelling by bike and public transport, and we're vegans. I gave up alcohol a year ago; it just doesn't agree with me, makes me violent and mad. I've learned to thoroughly enjoy sex; yes, there's lots of passion here, and fun. It's a roller-coaster ride which exhilarates and relaxes and it's a laugh. I'm often so earnest and intent on doing good, I too often forget about fun. That's where my partner comes in and I can legitimately call him that since my wedding ring dropped off two weeks ago, never to be replaced. The pets, two dogs, a cat and guinea pigs, are fun too. They keep me company and are very funny and sweet.

I lobby my MP, I'm always writing letters. I'm a Labour councillor. I left the party briefly when Tony and George did their first bombing spree together in the no-fly zones of Iraq, but I've learned that Tony Benn's advice suits me best: Fight from within.

Whatever you believe in, do it with complete commitment. I've learned that from my partner. If you want to eat healthily, eat organic. If you know carbon dioxide causes the greenhouse effect, don't drive. If you believe socialism, co-operation and sharing to be the best way, don't accept inheritance money, and up with the workers not the managers. All these lessons have been hard for me, brought up by *Daily Mail*-reading, Tory-voting parents. But every day's a challenge. Yesterday, on my own Easter Sunday evening, I somehow lost faith, through tiredness and loneliness perhaps. Today, I've been reminded, by a 95-year-old ex-Communist Quaker, of the day I met my guide who taught me faith and is teaching me every moment to listen and love from my heart.

STOP OUR DEVELOPMENT JUGGERNAUT!

Tracy Worcester

Tracy is an activist, environmentalist and writer living in Badminton, Gloucestershire

The western hemisphere describes itself as developed and 'first' in the civilisation race, and yet in many ways, so-called backward (i.e. Third World) rural cultures have it better.

Progress in the west is measured in terms of a country's economic growth, literacy and increased standard of living. Of course wealthy northern economies are way ahead of the south in all these, and yet, are we happier? Most of our houses are full of modern products; most of us have a job and can afford a car and a holiday abroad once a year. But do we smile, sing, or work with and for our family? Are we living within the ecological limits of our fragile planet as many do in the so-called impoverished Third World? Have we exchanged our quality of life for a higher standard of living?

To be part of the consumer culture, Third World people must abandon what was once a self-sufficient culture and join the workforce to produce and consume to serve a growth economy. Government taxes can now be raised and loans from foreign banks sought to invest in energy and transport infrastructure and invested into research and development to promote and facilitate high-tech industries and agriculture. Schools must be provided to mould future generations to abandon farming and seek their fortune in urban centres. They are not told, however, that mechanisation has replaced labour and only a tiny fraction of urban dwellers will actually find a job. Most will end up living in rented cardboard and corrugated iron hovels, scraping by doing menial labour, unable to afford the bus ticket back home. Is the desire to consume a human weakness? Or is it exploited by the very best psychiatrists, who manipulate our minds to think we are worthless and unfashionable unless we buy their product?

The United Nations says that the number of people living out their days in the squalor of a slum is almost a billion. Without radical changes, it believes, that number could double in 30 years.

Yet farmers across the world are deemed inefficient unless they can compete with grain from the United States and European Union that floods their markets due to distorting terms of trade, subsidies and intensive industrialised farming. Though cheap, consumers increasingly don't trust food from intensive systems, and the cost to agriculture, beyond mass bankruptcies, has been expensive disasters from mad cow disease and the mass slaughter of cattle with the curable foot and mouth disease to bird flu and salmonella outbreaks. If the external costs of intensive faming were internalised, small scale would be cheaper.

Outside of financial considerations, most rural cultures have a quality of life that many of us can only dream of living; loving extended families that live in close proximity to their work and are thereby present to guide their children. Supportive communities whose interconnectedness ensures most needs are answered in the locality.

The good news is that an increasing number of people in both developed and undeveloped countries are waking up to the impact of unfettered global trade—a system that breaks up family and community, steals land and resources and exploits labour to be competitive—as Clinton once boasted, 'America will win the global competition.' Who cares for the losers?

The political divide is no longer between the right (i.e. neo-liberal) and left (i.e. socialism), but between those who support the centralised global policies of both. They are both fighting for the so-called middle ground to facilitate economic growth for both corporations and banks competing in the global economy.

The modern economy is incapable of surviving without constant growth—it simply cannot stabilise—because our monetary system is founded on debt and our entire economies are propelled forward by this ruthless financial system.

On the other side, but not represented in mainstream politics, is the increasing number of people who see the growth economy perpetuating social and environmental breakdown. They want decentralisation, the relocalisation of every sector; economics, democracy, trade and banking. Many want money to return to being a means of exchange controlled by the people for the people. Usury (i.e. interest making money out of money), is reviled by every religion and many great political leaders. Thomas Jefferson and many leading politicians and bankers have recommended that the state should print and distribute the nations' means of exchange, not private banks.

The focus of democracy, trade and money should be based as close to

308

home as possible. The people should control their government, not government dictate to people, and development should be shifted from global dependence to local interdependence.

The skills of an African 13-year-old are no less sophisticated than my son's. One has spent time with his parents providing for the family, the other in a classroom learning the same curriculum the world over. We have been homogenised to serve the consumer culture. The African child knows how to find food, medicinal plants, and water in arid places; how to cure common ailments, help his mother build and cook, look after camels and cattle, sing and recount the hundreds of songs and stories that are passed from generation to generation. 'Appropriate' education needs to enhance human and ecological needs and interconnect subjects, as opposed to the reductionism and specialisation taught in schools today.

Contrary to popular ideas in the West, rural women in the Third World have dignity and authority. They work together to grow, harvest, preserve and cook, while the old tend to the very young. Work is at a convenient pace and supports and provides for loved ones, so it is a pleasure, not a chore. Yes, there are too many violent conflicts. However, most diverse religions have lived in harmony until one side is fuelled to hate the other by misinformation from outside geo-political interests.

In Ethiopia the whole community takes part in building a newlywed couple's home on inherited land. While talking, laughing and singing, a dozen men precariously balance on the woven roof frame while women hand up materials and booze. The atmosphere is more like that of a party than a construction site. All the materials are gathered locally. Similarly in Turkey, a modern concrete home is built with loans from the extended family, which, without the compounding interest of mortgages, can be repaid within a few years.

All this is in striking contrast to my dentist's receptionist here in the UK. She tearfully described her obligation to leave her sixteen-week-old baby at a kindergarten in order to return to work to help her husband meet mortgage payments on their £100,000 two-bedroom flat in the suburbs of Bristol.

What does it all come down to? *Think globally, act locally. Value our roots and culture, and cultivate self-sufficient communities. Cherish the family and community and relearn how to live in harmony with our surroundings.*

ABOUT THE CONTRIBUTORS TO
A WOMEN'S GUIDE

SUSANA AGER
Susana lives with a menagerie of animals in Somerset. She moved there in the late 1970s with her husband and four children. They were impressed by the writings of John Seymour (expert on self-sufficiency and sustainable living) and bought a home with outbuildings and land in order to try to emulate his path. The family took on a small milking herd, and raised rare breeds of sheep, pigs, chickens and goats. Eventually the children flew the nest, her husband died suddenly, and Susana now tends her large garden and cares for 'rescue' birds and a variety of other animals on her own.

THEA ANDERSON
Thea was brought up in Leicester but now lives in Brighton. Her previous occupation involved community work for the local council; now she's planning to work and train in psychotherapy.

JUDY BAKER
Judy was born to a Swedish father in 1948 in California and raised in Illinois. Her mother's side of the family were Michigan farmers. She particularly remembers her artist-father's cherry-flavoured pipe smoke as he worked in his studio and is sure she absorbed her own artistic bent through osmosis. She later did four years of art school and eventually received a Bachelor of Fine Arts degree and a teaching credential. She went on to earn a masters degree in creative art therapy and clinical psychology and spent many years being involved in art therapy programmes. She and husband John moved from Arizona to the Sierra Nevada foothills in California. She has become a grandmother and is a keen practitioner of sustainable living.

ELIZABETH JANE BALDRY
Elizabeth was born in Hampshire. She read music at Exeter University, and travelled to the Royal College of Music in London for her harp studies. She has been a professional harpist since 1994 and gives around 100 performances a year. Her compositions have been used by ITV and

the BBC and by Irish, Japanese and Canadian film, radio and television. She enjoys philosophy, art history and browsing around flea markets in Brighton. She is the 'muse' of composer Paul Lewis and the mother of two musical teenage boys. She is based in Devon.

IRENA BASHAM
Irena was born in Sheffield of Polish parents. She grew up in Sheffield and later spent two years in Australia. She has two grown sons and works as a receptionist for the ethical Triodos Bank in Bristol. She feels the greatest thing is to love and be loved in return and is passionate about environmental concerns.

MARGARITA MARINO DE BOTERO
Margarita was born in Colombia where she studied philosophy. In the 1980s, she became head of that country's National Institute for Natural Resources and the Environment. She also developed a national programme called 'The Green Campaign', which resulted in 600 green councils in 600 municipalities all over Colombia. She has travelled the world as a consultant to the UN Environment Programme and later became one of the Latin American members of the World Commission for Environment and Development. She is a member of many academic boards worldwide, and has devoted the last 20 years to creating and developing El Colegio Verde, a school for thought on environmental culture in Villa de Leyva, a small colonial town in the Andes.

ELISE BOULDING
Elise was born in Norway two years after the First World War and moved to New Jersey at the age of three. In college she majored in English Literature, played the cello in quartets and orchestra and learned to speak German and French. She eventually became a Quaker and married fellow Quaker, Kenneth Boulding. Their early life together included work for the League of Nations. She went to graduate school and earned an MA in sociology, became the mother of five children, started the International Peace Research Newsletter, later headed the Sociology department at Dartmouth College and went on to author several books. Husband Kenneth composed the Nayler Sonnets, which contain one of Elise's favourite quotes: 'Know this: though love is weak and hate is strong, yet hate is short, and love is very long'.

312

ROSIE BOYCOTT

Rosie was the founder of *Spare Rib* and Virago Press. She edited *Esquire*, *The Independent on Sunday* and the *Daily Express*. She has presented both radio and TV programmes. She is the author of *A Nice Girl Like Me* and her latest book is titled *Our Farm: A Year in the Life of a Smallholding*.

ELAINE BROOK

Elaine was born in London, grew up in Gloucestershire, and became involved in ecological work at an early age. She is a writer/photographer whose books include *The Windhorse* and *In Search of Shambala*. Her work reflects her travels in remote mountain areas of the world and the insights gained from being part of the extended family of a Himalayan shaman. She has developed an eco-home on the Welsh Borders where she gives talks and workshops on 'one-planet living'.

KATY BRYCE

Katy was born in Welwyn Garden City, Hertfordshire. She spent her early days roaming around green spaces and being fascinated by what came out of the earth. She earned a degree in human geography and later applied that to shelter, especially in poverty-stricken areas. This focus evolved into a fascination for building with 'cob'. She and her husband Adam Weisman have set up their own eco-building company, Cob in Cornwall and are authors of *Building With Cob: A Step-by-Step Guide*.

MONIQUE CADDY

Monique was born in The Netherlands in 1952. At the age of 9 she wrote her first play. After leaving the educational system, she worked with animals, drug addicts and the elderly before travelling throughout Europe for ten years. She then settled down with an English husband (poet, critic and editor of the poetry journal, *Tears in the Fence*) in Dorset where she works with the mentally disabled. While her children matured, she wrote poetry, gave readings, and was published in a variety of magazines and journals. Of late she has turned her attention to scriptwriting.

HELEN DE CASTRES

Helen is originally from Australia and now lives with her cat, Lottie, on Dartmoor where she works from home, using a process of self-discovery called Voice Dialogue. She creates sculptures which celebrate the sacredness of life. Her spirituality incorporates a wild blend of pagan, goddess, Jesus-loving, Buddhism, and simple devotion to love.

JILLY COOPER

Jilly was born in Hornchurch in 1937, but comes from Yorkshire and spent most of her childhood in Ilkley. She married Leo Cooper, the publisher, in 1961 and has two children, Felix and Emily, and two lovely grandsons, Jago and Lysander. She is a journalist and writer; the author of many best-selling novels, including *Riders*, *Rivals*, *Polo*, *The Man Who Made Husbands Jealous*, *Appassionata, Score!* and *Pandora*. She lives in Gloucestershire with Leo, her greyhound Feather, and five cats. She was appointed OBE in the 2004 Queen's Birthday Honours List for her contribution to literature.

SARAH DAWES

Sarah was 14 at the time she wrote her story and lives in Surrey. She's a student and would love to become some sort of an artist—because she's talented and people like her style.

POLLY DEVLIN

Polly is a broadcaster, writer and conservationist. Her first book, *All of Us There*, written in 1983, has been republished as a Modern Classic by Virago. She has received an OBE for services to literature. She makes her homes in Somerset and London.

KATE DEWES

Kate was born in New Zealand, is the mother of three daughters, and is a peace educator and anti-nuclear campaigner living in Christchurch. She has been a part-time lecturer in Peace Studies, an advisor to government and the UN on disarmament issues, and is an active member of many local, national and international peace groups.

TANIA DOLLEY

Tania grew up in the south of England and after completing a degree in environmental studies, spent time travelling and studying in India and teaching English in Thailand. Her desire to understand links between environmental problems and human behaviour led her to train as a Hakomi therapist and teach an MSc module in eco-psychology. She currently works as a counselling psychologist and eco-psychologist and lives in Wales, where she is also involved in various local community initiatives to promote sustainable living.

SISTER DORAH
Dorah was born in the Solomon Islands. She is a nun and member of the religious order called Sisters of the Church, a community formed by an English Anglican woman. She has worked in the Community for ten years, and when she's not in the Solomon Islands, lives at St Michael's Convent in Richmond, Surrey.

BUNTY DOWELL
Bunty was born in 1924 at Coombe Farm, Bradninch, Devon. She married Harry in Ilminster, went into nursing and became a Sister at Taunton General Hospital. She and Harry came to live in Coventry where they both became Quakers, had two children and Bunty continued to work in nursing. They then lived in Minehead (Somerset) until Harry's death in 2003, when Bunty moved back to Coventry where she still attends Quaker Meetings.

MARGARET DRABBLE
Margaret was born in Sheffield in 1939 and educated at a Quaker school, The Mount, in York, and at Newnham College, Cambridge, where she studied English Literature. She had a brief career as an actress with the Royal Shakespeare Company before becoming a full-time writer. She has published 15 novels, all currently in print with Penguin books. She has also published various works of non-fiction, and edited the fifth edition of the *Oxford Companion To English Literature*. She has travelled widely and lectured in many countries, often for the British Council.

ANN DRYSDALE
Ann was born near Manchester, brought up in London, married in Birmingham, raised her three children on the North York Moors and now lives in Wales. She has taught creative writing to undergraduates in Cardiff and Bristol. Describing herself as 'poet and peasant', she has been a writer since around the age of six. For many years she was also a journalist doing a column for the *Yorkshire Evening Post*. She has published four volumes of prose and four of poetry; her ninth book uses both, and is the result of her 'two voices learning to sing in harmony'.

SALLY EAVES
Sally was born in Manchester in 1950, 'a mere five years after the D-Day Landings'. Her father was one of those men who was shown jumping in the water and her mum delivered bottles of blood via ambulance through

the streets of Manchester. Sally's childhood was spent mainly in Devon and on the Sussex coast. As an adult she has lived in Bristol, West Wales and North Devon, where she currently teaches. She has a grown son.

MORAG EDWARDS

Morag was born in Dufftown, Scotland, and is the mother of three children. She's a volunteer worker for the RSPCA and has lived in Somerset for more than 25 years where she finds herself generally surrounded by numerous dogs, a flock of chickens, and at least one cat. She is also a performing member of the Bleadon Players, an amateur theatrical society.

MARTHA EKINS

Martha is 13 and lives in a village on Dartmoor. She attends school at Okehampton College and has a flair for mobilising the children in the neighbourhood to play outside instead of sitting in front of their tellies. She also rides her bicycle whenever she can and picks up litter.

SCILLA ELWORTHY

Scilla was born in Scotland in 1943, studied at college in Ireland and lived in Southern Africa for ten years working mainly in nutrition education. She was married there and had a daughter, Polly. Scilla has been nominated for a Nobel Peace Prize three times for her work with experts, analysts and others opposed to nuclear weapons. She has a private pilot's licence and made her first parachute jump in 1983. She has a PhD in political science from Bradford University, is the author of *Power & Sex* (translated into seven languages), founded the Oxford Research Group, established Peace Direct in 2000 to help develop knowledge of non-violent conflict prevention and resolution, was awarded the Niwano Peace Prize in 2003, and has been closely involved in many peace and negotiation delegations around the world. A near fatal attack of encephalitis in 1974 led her into psychological enquiry and spiritual practice. She now works with one of the world's leading entrepreneurs on an initiative to restore wisdom to global policy-making. She currently lives in Oxfordshire.

LIZ EVANS

Liz says she was born a long time ago to very average parents in a very average house. She insists she is a 'mongrel', a cross between a doormat and a scraper, as her father was a Yorkshireman, her mother Welsh. She was married for 25 years and has two children. One day she wandered into a local Job Centre to get out of the rain and wound up working in animal welfare and later co-managing Happy Landings Animal Shelter in Somerset where she claimed to have no social life, no spare time, and to be supremely happy.

JOSIE FELCE
Josie was born in London at the end of World War Two. Her parents were Quakers and her father a conscientious objector. She was the first person in her family to go to university, but after completing her studies, headed for the wilds of North Wales where she listened to traditional stories from the 'Mabinogion', and later made them into simple puppet shows to take into schools and to enliven historic castles. Puppetry grew into storytelling and she now tells stories in schools. In between, she has taught maths in the Seychelles, English in Malaysia and handwork in a Steiner school near Stroud, her present home.

MOLLY FISK
Molly was born and raised in San Francisco, and now lives in the Sierra Nevada foothills in Northern California. She teaches writing to cancer patients and sixth graders, runs an on-line workshop called Poetry Boot Camp and is a widely published poet. She also gives talks about women and culture that include: 'Does Curling Your Eyelashes Slow Down the Revolution'? She can be reached at mollyfisk.com.

MANDY-LOUISE FLETCHER
Mandy was born in Portsmouth, Hampshire in 1962. She works as a teacher of meditation and has a degree in world religions. She has spent many years studying what connects people and showing the way to their own happiness. Her central theme is *Love is all*.

ROSE FLINT
Rose is a poet, artist and art therapist. She teaches creative writing in schools and colleges, and uses poetry in health care settings such as hospitals, where she has worked in a wide variety of wards and units. She has been 'green' for many years and worked with the Green party in the 80s. She was brought up in the Midlands, lived in London as an art student, and is now at home in Wiltshire with her husband. Several collections of her poetry have been published.

HELEN GEE

Helen is a writer and environmentalist living in south-eastern Tasmania. She is a founding member of The Wilderness Society (Australia), a councillor with the Australian Conservation Foundation, and convenor of the Lake Pedder Restoration Committee. She has edited three major books dealing with the Tasmanian wilderness and forest campaigns.

JULIET GELLATLEY

Juliet was born in Cheshire and is the founder and international director of VIVA! (Vegetarians' International Voice for Animals) based in Bristol. She orchestrates campaigns against factory farming and is constantly agitating for improvements in animal welfare and farming conditions. She is married to writer Tony Wardle, is the mother of twins and lives in Bristol.

BETH GLOVER

Beth is an Anglican priest and vicar of St. Mary's Eastham on the Wirral. She is married to Gordon and has two grown sons. She was previously a lecturer in English and a trained 'deed' nurse. She is also one of the leaders of the Companions to the Melanesian Brothers in Chester diocese.

ARUNA GNANADASON

Aruna was born in India in 1949. After completing her MA in English Literature and teaching at university in Bangalore, she became involved with the National Council of Churches in India before moving to Geneva. She has since acquired a string of degrees, is the author of a book titled *No Longer a Secret*, and has written essays for several leading journals throughout the world. She is presently active in Asian and Third World theological networks and coordinates the work on justice, peace and creation for the World Council of Churches and is also responsible for the Women's Programme of the WCC. Her primary focus is on overcoming violence against women and children, women and economic justice, and drawing together women's voices and visions of the church as an alternative community.

ANGELA GOODMAN

Angie was born in Reading and did English and European Literature at Warwick University, cobbled together an art foundation course in London, and travelled to various parts of the world before finally settling in the Bristol/Bath area, where she is married (her husband is a mathematician) with her two children still living at home. She has illustrated two books (wrote her first book, a story about a car, at the age of five), sings with a choir, paints whenever she can and is currently employed by the Hospital Education Service as a teacher working with children who are at home, and periodically in the Children's Ward. Would love to spend all her time painting and writing.

CLARE MARYAN GREEN

Clare was born in 1964 in Surrey. She fell in love with Exmoor as a child and has spent half her life there in Somerset. She has been making stained glass for 20 years and is at home in Lynton with her dog and cat. She did an apprenticeship in glass blowing, but is essentially self taught and sells her work through word of mouth and a variety of outlets. She is currently studying life drawing, teaching stained glass at East Devon college and collaborating with an apprentice from Japan. Ultimately she wants to be recognised as an eminent artist producing quality work that will endure through time.

JENNIFER GRIERSON

Jennifer was born in Bulawayo, Southern Rhodesia (now Zimbabwe) in 1942. For a time she was warden of a Quaker Meeting House in Bridport, and now lives in Lyme Regis. Her life work lies in expressing her primary concerns of spirituality/people/creativity/ecology through textile artistry and art therapy. She sees herself as a 'community artist'.

SARAH GURTEEN

Sarah was born in North London and is 26. She lives with her boyfriend in Cambridgeshire and is employed by *The Times* Book Service. She loves horses.

JULIA HAILES

Julia works from her home in Somerset and has written nine 'green' books, the latest being *The New Green Consumer Guide*. She wears many different hats, all of them green, though her primary job is as an environmental consultant advising multinational companies. Her aim is to show us all how we can make a difference. She currently lives under the shadow of the iron age fort of Ham Hill with her three boisterous boys who don't always remember to turn the lights off in their bedrooms.

ALYSON HALLETT

Alyson was born in Somerset in 1963 and has lived and worked in many parts of the UK, including in mental health work in Glasgow, as a postwoman in Norwich and as Abbey housekeeper on Iona. In the 90s, she earned an MA in creative writing, has published poetry and short fiction, and written drama for Radio 4. In 2001 she was writer-in-residence at South West Arts, went on to be visiting writer at the University of the West of England, and is currently employed by the Small School in Hartland, Devon.

CLARE HAMON

Clare was born in Canada in 1956 and moved to England at the age of 12. She studied medicine at Cambridge and qualified as a doctor. In 1984 she became a GP with a special interest in home births. After a marital separation and her son's death from cancer in 1994, she moved to Plymouth, became a Quaker and studied for a Certificate in Theology. In 2006 she became a part-time GP, and took up voluntary work, including chairing the Plymouth Global Justice Group. Other interests include cycling, reading and theatre.

JEAN HARDY

Jean was a university teacher for some 30 years and has also been involved in many practical organisations for social change. She is past editor of *GreenSpirit* journal and takes part in many of the activities at Dartington Hall and Schumacher College in Devon. She is now most active as a writer and speaker.

MADDY HARLAND

Maddy is the editor of England's *Permaculture* magazine, offering solutions for sustainable living. She is co-founder of a company dedicated to publishing solution-orientated practical books. She lives and works in Hampshire with her husband Tim and their two daughters.

TANYA HAWKES

Tanya was born in Gloucester, but now lives in Wales with Maya and Doris (her daughter and dog, respectively) where she works for CAT (Centre for Alternative Technology) and writes for their *Clean Slate* magazine. She also sometimes writes for a punk rock fanzine called *Suspect Device* under the title 'Hairy Legs'.

ELAINE HELLER

Elaine once worked for The British Tourist Authority in London, but is now a healer. She makes her home in Bristol when not travelling to various parts of the world in the course of her work.

ELIZABETH HELLMICH

Elizabeth is a Bradfordian grandmother with two grown daughters. She has childminded more than 150 children and fostered 123 young people and is a nursery nurse by trade. She helps as a wardrobe mistress, scenery and costume designer for Stage 84, a children's stage school in Bradford. Her role as a Neighbourhood Watch coordinator has led to serious involvement in community volunteer work.

VERITY HESKETH

Verity is 13 and lives in South Devon. She loves to walk, swim, write, read, dance, talk, go to the cinema and theatre and get an eyeful of amazing views. She also loves gardening and doing still life and landscape drawings. She is passionate about wanting peace and an end to pollution.

JAIN HOPKINS

Jain was raised in Yorkshire in a farming community. Since then, she has lived in Cornwall and London and currently resides in Brighton where she works as a 'healing' psychologist. She has experience in using Osho inspired therapy, offers transpersonal work, physical therapy, meditation, and is currently inspired by the Hoffman Process.

REBECCA HUGHES

Rebecca was born in Hereford and grew up in 'lots of places'. She has worked in publishing and is the author of several non-fiction books. She campaigns for animal rights and co-founded Writers for the Abolition of Vivisection. She promotes positive thinking and non-violence through her postcard production company and is now a playwright and scriptwriter living in London and Gloucestershire.

LEONIE HUMPHRIES

Leonie grew up in the Norfolk countryside and attended the same primary boarding school as Princess Diana. She studied biology up to HND level, then worked for Bob Geldof's Band Aid Trust in the 80s. She has since studied philosophy and economics in London and is currently undertaking an Open University degree in International Studies, concentrating on environmental issues. She is married with two children and lives in Dorset.

JEMIMA KHAN

Jemima grew up in London and lived in Pakistan for ten years. She is trying to write a book, as well as working on a play with Gillian Slovo. In the past, she set up and directed a charity for Afghan refugees in Pakistan and ran a fashion business/Women's NGO in Pakistan for several years. She has a Master's degree in Islamic Societies and Cultures. She is the mother of two children, aged eight and ten.

PAULINE KIDNER

Pauline was born in 1950 in Kent; a policeman's daughter who gained her love of animals from her mother. She and husband Derek (they have three children) initially ran a dairy farm in Somerset that eventually developed into an 'open' farm with goats, sheep, chickens, guinea pigs; just about everything you could name. They decided to open to the public and gradually evolved into a full time wildlife rescue centre called Secret World set on 18 acres just off the M5 north of Bridgwater. Now, every year some 3,000 needy or injured wild animals pass through—the latest being an albatross—and the centre's far reaching goal is to help people understand wildlife and nature. Pauline has written three books and occasionally works with the BBC.

LUCY LEPCHANI

Lucy was born in Bromley, Kent. Her father is an immigrant of Sikkimese descent (Lepcha tribe) and her mother is descended from a long line of Cornish and Irish seafaring families. Lucy works for schools and with community groups and occasionally writes copy for businesses and individuals. She has won several writing awards and has been published in various magazines and anthologies. She is the mother of four and is completing a degree in Humanities. She lives with her husband Sean and youngest child Natasha in Ashburton, close to Dartmoor in Devon.

INGRID LEVER

Ingrid was born in 1953 in Waterloo (Liverpool, not the station!). As an only child, her early years were spent on the Wirral peninsula where she revelled in nature. She studied English at Durham and Landscape

Architecture at Sheffield University. She works in Bristol for local government in a capacity that gives her the chance to get new trees planted along the streets and to 'green' new development. She lived in a village near Wells with her cat and sheep before moving to Cumbria.

MARY LIDGATE
Mary was born in London and grew up at a boarding school in Newton Abbot. She has two daughters and lives with her partner. Her lifelong passion has consisted of dealing with people, the theatre, relationships and the stimulus of social groups. She feels the primary relationship we've let go of is with the environment. 'We've forgotten the creatures we are.' She loves being in, on and around the sea, and currently works in an all-women partnership called Theatre4Business.

CAROLINE LUCAS
Caroline grew up and was educated in Malvern. She has been a Green Party member since 1999 and spends much of her time in Brussels. She came to Green politics after active involvement in the Snowball Campaign against US bases and continues to campaign on peace and anti-nuclear issues. Her other main focuses are climate change and energy, food, and international trade. She is a widely published author, and works with a range of organisations, including the RSPCA and CND. She has two sons.

KARALINA MATSKEVICH
Karalina was born in 1966 in Minsk, Belarus. In the 90s she was co-editor of the first Belarusian religious and philosophical journal, *Unia*. She studied theology in London and Paris and now lectures in Old Testament and Hebrew at the Missionary Institute in London. She lives in Surrey with her husband and two daughters.

BARONESS SUE MILLER
Sue started her working life in book publishing. When her two daughters were young, she became increasingly concerned about many issues, and subsequently got involved in direct action and politics. As a Liberal Democrat, she was nominated to the House of Lords in 1998, where she is currently spokesperson on the Environment, Food and Rural Affairs. She lives in Devon where she and her husband Humphrey like to spend time sailing, gardening and walking.

HEATHER MILLS

Heather was born in 1968 in Washington, near Newcastle-upon-Tyne. In 1993 her life changed forever when she was involved in a road accident with a police motorcycle that resulted in the loss of her left leg below the knee. One year after her accident, she arranged for the first convoy of artificial limbs to be sent to Croatia. Now she voluntarily counsels people from around the world who have lost limbs through natural disasters, accidents and terrorist attacks. She is a patron of Viva! and campaigns to end animal cruelty, environmental destruction and for a healthy future. She has campaigned for over 15 years to raise funds and awareness to rid the world of landmines. She and her young daughter live in Hove, Sussex.

MARY MORTON

As the daughter of a Royal Navy officer and the wife of another (she was six years old when they met), Mary has spent most of her life on the move. Since the death of her husband, she has retired, and lives in a snug granite cottage on the fringes of Dartmoor where she maintains an active part in community activities and is deeply connected to the families of her beloved offspring. Drama and poetry play an important role in her life and she is a writer-member of Moor Poets. She is a committed Christian and looks to her faith to save the world.

MO MOWLAM

Mo was a former secretary of State for Northern Ireland and after her tenure there, worked as a writer and broadcaster. She was originally from London. (Sadly, Mo died on 19 August, 2005 at the age of 55, without having a chance to enlarge on her contribution to this book.)

ELIZABETH NATHANIELS

Elizabeth was born in Salisbury, educated 'all over England' and wound up at a Maltese convent. She was offered a place at Oxford but had to turn it down because her brother 'needed it more'. Eventually she became a student at the Slade School of Art and University College, London. She left in the middle of it all to get married and move to the Bahamas where she worked as a journalist and interior designer. Twenty-six years and three children later, they were still there. She then went to Harvard, and on to Cambridge where she earned a degree in social anthropology. She now resides in Hastings and is working on a biography.

HELENA NORBERG-HODGE

Helena is a leading analyst of the global economy on cultures around the world. A linguist by training, she was born in 1946 and educated in Sweden, Germany, England and the United States, and speaks seven languages. She has lectured and taught extensively around the world: from the Smithsonian Institute to Harvard and Oxford universities. She is the founder and director of the International Society for Ecology and Culture (ISEC), and also directs the Ladakh Project, renowned for its groundbreaking work in sustainable development on the Tibetan plateau. She and her partner live in Dartington.

MARIAN PARTINGTON

Marian grew up near Cheltenham. As an adult, the loss of her sister, Lucy, as a victim of Fred and Rosemary West in Gloucester, led to deeply introspective soul-searching and later, her current work in 'forgiveness' and prisoner rehabilitation, which includes writing a book on the subject. She has three children and a stepson and lives in Wales with her husband. She is a Quaker and practices meditation.

SISTER PHYLLIS

Phyllis Margaret Sau comes from San Cristoval (or Makira) in the Solomon Islands where she was one of nine siblings. Around 1980 she went to a Church Training Centre to be trained as a lay reader in the church and eventually decided she wanted to be a nun. In 1982 she travelled to another island to join the Community of the Sisters of the Church and has been a member ever since. In 2001 she came to England to study and live with the Sisters at St. Michael's Convent in Richmond. In 2002 she went to Trinity College in Bristol and graduated with a certificate in theology. Now she wants to go home and put into practice what she has learned.

LUCY PINNEY

Lucy was born in Hammersmith, London. She has written two novels, composed a country column for *The Times* for six years, and has contributed articles to numerous newspapers and magazines. She has three children and lives on a small farm near Honiton (Devon) with her partner.

SUSANA PIOHTEE

Susana is 62 and has a delightful relationship with her twin daughters. She lives in Herefordshire, where for the past 20 years she has been a therapist and participant with the Independent Therapists' Network. She currently works as a Community Liaison Officer for a Housing Association in Hereford.

PENNEY POYZER
Penney is 47, was born in Suffolk, and is a writer and broadcaster on green issues, and has two daughters. She and husband Gil own the Nottingham Eco-home, recognized as a pioneering eco retrofit showing how housing stock can be transformed. She is currently working on her second book and makes a reasonably ethical living eco-ranting on a regular basis.

LIZ REASON
Liz is from Charlbury in Oxfordshire. She's an experienced policy analyst specialising in energy and climate change. She is currently director of Reasons to Be Cheerful, a consultancy vehicle for assisting the implementation of effective policies aimed at mitigating climate change. Meeting Daisy the Cow in King Street, Cambridge inspired her to dedicate her life to lightening her footprint on the planet and to helping others understand why it is important to do the same.

PHILIPPA REYNOLDS
Philippa was born in 1931 in Invercargill, New Zealand and graduated with an MA in Geography from the University of Canterbury. After teaching for many years, in 1965 she travelled by ship to England, where she met and married a Devon farmer. She now lives in Chagford on Dartmoor and is busy with an allotment, choir, church, Chinese brush painting, playing badminton and being active in a peace group.

DAME ANITA RODDICK
Anita was born in Littlehampton. James Dean was her schoolgirl idol. She trained as a teacher but after a stint in a kibbutz in Israel wound up on an extended working trip around the world. She later married Gordon Roddick and the couple first ran a restaurant, then a hotel in Littlehampton. In 1976, without training or experience, she started The Body Shop. She has been involved with Greenpeace and many campaigns aimed at righting social injustice and travels frequently throughout the world checking on Body Shop projects. (Sadly, Anita died on September 10, 2007.)

JEAN SCHULZ

Jean was born in Mannheim, Germany and has lived for many years in California where she was the wife of Charles Schulz, inventor of the *Peanuts* (aka *Charlie Brown*) cartoon strip. She is a longtime member of the League of Women Voters, and helped develop the Meals on Wheels programme. She is a board member of Canine Companions for Independence and produced a documentary: *What a Difference a Dog Makes*. She holds a pilot's licence and has flown two Powder Puff Derbies (a transcontinental air-race).

KAREN EBERHARDT SHELTON

Karen was born and raised in northern California where her teacher mother was awarded a Fulbright teaching scholarship that took the family to England, the land of their ancestral roots. Many countries, one son, two marriages and one adopted child (from India) later, Karen moved permanently to England, worked as a journalist, had a book of poetry published, and one bright day at her then home in Porlock, Somerset, embraced the concept of this book. She now aspires to set up a multi-purpose Trust in her mother's name and gather creative minds eager to collaborate on solutions to some of the world's problems; in a solar-powered and organically maintained environment.

CLARE SHORT

Clare was born in Birmingham in 1946 and studied at the universities of Keele and Leeds. She graduated as Bachelor of Arts with Honours in Political Science. In 1983 she entered the House of Commons as an MP for Birmingham Ladywood. Among a variety of other posts, she has been Opposition spokesperson on Environment Protection, Social Security and Employment. In 2004, her book, *An Honourable Deception? New Labour, Iraq, and the Misuse of Power* was published. She is widowed, with one son, and lists swimming and her family as her favourite leisure pursuits.

PENELOPE SHUTTLE

Penelope was born near London but has lived in Cornwall since 1970. She is a poet and the widow of poet Peter Redgrove. She has published eight collections of poetry and her 2007 publication, *Redgrove's Wife*, was shortlisted for the Forward Prize and the T S Eliot Award. Penelope is a Hawthornden Fellow and tutor for The Poetry School and has given numerous readings at festivals such as Aldeburgh, King's Lynn, Poetry-next-the-Sea and venues that include The Wordsworth Trust.

SHANNON SMY
Shannon was born in Sheffield in 1965. Her mother was a nursery nurse, her father an itinerant pop star whom she never met. She started her education in Kent, and moved every couple of years with her mother and stepfather to Hampshire, Northamptonshire and Derbyshire. She studied economics and politics at Warwick University, but dropped out to concentrate on political activism. She became a founder member of the Geese Theatre Company before deciding she wanted to start her own band, hence The Passionground, an all-women four-piece rock band which played with Chumbawamba, Danny Sensible and Danni Minogue, among others. She left to start Seize the Day with partner Theo in 1996 during the Newbury bypass protest. She now lives with him and young daughter Rosa at Kingshill in Somerset.

MARY TAYLOR
Mary was born in 1951 to Irish parents in Bath. In 1970 she married an Englishman and they lived in Samoa. She now resides in Fiji and works in plant genetic resources, with a specialty in tissue culture (putting plants in tubes to conserve them or make them multiply faster). She loves being in nature and is a keen gardener and walker.

NANCY TODD
Nancy is an environmental writer based on Cape Cod. She is currently editor of *Annals of Earth*, published by Ocean Arks International. She and husband John are the co-founders of The New Alchemy Institute in Massachusetts. She has lectured at a number of universities and colleges in the U.S., Canada and Europe and is the author of several books dealing with a variety of approaches to eco-cities, bioshelters, city farming and ecological design. She and John have three children and a lovely little flock of multi-racial, multi-ethnic grandchildren. When relaxing at home she reads, writes, runs, gardens, dances and picnics.

ANNA MARIA VALLARIO
Anna Maria was born of Italian parents and grew up in south Wales. She married in her early 20s, had three children, and six years later left an unhappy relationship and became a single mum. She got through four years of a B.Ed. Hons degree and went into teaching at 34. She currently resides on the outskirts of Bristol.

ELSIE WALTON
Elsie, now deceased, was an 84-year-old widow living in Milverton, Somerset where she was once head of the village primary school. She was born in Sheffield where, during the final years of the war, she was a secondary school teacher. She and her husband had three children. She became a Methodist Local Preacher and worked ecumenically with the parish church.

FIONA WALTERS
Fiona was born in Cheshire in 1960, educated at Moreton Hall in Shropshire and subsequently, Rose Bruford College, Kent. She recently read Law at Exeter University and after successfully passing exams to become a solicitor, works in a criminal litigation practice in Exeter. She is married with a daughter and has lived on Dartmoor for over 20 years. She has restored an ancient apple orchard and makes cider from its fruit.

JILL WESTON
Jill is in her 50s and lives in Welwyn Garden City, Herts, with her musician partner and various pets. She has a son and daughter. She has worked as an artist's model, a home tutor and an English and Special Needs teacher. In 1991 she became a Labour councillor and was chair of the Environmental Strategy Committee. She has been a peace activist since the early 1980s and was a CND volunteer. She is a Quaker who likes to garden, read, cycle, run, dog-walk and listen to music.

TRACY WORCESTER (Marchioness of Worcester)
Tracy was born in London but grew up in Oxfordshire where she abandoned her education and went to live in Paris. She took up modelling but loathed it, so lived in Italy for a time with her mum before studying History of Art at the Royal College of Art. She did volunteer work at Friends of the Earth, acted in *Cat's Eyes* (TV series), then turned to public speaking, writing and fund-raising focused on bringing politicians together with ecologists. She is now making sociological and environmental documentaries questioning the benefits of development. She is married, with three children and lives in Gloucestershire.

WOMEN OF ACCOMPLISHMENT THROUGHOUT HISTORY

As a kind of template for *A Women's Guide*, I've gathered names of women through the ages who have made a significant social contribution, a betterment of some note, or offered an insight into the human condition. Only a small minority have had to deal with the kinds of global change we're facing now. How few women are currently making a difference and how few in comparison with men. The names assembled here (with a little help from friends) by no means represent a complete list.

Anne Frank	Helen Keller
Elizabeth Fry	Sarah Emily Davies
Beatrix Potter	Dian Fossey
Anna Freud	Mother Teresa
Eleanor Roosevelt	Golda Meir
Barbara McClintock	Indira Gandhi
Mary Magdalene	Hildegard Von Bingen
Marie Stopes	Florence Nightingale
Nefertiti	Joan of Arc
Harriet Beecher Stowe	Helen Caldicott
Marie Curie	Emmeline Pankhurst
Jane Goodall	Maria Montessori
Virginia Woolf	Charlotte Perkins Gilman
Wangari Maathai	Betty Friedan
Queen Victoria	Pearl Buck
Anita Desai	Elizabeth Garrett Anderson
Catherine of Sienna	George Eliot
Rosa Parks	Brigid of Kildare
Edith Cavell	Mary Slessor
Rachel Carson	Arundhati Roy
Elizabeth Kenny	Jane Austen
Maya Angelou	Annie Besant
Mary McLeod Bethune	Dame Myra Hess
Frances Moor Lappe	Boadicea
Amelia Earhart	Ann Morrow Lindbergh
Queen Elizabeth I	Eleanor of Aquitaine

331

Anita Roddick
Beryl Markham
Margaret Mead
Julia Ward Howe
Theodora (wife of Justinian I)
Germaine Greer
Margaret Bourke White
Grace Cook
Lucretia Mott
Queen Wilhelmina
Ida Wells-Barnett
Freya Stark
Pocahontas
Octavia Hill
Vera Brittain
Han Suyin
Hilda Bernstein
Rosamund Carr
Angela Merkel
Mary Seacole
Bella Abzug
Dame Cicely Saunders
Hypatia
Mary Shelley
Emma Willard
Rosalynn Carter
Denise Levertov
Bess of Hardwick
Vanessa Redgrave
Anne Clough

Julian of Norwich
Emily Greene Balch
Alice Hamilton
Alva Myrdal
Dorothy Day
Jacquetta Hawkes
Mary Leakey
Aung San Suu Kyi (Burma)
Dorothea Lange
Lady Astor
Mary Ann Girling
Margaret Sanger
Elsie Widdowson
Martha Gellhorn
Simone Weil
Alice Paul
Grace Paley
Tillie Olsen
Elizabeth Gaskell
Eleanor of Arborea
Susan B. Anthony
Emma Lucy Braun
Aphra Behn
Eva Peron
Gerty Cori
Jane Addams
Margaret Ursula Mee
St Clotilda
Dame Catherine Anne Tizard

'Rationality cannot flourish without the presence of the feminine.'
Hildegard von Bingen 1098–1179

ASSEMBLING A WOMEN'S GUIDE

Exploring the Path It Took Me Along

Karen Eberhardt Shelton

Focusing on this final piece of my cherished project has been very strange. Even now, with a deadline ticking, I have to *force* myself to sit down and finalise thoughts and feelings on what it has been like assembling this book – and I'm not sure why this is so. It's a bit like saying goodbye to a child or parent I might never see again. *A Women's Guide* has been an intimate part of my everyday life for more than five years; a kind of piston pumping away inside affecting my energy levels, my attitude toward society, how I spend my time; a kind of gargantuan inner journey that has led me into brick walls, up to the tops of mountains, down into dark troughs, across turbulent passages, and into labyrinths that seemed to have no beginning or end. But ultimately, the long and difficult process of assembling everything here has slowly turned into a beloved old friend and companion that has been breathing into my ear, fuelling my heart, holding sessions with me over how I see life, the world, the whole of creation – and I'm finding it painful to finally let go.

In 2002 I was living in Porlock, Somerset and my writing for *The Western Daily Press* in Bristol had slackened. I needed to put my concerns for the decline of Planet Earth into some kind of perspective and one night, after a few glasses of wine and finding a lost hedgehog in the car park, in some mysterious way the essential idea for *A Women's Guide To Saving The World* came into being. '*If I could wave a magic wand and make the world a better place, and offer that wand to other women to do the same, what might come of it all?*'

Putting this book together has been like raising eighty puppies from birth to adulthood, building a village from scratch, going around the world without a map. I thought perhaps in the vein of the 100th Monkey Syndrome, if I could persuade various women I encountered to 'speak up' about how they'd put that wand to good use, some modest movement for change might be set in motion. I had no plan, no agenda; just a great need to apply myself to a worthwhile collaborative project. I started with women I knew and slowly branched out to recommendations and obvious choices – offering the Magic Wand concept to each. I didn't stipulate length or subject matter. I simply asked that they speak from the heart, be passionate, avoid formality and try to avoid sounding *academic*.

I knew a literary agent in London, so approached him with the idea and the first few stories. He was enthusiastic, but showed what I'd put together to a big-time publisher woman, who in the manner of that mainstream money-making, sales-conscious business mode, found all kinds of things she considered flaws. She even criticised my *'women who've made social contributions throughout history'* list. So I shifted my focus and pushed on. Of course, in the early stages, there were no famous women in the book, so it was of no interest to literary agents, let alone publishers. In the end, 24 publishers and 7 or 8 literary agents said no (I wish I could list them all here.) Virago in particular were a disappointment because they kept me dangling for close to a year.

Eventually I reached a point of 'no return'. Too many women were involved for me to lose faith or drop the whole thing. It became not my, but *our* book, *our* collective voice speaking up for change. I accepted that no matter how tough, frustrating or time-consuming it might become, I'd stay with it no matter what; even when I felt like pulling my hair out, went cross-eyed from staring at the computer screen, my phone bill sky-rocketed, and I turned into a completely stressed-out, snarly old woman. After all, explorers and social reformers also have their ups and downs, false turns, dead ends, but it's that *complete* story that encourages and inspires others even if it includes half the crew dying of scurvy, your climbing partner falling into an inescapable crevasse or the wildlife you've been protecting at Chernobyl getting hit by a meteor. The story doesn't work on all levels if the problems and tough bits are left out. How others meet challenges can encourage one to hold on when the task appears to be hopeless. This is how my thinking sometimes ran when I received another rejection letter or 10 women in a row said 'no thanks'.

As the number of stories increased, I shifted the parameters slightly to include contributions from women in other countries. (While at a special church function in Gidleigh on Dartmoor, I connected with two of the Polynesian women guests and they are in this book.) The little biographies I asked for were at first pared down descriptions of 'self', but strangely, later turned into quite lengthy affairs. *'Tell me who you are, where you're from and what you do – so that every woman in the book will have an identity.'* (I probably began to probe deeper and ask more questions.) Because it took so much time to compile this collection, naturally a great many details and circumstances altered over that period. Women from the earlier stages in some cases moved away, died, divorced, changed jobs, left school, and so on. With 80-plus women to account for and keep track of, I would have found it impossible to reconnect with each one in order to bring her bio up to date. Thus I hope you will take each woman as you find her, even though in fact, where she is in the 'now' may have little in common with where she was when she first wrote her piece.

In the course of various travels to conferences and workshops, a visit here, a look in there, if I encountered a woman who struck me as a *thinking* individual engaged in something interesting, I asked if she'd write for the book. Even if I got a *yes*, frequently nothing came of that initial assent, so I'd have to nag-nag-nag via email, phone or letter. Often it was a real grind persuading someone to deliver, though in a majority of cases the response was timely and appropriate. In every instance, I learned *something* about each individual woman's character, and the cumulative effect of interacting, sometimes over long periods of time, with so *many* different women – plus secretaries, personal assistants, relatives, husbands, lawyers, friends and even dogs and parrots – could probably constitute a book in its own right.

In the end, there were considerably more 'no's than 'yes's or 'maybe's and I almost wish I could include those 'no's as representing another aspect of the whole journey, including the time factor. I found it interesting to note that lack of interest, involvement in other projects, bad timing, didn't suit their agenda, and mostly 'too busy' were the primary barriers to participation. In the case of well-known women, I suspect secretaries and PAs of sometimes making a choice for them and wonder how many big names never knew I'd knocked on their door. (I was told by Annie Lennox's office she was writing a piece, but after 4 months and many phone calls, nothing showed up and I stopped trying.) In the end I had to accept that yes, we all prioritise, and what is a big ship coming in to one is a small canoe on the horizon to another, and thus we choose which paths to follow. I do know that countless women have been *silenced* throughout the ages, and that's why I highlight the struggle, the mental and emotional geography I've traversed to reach this point; to break out of that *silence* and relate my story.

Time passed, the book evolved, support came from unexpected sources, details became more numerous and hard to keep track of. I wound up having to convert emailed stories into properly formatted text and did more editing (most of it minor) than anticipated. Ultimately came the task of tracking every woman down in order to supply her with a 'consent' form to be signed giving the publisher permission to use her piece. (Whew! I wouldn't want to go through that again.)

Now here we all are, linked in this common endeavour; our unique window from which to appeal to a wider collage of those who make up Society. I could never have stayed with this venture through all its rejections, prevarications, no-shows, and elusive promises were I not so committed to capturing the essence of current women's thinking in terms of what conditions and priorities are like in the world *now*, while realising that fifty or one hundred years on, this collection may well constitute a descriptive diary anchoring our place in time. I am quite literally astonished by the finished product and filled with a kind of grateful love for everyone who participated. In a way, it feels as though I've become enmeshed within a very large and convoluted family, moving forward as spiritual colleagues in our touching mixture of callings to make the world a better place. Now, more than ever, whatever care and concern we feel inside needs to be expressed outwardly; Being and Doing can be balanced by the type of Speaking Up that makes a difference. Most of all, may that *balance* come to include profound harmony between women *and* men working together to save the world.